LIFE *in* CHRIST

Practicing Christian Spirituality

JULIA GATTA

CHURCH
PUBLISHING
INCORPORATED

Psalm citations contained herein are from The Psalter of The Book of Common Prayer (1979). Unless otherwise noted, the Scripture quotations contained herein are from the Revised Standard Version Bible, copyright © 1973 and from the New Revised Standard Version Bible, copyright © 1989 by the Division of Christian Education of the National Council of Churches of Christ in the U.S.A. Used by permission. All rights reserved.

Church Publishing
19 East 34th Street
New York, NY 10016
www.churchpublishing.org

Cover art: The painting of an icon of the Anastasis was commissioned as a gift in honor of the Very Rev. William S. Stafford, dean emeritus of the School of Theology, upon his retirement. It was painted by the Rev. Peter Pearson. It hangs in the Chapel of the Apostles, Sewanee.

Cover design by Jennifer Kopec, 2Pug Design
Typeset by Rose Design

Library of Congress Cataloging-in-Publication Data

Names: Gatta, Julia, 1947– author.
Title: Life in Christ : practicing Christian spirituality / Julia Gatta.
Description: New York : Church Publishing, 2018. | Includes bibliographical
  references.
Identifiers: LCCN 2018003297 (print) | LCCN 2018020807 (ebook) | ISBN
  9780819233127 (ebook) | ISBN 9780819233110 (pbk.)
Subjects: LCSH: Spiritual life—Episcopal Church.
Classification: LCC BV4501.3 (ebook) | LCC BV4501.3 .G38 2018 (print) | DDC
  248.4/83—dc23
LC record available at https://lccn.loc.gov/2018003297

Printed in the United States of America

For my daughter
Mary

CONTENTS

Preface vii

Introduction: The Heart's Longing xi

1. Reliving Christ's Death and Resurrection 1

2. Communion with Christ 37

3. Sanctifying Time through the Liturgical Round 87

4. Prayer in Solitude 128

5. Practices for the Journey 179

PREFACE

This book had its genesis in a course that I have been teaching, in various permutations, for most of my adult life. I am grateful to Robert Taylor, then vicar/chaplain of St. Mark's Episcopal Church in Storrs, Connecticut, where I was a parishioner, for inviting me in 1976 to create a course for adult inquirers. I did, and we subsequently had the pleasure of teaching it together for several rounds. We used only two books as our texts: the Bible and the Book of Common Prayer. Although our students were regular worshippers at the parish, we watched them light up as they discovered the essential nexus between the gospel proclamation of Jesus's death and resurrection and the *experience* of those saving events through the liturgy and sacramental life of the church. We dug into the theology and history of baptism and the Holy Eucharist, moving between Scripture and liturgical text. The layers of significance undergirding the familiar Sunday Eucharist came as a surprise. They began to feel the same engagement with Christ through the sacraments that St. Ambrose of Milan described: "You have shown yourself to me face to face, O Christ: I meet you in your sacraments." Within such a vision of faith, sacramental life ushers in mystical encounter. Other topics were of course covered over the span of those classes, but it was and remains my conviction that the communal, sacramental life of the church grounds our life in Christ. From that foundation the further exploration of prayer and meditation, witness and service, can spring. The experience of many a churchgoer, however, falls far short of this mystical depth even when there is hunger for it.

In the mid-1980s, on behalf of the Diocese of Connecticut and with the encouragement of its bishop, Arthur Walmsley, I revised the course in collaboration with Kirk Smith, now bishop of Arizona, for circulation among parishes. I continued to refine and teach the course for decades in the various parishes I served until my departure for Sewanee in 2004.

For the past twelve years, I have taught an introductory course in Christian spirituality to first-year seminarians at the School of Theology. Not surprisingly, I turned to the parish syllabus to structure the opening sessions of that course, which set out the sacramental foundations of Christian spirituality. The Bible and the Book of Common Prayer continue to be touchstone texts, although other volumes now add greater depth and breadth to the students' reading. Inevitably, within the first few weeks of teaching, a student will ask with some indignation, "Why didn't anyone ever tell us this before?" It is to facilitate the crucial task of connecting gospel, sacramental worship, and the practices of Christian spirituality that I have written this book. I am indebted to my students over the years, especially those at the School of Theology, who have enriched my thinking and teaching through lively discussion.

Because it is a community of both learning and prayer, Sewanee seems the ideal place to work on a book such as this. I am grateful to the University of the South for granting me a sabbatical leave in the 2017 Easter term for writing, and specifically to J. Neil Alexander, dean of the School of Theology, for making it possible. My colleagues have always been accessible and unfailingly helpful to clarify scholarly points.

Two colleagues in particular merit special thanks: Karen Meredith and Christopher Bryan. The initial impetus for this book came through conversation with Karen Meredith, executive director of Education for Ministry. In the three years since we first discussed it, she has offered wise counsel based on her years as a Christian educator and unflagging support of the project. I am honored that it will be used as an "interlude" book for EfM. Christopher Bryan, emeritus professor of New Testament at the School of Theology, gave meticulous attention to a draft of the manuscript, proffering both learned recommendations and graceful stylistic suggestions. The usual disclaimer about remaining mistakes and infelicities being entirely my own is more than apt.

I wish to thank two Sewanee students whose diligence helped me secure some of the illustrations for this book: seminarian Arthur Jones and student librarian Michael Rudolph.

Finally, I owe my husband, John, my deepest thanks. An exceptionally gifted writer himself, he has been my first reader for almost fifty years, always generously available and singularly astute.

Christopher Wells, editor of *The Living Church*, helped this project along by inviting me to write a series of short pieces on Christian spirituality for that publication. These appeared in the fall of 2015. I wish to express my thanks for that opportunity to refine my thinking as well as for permission to incorporate material from those articles.

I am grateful to Nancy Bryan, editorial vice president of Church Publishing Incorporated, for her enthusiastic endorsement of the project ever since Karen Meredith and I first proposed it. I am obliged to her and to Martin Smith, co-author of *Go in Peace: The Art of Hearing Confessions*, for permission to develop my presentation of confession from passages in our earlier book.

I am also indebted to Patricia Zline of Rowman & Littlefield for permission to draw on my book *Three Spiritual Directors for Our Time* (still in print through Wipf and Stock as *The Pastoral Art of the English Mystics*) in my discussion of apophatic mysticism.

INTRODUCTION

The Heart's Longing

"You speak in my heart and say, 'Seek my face.'
Your face, Lord, will I seek." (Psalm 27:11)

The current interest in spirituality, both within and beyond the church, is a healthy sign. It suggests that we have stopped repressing, at least in some quarters, those brushes with God that most people experience, at least from time to time. We have ceased denying the ache of the human heart for something transcendent. Many people do in fact have vivid experiences of God, more often than they might be prone to admit. These encounters with holy mystery sometimes occur in quite ordinary circumstances—walking to work, doing the dishes—as well as in more typically liminal settings. People frequently find themselves overcome by a sense of divine Presence in nature, God's first gift to us. Gazing up at the night sky while setting the household trash by the curbside can suddenly open us up to "the love that moves the sun and all the stars," as Dante put it. If we allow ourselves to reflect on these moments, we may become curious about them. What was *that* all about? Could such an experience happen again? How might I prepare for it?

Embarking on a spiritual path requires us to pay attention to such episodes and to the deep longings of our hearts that may be awakened by them. But what do we really want? Do our yearnings tell us anything about ourselves or the horizons of the world we live in? Consider young children. From the first, human beings are a bundle of desires. Even before they can speak, babies cry for what they want and, just a little later, point to what they demand. As we grow, so does the span of our cravings. Some are rooted in our need to survive and prosper physically; others, in our emotional need for security, respect, and love. From an early age, we are driven by an intellectual hunger to comprehend the world we live in and to take delight in beauty. In time, we develop moral passions: for fairness and honesty, for example. We want to find work that draws upon our best gifts, and relationships that address our need to be understood and, if possible, to love and be loved. Many of our desires are salutary and innocent, but some are not. Sometimes our desires conflict with one other and tear us apart inwardly. Some are dangerous and destructive to ourselves, others, and the fabric of society. A consumer culture tries to inculcate artificial desires for many things we could easily do without, often appealing to our insecurities or greed, reinforcing indifference to our neighbor's more pressing needs or the limitations of our planet.

But underneath all these desires is a profound longing for something we can scarcely describe. Indeed, until we begin to notice that our desires really have no bounds—that they signal an infinite longing woven into our very humanity—our cravings are apt to multiply exponentially, pull us in all directions, and inevitably disappoint, even when we get what we thought we wanted. We begin to mature when we start to notice how manifold—and sometimes contradictory—our wants can be. Of course the fulfillment of some desires brings considerable contentment and joy: satisfying work or a harmonious marriage, for instance. But even these blessings cannot fill up that ceaseless yearning in us for something more, something beyond ourselves, something infinite and absolute. Spiritual growth requires us to drill down to the source of these desires, attempting to name and embrace it.

"God, of thy goodness, give me thyself. For thou art enough to me," cries the fourteenth-century mystic Julian of Norwich. When we allow ourselves to feel the full force of our perpetual yearning, we may discover that God is at the bottom of it. For it seems that God has instilled this infinite desire in us precisely so it might lead us back to Infinite Love. When Julian of Norwich says that "God is enough" for her, she is not pretending she has no other needs. She is not denying that she, like every other human being, requires many things. She is instead recognizing that all our true needs and desires fall under the scope of God's care. When our desire for God is acknowledged, when we boldly pray as Julian does for the reality of God to take hold and move us into the vast abyss of divine love, these other legitimate but subordinate desires gradually fall into place. "Strive first for the kingdom of God," counsels Jesus, "and all these things will be given to you as well" (Matt. 6:33).

Many of the psalms express our universal thirst for God: "As the deer longs for the water-brooks, so longs my soul for you, O God" (Ps. 42:1). Psalm 27 speaks in another vivid metaphor about seeking God's "face." But here the psalmist goes further, pressing his own seeking back to its source. He attributes his pursuit of God to God's pursuit of him: "You speak in my heart and say, 'Seek my face.'" So here is a surprise: it is ultimately God's desire for us that animates our desire for God. The psalmist finds his heart resonating with the word God speaks within it, calling him forward. His search for the face of God is but a response to God's word already sounding in the depths of his being. Naturally, we start with our own feelings. We are most cognizant of our own longings, including our longing for God. Yet in time we may sense, as does the psalmist, that God actually initiates this game of seeking and finding. Or as the First Epistle of John puts it, "We love because he first loved us" (1 John 4:19).

How do we respond to this divine love? Like many people of other faith traditions or none, Christians have lately been awakening to the call to pursue spiritual depth. Just "going to church" is not enough, nor should it be. Yet few people, whether churchgoers or simply spiritual seekers, ever turn to the parish church for guidance in spiritual practice. How many parishes expect their members to become proficient in these things? Since the teaching of meditation and other spiritual disciplines seems to be most available to North Americans in Buddhist or other non-Christian meditation groups, that is where serious seekers usually turn. Yoga classes offer opportunities for physical training coupled with enhanced mind-body integration, often leading to a sense of wellbeing and peace. These are good things. Yet it has been a grave failing in the Christian church to have permitted collective amnesia of its own contemplative tradition, preserved until recently only in monasteries and a few other religious circles. Fortunately, this is beginning to change.

Christian spirituality, however, cannot be reduced to learning a few meditative techniques or to cultivating certain habits aimed at achieving inner tranquility. It is far more encompassing than that. The Christian spiritual path is life itself, lit up by the Holy Spirit. It is linked to moral theology and the cultivation of virtue. It aims for the transfigured life of holiness and is expressed in self-giving service. It is critically shaped at every turn by the vision of faith and sacramental community of which we are a part. There are indeed centuries-old traditions of Christian meditation and other ascetical practices, the topic of later chapters, which we urgently need to recover. But these practices are not free-floating. They find their grounding in another set of practices: the ordinary sacramental life and communal worship of the praying church. But we cannot be content with mere outward observance; it is crucial to grasp the mystical depth of Christian sacramental life. So that is where these reflections begin.

All the practices of Christian spirituality are enmeshed in a distinctive theological vision: a particular way of seeing things, revealed over centuries to Israel and, decisively, in the gospel of Jesus Christ. From this angle, Christian spirituality is concerned with how to make sense of life at its most crucial junctures: death, guilt, forgiveness, and hope. But if Christian spirituality is more than a set of disjointed practices, it is also more than a set of abstract beliefs. Faith reaches into the heart, the existential core, and transforms everything: what we believe and how we live into those beliefs.

It is a mistake to suppose that the practices of Christian spirituality are reserved for a spiritual elite in the church. As we will see, Christian baptism itself implies embarking upon a whole set of practices, both communal and personal, designed to foster union with God and communion with others. These practices are concerned with how we experience God, day in and day out, and become transformed in the process. Christian spiritual practice is thus not an addendum to gospel faith; it springs from it and is integral to it. There exists, of course, considerable variety and richness across centuries, cultures, and traditions in the church about how all this is worked out. Yet underneath this diversity there subsists a basic pattern that can be traced to the earliest generations and which, in one form or another, has been maintained in churches of a catholic character, including the Episcopal and Anglican tradition that informs this book. We begin, then, at the beginning: with baptism.

CHAPTER ONE

Reliving Christ's Death and Resurrection

"What do you seek?"
Answer: "Life in Christ."
—Admission of Catechumens[1]

L ife in Christ begins with baptism. With this sacrament, which many of us received as infants or children, the goal of the mystics—union with God—is already given to us, at least germinally. Yet living into this grace and letting it mold us over the course of our lives will cost us, as T.S. Eliot once said of the mystical way, "not less than everything." And a mature Christian spirituality demands nothing less than making the baptismal identity we received, at whatever age, our own. It requires us to embrace its astounding grace and its demanding commitments day after day and year after year. As we begin our exploration of Christian spirituality, we need first to plunge into the mystery of baptism to experience its depths. Before we can see why baptism shapes Christian life as definitively as it does, we must peel back the layers of cultural conditioning that trivialize it. Many people regard baptism as merely the occasion for a family celebration of a baby's birth—a worthy enough sentiment in itself, but one that falls far short of the spiritual reality of baptism. We have to overcome the impression that the rite of baptism simply issues a membership card in the church, without pondering what it means to become a living member of the living Christ.

---

1. Preparation of Adults for Holy Baptism: The Catechumenate in *The Book of Occasional Services* (New York: Church Publishing, 2004), 117.

Many religions have developed rites involving water. Rituals designed to enact, one way or another, an aspiration for interior purification have often drawn upon the inherent symbolism of this cleansing agent. By the time of Christ, elements within Judaism seem to have evolved forms of proselyte baptism: that is, as part of their initiation into the Covenant people, Gentile converts underwent a ritual bath, by which the filth of paganism was symbolically washed away. When John the Baptist appeared offering a "baptism of repentance," he was most likely building upon this and other ablutionary precedents. Yet the baptism he urged upon his contemporaries also differed significantly from these earlier models. For John's baptism was not intended for Gentiles but for Jews, at least for those who were aware of their need for inner cleansing and renewal. Above all, John's baptism was preparatory and temporary. It was a baptism full of expectation, anticipating its own fulfillment in another, messianic baptism: "I baptize you with water for repentance, but one who is more powerful than I is coming after me. . . . He will baptize you with the Holy Spirit and fire" (Matt. 3:11).

It is remarkable that Jesus begins his public ministry by submitting to John's baptism of repentance since the New Testament and subsequent tradition never attribute personal sin to Jesus. What is Jesus doing in such a compromising situation? He is emphatically taking his stand with human beings in their sinfulness. He is defining the radical scope of his ministry from the outset. It is a position that will elicit criticism throughout his life as Jesus dines with public sinners and, finally, suffers a shameful and ignominious death, crucified between two criminals. His life and ministry and, at the last, his death address our desperate plight: "Those who are well have no need of a physician, but those who are sick" (Matt. 9:12).

When at his baptism Jesus embraces humanity in its sinful condition, the Father embraces him: "You are my Son, the Beloved; with you I am well pleased" (Mark 1:11). The voice from heaven identifies Jesus as Son and beloved servant (Is. 42:1), thus ratifying all that is about to happen in Jesus's ministry. The descent of the Spirit tells us that with the coming of Jesus a new creation is springing into life, even as the Spirit of God moved over the face of the waters in the beginning of creation (Gen. 1:2). The baptism of Jesus is thus both a commencement and a completion. It begins Jesus's public ministry in an electrifying Trinitarian epiphany as God the Holy Spirit descends on Jesus and God the Father manifests him as the Messiah, the Christ. And it brings stunning fulfillment to all the messianic expectation bound up in John's preaching and baptism. The baptism with the Holy Spirit foretold by John is here revealed and established.

Jesus fulfills the course presaged in his baptism through his death and resurrection. After his glorification, the Spirit is released upon Jesus's disciples, transforming them. Having accomplished the mission for which he was sent into the world and anointed at his baptism, Jesus's own pattern of baptism in the Spirit/death/ and resurrection becomes the paradigm for his followers: To be a Christian is to live the Christ-life, share the Christ-death, and enjoy eternal communion with the Father and the Spirit.

"Repent, and be baptized every one of you" (Acts 2:38)

Several New Testament texts work out various implications of participating in Christ's new life through baptism. These passages, written in the middle or latter part of the first century, were enriched by the experience of the church, which had already been living into this reality for a generation or two. A key text for understanding baptism, and an obvious place to begin, comes from St. Luke's description of the very first post-resurrection baptisms in the church (Acts 2). It is significant that these occur on Pentecost Day and are intimately tied up with a series of events that, as they unfold, establish enduring patterns of grace and living.

The time is Pentecost or the Jewish Feast of Weeks. The place is Jerusalem, the holy city—the destination of pilgrims drawn from every quarter of the Hellenistic world. Luke first focuses our attention on the small community of disciples who, after the Ascension of the Lord, have gathered in prayer, awaiting the promised Spirit: the Twelve, certain women disciples, Mary the mother of Jesus, and Jesus's brothers. The messianic baptism by the Holy Spirit and fire foretold by John the Baptist suddenly comes upon them.

Violent wind and flames of fire convey the sheer power and burning intensity of the Spirit's interpenetration, a shared experience of God. Those assembled will never be the same.

What had been a personal event for Jesus at his baptism now becomes communal. With a kind of ripple effect, the grace of Pentecost presses beyond even the original community of disciples. The apostles immediately leave their shelter and begin preaching about Jesus—a very risky business. Something has happened to them: the entirely natural fear of death, common to all sentient beings, has lost its power. Peter, spokesman for the group, explains the new situation. He recalls the crucifixion of Jesus, a well-known event that took place a mere fifty days earlier at the time of Passover. But then Peter announces, for the first time in a public forum, the heart of the gospel: "This Jesus God raised up, and of that all of us are witnesses" (Acts 2:32).

Here is a transformation within a transformation. The disciples are now fearless in the face of death because death has, as St. Paul would put it, lost its sting. The resurrection of Jesus changes everything. Life is no longer confined to the familiar cycle of birth, growth, decay, and death. Something utterly new has happened. Across centuries and cultures there have evolved innumerable myths of death and resurrection, beliefs in reincarnation or the immortality of the soul, and stories of the "afterlife"—all of which attest to a profound human longing. We might cynically or resignedly dismiss these yearnings as mere wishful thinking or the stuff of fairy tales. But in the resurrection of Jesus, God reaches into our deepest hopes and fears. Death does not have the final word. The risen body of Jesus, radiant prototype of the new creation, leads the way.

The raising of Jesus also illumines our moral state of affairs. Surveying the ascendancy of power over justice and privilege over fairness, we might well conclude that "good guys finish last" and wonder along with Jeremiah, Job, and many of the psalms, "Why does the way of the guilty prosper?" (Jer. 12:1). Yet the Bible consistently affirms that God is just. The justice of God is played out in the Pentecost scene when Peter confronts his listeners with their role in Jesus's execution: "This man . . . you crucified and killed by the hands of those outside the law" (Acts 2:23). There must be moral accountability. Like the apostles themselves, who abandoned or denied Jesus, the crowd gathered in Jerusalem cannot pretend innocence. And so Peter's announcement that "this Jesus God raised up" simultaneously convicts and liberates them from both personal guilt and shared culpability. What is more, God's action in raising Jesus is harbinger of the final undoing of injustice and the ultimate defeat of evil. Thus when Martin Luther King Jr. confidently asserted that, "The arc of the moral universe is long, but it bends towards justice," his reading of history was shaped in part by this vision of faith.

What Acts goes on to relate is a blueprint of the conversion process. First, the gospel is proclaimed, and this proclamation has a transforming effect. The crowd is stirred, indeed pierced, by the gospel message: "Now when they heard this, they were cut to the heart" (Acts 2:37). The Spirit, which had invaded the disciples, now moves the assembly to compunction of heart, a rending conviction of sin. Yet they do not stay there, paralyzed by remorse and immobilized by sorrow. They immediately ask the apostles an eminently practical question: "What should we do?" What to do about guilt? What to do about this resurrection? How do we connect with it? Peter replies with a fully practical response: "Repent, and be baptized every one of you in the name of Jesus Christ so that your sins may be forgiven; and you will receive the gift of the Holy Spirit" (Acts 2:38). This is where Christian life—life in Christ—begins: with baptism. It addresses the most crucial issues that confront human beings: life and death, sin and guilt, justice and injustice, forgiveness and hope.

The gospel is proclaimed and the people respond. Baptism is the way forward. This is how we take on a new identity: the paschal mystery of Christ's death and rising becomes ours. So baptism is both a gift of God and our faithful response to the pressure of the Holy Spirit who leads us to conversion in the first place. Is baptism God's work or ours? It is both. God initiates, yet does not override our free response as human beings who have been invited to cooperate with the divine action. This dynamic synergy of God's grace coupled with our effort, which begins at baptism, characterizes all of Christian life. In many cases, we are more aware of one side of this partnership than the other. Sometimes hard human labor or struggle seems paramount. At other times, we can seem almost carried away by grace. But even then, grace needs to find a receptive home. Like a double helix, divine action and human response are inseparably intertwined.

In the case of adult baptism—certainly the typical situation envisioned in the New Testament and early centuries of the church—baptism entails a deliberate personal commitment to Jesus Christ springing from faith in his saving death and resurrection. In the baptism of an infant or young child, the gracious gift of God towards one who cannot yet make a personal response of faith is evident. Yet faith remains an essential component in infant baptism as well. Here it is the faith of the believing community, embodied above all in the covenant promises of the parents and sponsors, which creates the pastoral milieu in which this sacrament can be responsibly administered.

In every case except emergency baptism, the church requires prior catechesis of all parties: whether adult candidates, parents, or godparents. This instruction involves basic teaching: "Conversion of mind" or the capacity to view everything afresh with the eyes of faith is one aspect of conversion. Catechesis also begins the process of learning distinctly Christian habits, practices, and virtues. This formation cannot be hurried. It takes time to learn a new way of thinking and to unlearn old habits of mind and behavior. New Christians and their sponsors need to understand the faith articulated in the creeds, grasp its internal coherence, and experience this faith from the "inside"—as an inner dynamic creating order, insight, beauty, and direction in one's life. Christian formation also entails shedding obsolete and defeating patterns of thought and conduct.

St. Paul insists that baptism forges a union with Christ in his death and resurrection: "Do you not know that all of us who have been baptized into Christ Jesus were baptized into his death? Therefore we have been buried with him by baptism into death . . . so we too might walk in newness of life" (Rom. 6:3–4).How did Paul come to think of baptism as a "burial" with Christ? The metaphor of death and burial would have suggested itself naturally enough since all baptisms at the time took place

Baptism of Christ, fifteenth century, Tver School. *Used with permission.*

by immersion in "living water"—a lake, river, or stream. When the church expanded into climates and regions in which baptism in natural bodies of water was no longer practical, for many centuries churches still built baptisteries (some of them very beautiful) so that baptism could continue to take place with complete immersion of the candidate. Baptism by immersion can be frightening, as the candidate "goes under" three times in a symbolic dying with Christ. Fortunately, some churches have maintained this arresting tradition, including the Eastern Orthodox, and the practice is being revived in some places in the Episcopal Church. One parish church in rural England recently recovered from its neighborhood an old stone watering trough once used for horses, moved it in front of the church, and now uses it for immersion baptisms. The coffin-like shape of an animals' watering trough suits perfectly the action of being buried with Christ in baptism.

For tomb it is. Some traditional icons of the baptism of Jesus show him fully surrounded by dark waters, foreshadowing his own entombment. St. Paul contends that baptism into the "death of Christ" spells an end to the deathly grip of sin over a believer's life, its power to control our choices and actions: "We know that our old self was crucified with him so that the body of sin might be destroyed, and we might no longer be enslaved to sin" (Rom. 6:6). If St. Peter counseled those assembled in Jerusalem on Pentecost to "repent, and be baptized every one of you . . . so that your sins may be forgiven," Paul presents the repentance enacted in baptism as a crucifixion of sin. The language of crucifixion, of course, underscores the spiritual union with Christ in his particular form of death that is accomplished by baptism. What Christ achieved on the cross for our salvation is now part of the believer: he or she has been immersed in this grace. Crucifixion language also highlights the suffering entailed in renouncing sin and struggling against it daily. Repentance is no easy matter. There are layers and layers to sin and thus to repentance, many of which we discover only after years of effort, and countless humiliating lapses. Baptism begins the process of a "death to sin," but it is a death Christians feel every day.

Baptism thus sets us on the "purgative way," a painful cleansing from sin that lasts a lifetime. Writing of the petition "Thy kingdom come," Evelyn Underhill insists that its advent demands costly inner purification: "None can guess beforehand with what anguish, what tearing of old hard tissues and habits, the Kingdom will force a path into the soul, and confront self-love in its last fortress with the penetrating demand of God."[2] As the Spirit gradually sets us free from destructive patterns of "thought, word, and deed," we come to realize just how bent we actually are, and how all-embracing and utterly necessary to us is the gift of grace. Indeed, it is only by grace that we can even begin to see sin for what it is and how deeply its malignant roots penetrate us. Life itself has a way of repeatedly holding a mirror

2. Evelyn Underhill, *Abba: Meditations Based on the Lord's Prayer* (Cincinnati: Forward Movement Press, 1982), 32.

up to our disordered desires and habitual failings. So as we move out of the pseudo-innocence characteristic of the secular mindset, our awareness of the distortions of sin—in ourselves and in the world around us—grows rather than diminishes. Even though our personal entanglement in sin may become objectively diminished over time, grace clears our vision to see things as they are.

The way of purgation is the first component of the ancient threefold path of Christian spirituality: purgation, illumination, and union. All three aspects of this graced paradigm are present, at least in germinal form, in baptism: the renunciation of evil and ongoing death to sin (purgation); the profession of faith and turning towards Jesus as savior (illumination); and participation in Christ's death and resurrection (union). In this context "illumination" means nothing other than the Light of Christ, signified by the paschal candle prominent at every baptism. The radiant truth of Christ now shines upon our entire landscape, revealing its shadows and its beauty. As we continue on the illuminative way, we grow in *insight*: into ourselves, others, and God, perceiving both distinctions and connections. Illumination is intertwined with purgation when our degraded and alienated state becomes painfully clear. But it also opens up the vision of God in Christ. The profession of faith in the Creed is both a summary of this vision and an entry into its continuous unfolding. The grace of illumination bears fruit in such gifts of the Spirit as wisdom, greater understanding of the mysteries of the faith, and discernment. It is, finally, a transformative vision. As St. Paul says of the vision of Christ apprehended in faith: "All of us, with unveiled faces, seeing the glory of the Lord as though reflected in a mirror, are being transformed into the same image from one degree of glory to another" (2 Cor. 3:18).

Our baptismal union with Christ in the paschal mystery unites us, through Christ, to God. We wade deeper into this divine life by love: "Those who love me will keep my word, and my Father will love them, and we will come to them and make our home with them" (John 14:23). Because God is love straight through, we travel the unitive way by loving as Christ loves.

Eventually we come to love with Christ's own love. Not a shred of sentimentality is involved here, for Christ's love embodies self-sacrificial commitment: "This is my commandment, that you love one another as I have loved you. No one has greater love than this, to lay down one's life for one's friends" (John 15:12–13). As Jesus speaks these words at the Last Supper, he is poised to lay down his own life for us, his friends.

We lay down our lives bit by bit, day by day, in service and availability to others. It requires a high degree of vulnerability, connecting us once again to the Love that went to the cross. But as Paul astutely realized, what may appear to be sacrificial love may turn out to be the opposite: "If I give away all my possessions, and if I hand over my body . . . but do not have love, I gain nothing" (1 Cor. 13:3). What can pass as heroic service may spring from spiritual pride, pandering to self-image, or the presumptuous attempt to manipulate and control. Self-deception covers a multitude of sins. Hence the unitive path of love depends upon ongoing purgation of love. It requires the cultivation of what the desert tradition called *apatheia*, usually translated as "detachment" or "indifference." The "detachment" in question is not an icy distancing from others or the goodness of the created order. It rather signals a process by which we gradually become free from our ego-driven compulsions and disordered passions—our "attachment" to status, approval, self-gratification, and the desire to make others over in our image. Only detached love—a love utterly respectful of the mystery of the other—is pure. It alone produces the fruits of love: "Love is patient; love is kind; love is not envious or boastful or arrogant or rude. It does not insist on its own way . . ." (1 Cor. 13:4–5). What union with God entails, then, is not some special, unusual experience of God, however conceived. It is rather participation in the divine life (2 Pet. 1:4) and through that union, sharing in the divine attributes, the foremost of which is love.

The threefold path of purgation, illumination, and union has sometimes been construed as a sequence of stages leading to mature Christian holiness. According to that reading, we progress from purgation to illumination and, finally, to union with God. But as even this brief survey indicates, these facets of Christian life are interpenetrating and overlapping, and they all inform Christian life from baptism onward. Rather than thinking of them as a ladder with ascending rungs, we might conceive of them as a spiral: circling round and round, with one aspect or another strongly coloring our journey at different seasons, we always come back to the others, now experienced with greater intensity. In his comprehensive and wise theology of Christian spirituality, *Beloved Dust: Tides of the Spirit in the Christian Life*, Robert Hughes likens the threefold path to tidal currents: "As in a real ocean, these tides are concurrent, though one may predominate at any given moment in a person's life. This requires us to think and navigate in three dimensions, as it were: pitch, roll, and yaw."[3] Hughes appropriates the threefold way as "conversion, transfiguration, and glory"—terms more common in the Eastern Orthodox tradition—and organizes his treatment of Christian spirituality around these currents of grace.

DYING IN CHRIST: THE BAPTISMAL RENUNCIATIONS

In *The Voyage of the Dawn Treader*, book five in The Chronicles of Narnia, C.S. Lewis depicts a baptismal scene that illustrates both the pain and the grace of embarking on a new life. It occurs in a chapter about Eustace, the thoroughly obnoxious cousin of the Pevensie children, who are now back in the enchanted world of Narnia. In this episode, Eustace has wandered away from his companions and come upon a dragon's lair, full of treasure. In his greed, Eustace puts on a bejeweled bracelet, stuffs his pockets with diamonds, throws himself upon a pile of gold coins, and falls asleep. When he awakens from the pain of the bracelet that is now much too tight, he discovers to his horror that he has become a dragon himself. Eustace's sinfulness—his habitual selfishness, greed, and mocking cynicism—have made him less than human. When in his dragon state he returns to his cousins and others

---

3. Robert Davis Hughes, III, *Beloved Dust: Tides of the Spirit in the Christian Life* (New York: Continuum, 2008), 8.

he had formerly disdained, he appreciates the wholly undeserved comfort and practical help they offer him. His humil-
iation softens him, and for the first time he tries to be useful.
Thus prepared by the beginnings of a moral conversion, Eustace
encounters a mysterious lion, whom readers will instantly recognize as the Christ-like figure of Aslan, who will deliver him
from his plight. Aslan leads him to a mountain in which there
is a garden with a well in the middle of it. As Eustace later narrates to Edmond:

> "I knew it was a well because you could see the water bubbling
> up from the bottom of it: but it was a lot bigger than most
> wells—like a very big, round bath with marble steps going
> down into it. The water was clear as anything and I thought if
> I could get in there and bathe it would ease the pain in my leg.
> But the lion told me I must undress first. . . .
>
> "I was just going to say that I couldn't undress because I
> hadn't any clothes on when I suddenly thought that dragons are
> snaky sort of things and snakes can cast their skins. . . . So I
> started scratching myself and my scales began coming off all
> over the place. And then when I scratched a little deeper and,
> instead of just scales coming off here and there, my whole skin
> started peeling off beautifully. . . . In a minute or two I just
> stepped out of it. I could see it lying there beside me, look-
> ing rather nasty. It was a most lovely feeling. So I started to go
> down into the well for my bathe.
>
> "But just as I was going to put my feet into the water I
> looked down and saw that they were all hard and rough and
> wrinkled and scaly just as they had been before. Oh, that's
> all right, said I, it just means I had another smaller suit on
> underneath the first one, and I'll have to get out of it too. So
> I scratched and tore again and this underneath skin peeled off
> beautifully and out I stepped and left it lying beside the other
> one and went down to the well for my bathe.
>
> "Well, exactly the same thing happened again. And I
> thought to myself, oh dear, how ever many skins have I got to
> take off? For I was longing to bathe my leg. So I scratched away
> for the third time and got off a third skin, just like the two

others, and stepped out of it. But as soon as I looked at myself in the water I knew it had been no good.

"Then the lion said—but I don't know if it spoke—"You will have to let me undress you." I was afraid of his claws, I can tell you, but I was pretty near desperate now. So I just lay flat down on my back to let him do it.

"The very first tear he made was so deep that I thought it had gone right into my heart. And when he began pulling the skin off, it hurt worse than anything I've ever felt. The only thing that made me able to bear it was just the pleasure of feeling the stuff peel off. . . ."

"And there I was as smooth and soft as a peeled switch and smaller than I had been. Then he caught hold of me—I didn't like that very much for I was very tender underneath now that I'd no skin on—and threw me into the water. It smarted like anything but only for a moment. After that it became perfectly delicious and as soon as I started swimming and splashing I found that all the pain had gone from my arm. And then I saw why. I'd turned into a boy again. . . .

"After a bit the lion took me out and dressed me—"[4]

It is worth noticing that Eustace is not a wholly passive partner in his rehabilitation. Once Aslan brings him to the regenerative well, he requires further action from him. Eustace must take off his snakeskin three times, layers upon layers of his corrupted self, reminiscent of the three renunciations of sin in the baptismal liturgy. Eustace can make only limited progress, however, by his own exertions, and in the end he must submit to the still more painful stripping that Aslan alone can accomplish. It is an interplay of effort and grace with which every serious Christian is familiar. Eustace is "afraid of his claws," which indeed cut him to the heart, but desperation drives him to accept Aslan's more penetrating work of slitting and slashing. Imagery of being divested of old clothes and then reclothed in new ones runs through several Pauline texts: "You have stripped off the old self with its practices

---

4. C.S. Lewis, *The Voyage of the Dawn Treader* (New York: HarperCollins, 1952), 107–110.

and have clothed yourself with the new self" (Col. 3:9–10; cf. Eph. 4:24; Rom. 13:14). And it was an image compellingly enacted in the ancient baptismal liturgy when candidates were stripped completely naked before entering the font. A more effective way of dramatizing the abandonment of one's old life can scarcely be imagined, as candidates shared in the utter vulnerability and shame of Christ's own nakedness on the cross. When Eustace emerges from the well, Aslan dresses him in fresh clothes, just as the newly baptized were clothed in white garments, signifying their newly-minted innocence in Christ: "As many of you as were baptized into Christ have clothed yourselves with Christ" (Gal. 3:27). This is, of course, the origin of the white christening gown, and the baptismal robe continues in use as a liturgical undergarment: the alb.

With his "baptism," Eustace is "turned into a boy again," his humanity recovered. This is the goal of baptism: the restoration of a human nature that has been distorted by sin and doomed to death. Only in Christ, the "last Adam" (1 Cor. 15:45), is our humanity fully restored and transfigured. We do not leave the "first Adam" completely behind, however, not even in baptism, but it no longer limits and defines us. Those who are baptized thus share simultaneously in the inevitable mortality and propensity to sin characteristic of the "first Adam" and the resurrected life accomplished by the "last Adam," Christ. We move towards glory as Christ did: by entering the tomb of baptism and emerging into a new plane of existence. The baptismal renunciations and affirmations, which reverberate throughout Christian life, are key moments in this passage.

As Eustace sheds skin after skin, he experiences a sense of liberation and growing lightness. In the baptismal renunciations, candidates tear off allegiances which, like Eustace's snakeskins, are "hard and rough and wrinkled and scaly"—in fact "rather nasty." The renunciations move in a descending scale from the cosmic to the social to the personal: evil in its various guises.

The first question—"Do you renounce Satan and all the spiritual forces that rebel against God?"—sometimes causes consternation among contemporary people. Some might wonder whether the Christian faith demands subscription to literal belief in Satan or the devil. Christian faith requires belief in Jesus Christ and his saving power, as the affirmations attest. Since belief in Satan is not part of the creed, nor is any particular demonology required of Christians, this issue should not be unduly unsettling. Yet it is unwise to distance ourselves too far from the reality to which this mythic language points. From time to time we do encounter evil in raw form. In *The No.1 Ladies' Detective Agency*, the savvy protagonist of this novel finds herself at one point pursuing an African witch doctor. She suspects him of killing an eleven-year-old boy in order to concoct one of his potions:

> She parked the van and drew in her breath. She had faced down fraudsters, she had coped with jealous wives, she even stood up to Mr. Gotko; but this meeting would be different. This was evil incarnate, the heart of darkness, the root of shame. This man, for all his mumbo-jumbo and his spells, was a murderer.[5]

Yet to appreciate the first renunciation we need not go so far as to visit, imaginatively or otherwise, the world of witchcraft or the occult. There is plenty of enslavement to forces of evil much closer to hand. What family, for instance, has not been touched by the scourge of addiction, whether of alcohol, food, drugs, gambling, sex, the Internet, or work? Participants in twelve-step programs are familiar with a sense of struggling against fiercely ruinous impulses that seem to assault from within and without. Such powers feel larger than life, and their malignant energy and direction can only be termed "demonic."

Writing about the traditional baptismal renunciation of "Satan and all his works," theologian Kenneth Leech quite sensibly observes this about "evil spirits": "Whether they were non-human minds external to man, or disturbing forces within the psyche, the result was the same: a reduction of human freedom, and spiritual disturbance." It is thus a mistake to discount, belittle, or ignore such evil forces, no matter their precise location. Nor

---

5. Alexander McCall Smith, *The No.1 Ladies' Detective Agency* (New York: Pantheon Books, 2005), 223.

should we rule out the possibility that malevolent "non-human minds external to man" do in fact exist. Leech continues, citing Archbishop Michael Ramsey: "It is arbitrary to assume that we human beings are the only rational beings, knowing good and evil, in the universe, and it seems to be a reasonable assumption that there are, outside the human sphere, beings who can do good and evil."[6]

So while the first renunciation of evil does not require an unvarnished belief in Satan, it does presuppose our taking full stock of the power of evil. We must relinquish any lingering naiveté about its subtlety and strength. Exorcism characterized much of Jesus's Galilean ministry. Today we would attribute many of the ills ascribed in the first century to "demons" to physical and mental illness. But we miss the mark if we fail to see that Jesus exercised a ministry of deliverance from all forces operating in body, mind, and spirit that undermined human integrity. The traditional mythology of demons understands such forces as alien and non-human. It generously implies that evil does not spring from human nature, but rather afflicts it. The work of grace restores us to our true humanity, just as Eustace "turned into a boy again."

With the second renunciation we turn to the social arena: "Do you renounce the evil powers of this world which corrupt and destroy the creatures of God?" Contemporary development of the social sciences has helped us become more aware than ever of the many ways we are shaped by history and culture. There are some "evil powers of this world which corrupt and destroy the creatures of God" so blatantly that they cannot be missed. The fever of fascism in the decades leading up to the Second World War is an oft-cited example. We find ourselves amazed at its power to sweep up millions in its murderous fervor. Yet the twenty-first century has also been filled with blood and hate, stirred into motion by skewed political, social, and even religious forces, issuing in war, terror attacks, random killings, and gun

---

6. Kenneth Leech, *Soul Friend: The Practice of Christian Spirituality* (San Francisco: Harper and Row, 1977), 131.

violence. In some quarters, publically articulated ethnic bigotry, racial and religious prejudice, and misogyny have even become socially respectable. We seem willing to accept vast and growing economic disparities between rich and poor, in our own country and internationally, as if they were simply inevitable. Most people recognize the scientifically verified fact of climate change—arguably the greatest threat to all forms of life on this planet—but few are willing to contemplate the entirely feasible social and personal changes that would offset some of its more devastating effects. Surely those who cynically benefit from the short-lived status quo are among the most "evil powers of this world which corrupt and destroy the creatures of God." By renouncing them, we also renounce our own indifference and apathy.

Parents and teachers find themselves combating a tidal wave of "evil powers of this world" that seem bent on harming children. The advertising world turns toddlers into consumers and pre-teen girls into objects of sexual attraction. Adolescent peer pressure can take a sinister turn with the unlimited possibilities available in social media for exposure and mocking, leading in some cases to depression and suicide among its victims. The imaginations of children and adults are fed by an entertainment industry that capitalizes on violence, ridicules chastity, discounts honesty, and glorifies greed. What is most insidious about these evil powers is their confident, unquestioned presumption that this is the way the world is and must be. The unspoken message is: You're trapped. You have no choice but to conform. In baptism, we renounce that lie and all the others.

Precisely because we are so thoroughly conditioned by our cultural matrix, we often have difficulty seeing how aspects of our cultural formation may have warped us. Although we can never stand entirely outside our "social location," searching self-knowledge and vigilance can help us gain some perspective. This discipline entails a willingness to confront cultural assumptions, events, and changes in the searing light of the gospel. Sometimes it will mean stepping beyond our political comfort zone. It is easy for religious liberals to expose social sin and for religious conservatives to decry personal sin, and most of us know where we stand on that spectrum. We see the speck in our brother or sister's eye but not the log in our own. Can we learn from the well-informed and conscientious critique of Christians who, because they see things from a different angle, just might be able to identify our blind spots?

The final renunciation hits us where we live: "Do you renounce all sinful desires that draw you from the love of God?" Having renounced evil on the cosmic and social scale, we now tear away the snakeskin of personal sin. We are renouncing everything—all "thoughts, words, and deeds"—that compromise our total dedication to God. Jesus taught that we are defiled by what comes out of our hearts, from the welter of contaminated desires and motives that lodge there: "For it is from within, from the human heart, that evil intentions come: fornication, theft, murder, adultery, avarice, wickedness, deceit, licentiousness, envy, slander, pride, folly. All these evil things come from within, and they defile a person" (Mark 7:21–23). In the Sermon on the Mount, Jesus pressed his listeners to consider the interior dispositions that lie behind the Torah's various prohibitions. What gives rise to murder, for instance, except violent, hateful anger? To adultery, except the cultivation of a lustful imagination? (Matt. 5:21–22; 27–28). Jesus urges us to scrutinize our hearts and explore the landscape of our desires. Often what we will find there is not pretty. Our prayer will then echo the great penitential psalm: "Create in me a clean heart, O God, and renew a right spirit within me" (Ps. 51:11). By renouncing "all sinful desires" that draw us from the love of God we make a start. We express our intention, our direction. We will have to keep working at it. In the end, we will have to let Aslan make the most piercing cut into our hearts: what the ascetical tradition calls "passive purification." Like Eustace, however, we must desire this change and accept its pain. The deep-rooted impurity of our hearts has simply become too burdensome. We want to be free.

Another question soon arises to probe once more the depth of our repentance. In the course of the Baptismal Covenant, the candidate is asked: "Will you persevere in resisting evil, and whenever you fall into sin, repent and return to the Lord?" Although we have just renounced evil three times, we have not yet finished with it. Evil will be waiting to ensnare us just as surely as Jesus, after his own baptism, was driven into the desert to be "tempted by Satan" (Mark 1:12–13). Perseverance—not perfection—is the characteristic virtue of the maturing Christian. Growth in Christ demands persistence to keep resisting the great and small temptations that come our way each day. Perhaps even more importantly, perseverance requires that we "repent and return to the Lord" after each of our humiliating falls. We never outgrow our need for divine mercy; we are sinners to the end. A story from the desert ascetics of the third and fourth centuries relates how a visitor once asked a monk what the brothers did all day. He simply replied: "We fall down and get up, and fall down and get up." Getting up—abandoning self-contempt, despair, and the temptation to stay down—is hard. So we are asked, "Will you persevere . . . ?" In his final words about Eustace's conversion, the narrator closes off the chapter with a recognition that spiritual progress is a slow business:

> It would be nice, and fairly nearly true, to say "from that time forth Eustace was a different boy." To be strictly accurate, he began to be a different boy. He had relapses. There were still many days when he could be very tiresome. But most of these I will not notice. The cure had begun.[7]

So for us all in baptism.

RISING IN CHRIST: THE BAPTISMAL AFFIRMATIONS

With the affirmations we make an emphatic turn-around. In the fourth century in Jerusalem, this about-face was enacted literally as the baptismal candidate, having faced the west during the renunciations, was then turned towards the east for the affirmations. The sun was setting on the old life defined by sin; new life in Christ, "the morning star," was rising. The first topic for affirmation presents the most crucial question we can ever be asked: "Do

---

7. *The Voyage of the Dawn Treader*, 112.

you turn to Jesus Christ and accept him as your Savior?" Like the disciples at Caesarea Philippi, Jesus is asking us, "But who do you say that I am?" (Mark 8:29). Our answer to that question does not so much define *him* as it defines *us*. Here we take our stand with Jesus, accepting the salvation he offers. We regard him not simply as a prophet, a martyr, a teacher, or a healer: common enough designations in his time, and our own. We say that he is our "Savior." He is the one "who for us and for our salvation came down from heaven." It is worth noticing that when the Creed (whether the Nicene or the Apostles') narrates the work of salvation, it starts with the Incarnation. Salvation begins when the Son of God enters the human race by the power of the Holy Spirit, taking flesh from a human mother. Becoming human, he sanctified the whole of creation from the "inside," so to speak. Only two other people are named in the Creeds—Mary and Pontius Pilate—one instrumental in Jesus's birth; the other, in his death. These two personages anchor Jesus firmly in history with all its particularities. Yet the salvation he achieved—everything he accomplished through his life, death, resurrection, and ascension—is universal in scope. So by accepting Jesus as "our Savior," we embrace him as our "personal savior," to be sure; but we are doing more. We are acknowledging him as the savior of all.

With this affirmation, we are admitting that we need to be *saved from* something. But what? Those assembled in Jerusalem at Pentecost heard a twofold message of deliverance: from sin and from death. The proclamation of Jesus's resurrection released them from the crushing burden of complicity in an innocent death: "this Jesus whom you crucified." If God could undo that evil, there could be no bounds to God's power to forgive and recreate lives. They had only to "repent, and be baptized" for their "sins to be forgiven." Yet our need for forgiveness does not stop once the baptismal liturgy is over. It continues over the course of our lives. Again and again we will draw on the grace of the "one baptism for the forgiveness of sins," sometimes in desperate straits because of serious sin; more typically, because of everyday lapses or ingrained habits resistant to reform. The query about repenting "whenever we fall into sin" is utterly realistic. We never outgrow the need for forgiveness. We return to God over and over, and find an infinite wellspring of divine mercy awaiting us. By repeatedly jumping into this ocean of love, we become so saturated with divine compassion that we are able to "forgive those who sin against us" as we ourselves have been forgiven.

Forgiveness is inextricably intertwined with the Easter event. When on Easter evening the risen Lord appears to disciples who have barricaded themselves behind locked doors, his first word to this guilty and fearful band is "Peace be with you." Having in effect absolved them from their cowardly abandonment, he immediately sets in motion a ministry of forgiveness: "Receive the Holy Spirit. If you forgive the sins of any, they are forgiven them" (John 20:22–23). When Jesus later appears to the disciples by the Lake of Tiberius, he restores Peter to fellowship with himself, undoing his threefold denial with a threefold question and affirmation, "Do you love me? . . . Yes, Lord; you know that I love you" (John 21:15–17).

The strength to forgive even mortal enemies is one of the most convincing witnesses to the resurrection. Facing their own imminent death, the martyrs frequently offer such a powerful testimony. Jesus forgave his enemies from the cross (Luke 23:34). St. Stephen, the first martyr, echoes his words as he is stoned to death (Acts 7:60). In our own time, the martyred prior of a Cistercian monastery in Algeria forgave his killer in advance in an extraordinary letter only discovered after his death. In March 1996 he and six of his brothers were kidnapped by Islamic extremists during a civil war. Two months later they were killed under ambiguous circumstances. During the war, the monks had refused to take sides, maintaining a pacifist stance of love towards everyone. This position infuriated all contestants for power, and the brothers knew that their days were numbered. Still, they did not flee, but maintained the quiet witness of their common life of worship, prayer, and service to their Muslim neighbors. In his "testament" Dom Christian de Chergé, prior of the community, disclaims any pretense of personal innocence, aware that the evil of the world now convulsing his beloved

Algeria is part of him, too. In this same remarkable letter he also addresses his future killer:

> I have lived long enough to know that I share in the evil which seems, alas, to prevail in the world, even in that which would strike me blindly. I should like, when the time comes, to have a clear space which would allow me to beg forgiveness of God and of all my fellow human beings, and at the same time to forgive with all my heart the one who would strike me down. . . .
>
> And you, also, the friend of my final moment, who would not be aware of what you were doing. Yes, for you also I wish this "thank you"—and this *adieu*—to commend you to the God whose face I see in yours.[8]

The generosity of the martyrs towards their executioners springs from a transformed apprehension of death. We see a similar calm courage in many people facing terminal illness and the elderly who, aware that they are near life's end, are filled with gratitude rather than bitterness. The witness of a "holy death," while not universal among people of faith, is still very common, and it is always moving. But we do not have to wait for the deathbed to experience how faith in the resurrection of Jesus can change our experience. It permeates our present condition and alters the way we live now. Some people sneer at belief in the resurrection as "pie in the sky when you die." They charge that hope in eternal life fosters indifference both to the beauty of the world and to its suffering. Just the opposite is true. By freeing us from a crippling fear of death, the resurrection of Jesus enables courageous, prophetic, and compassionate action throughout our lives. Sister Constance of the Episcopal Community of St. Mary and her companions— the "martyrs of Memphis"—responded to the Yellow Fever epidemic of 1878 by caring for the sick and dying, knowing that it was only a matter of time before most of them would succumb as well. There are innumerable, similar examples of recognized and hidden service, undertaken at great personal cost, throughout

8. Christian de Chergé, "Last Testament," trans. Monks of Saint Bernard Abby, Leicester, England, *First Things* 65 (August/September 1996): 21.

Christian history right up to the present. Accepting Jesus as our "Savior" means stepping into a realm of ultimate freedom. What we are *saved from* is death and, in our lifetimes, the disabling fear of death. Death will certainly come to us, one way or another. But as Doris Westfall has said, "The Easter message is that the worst thing to happen to us is never the last thing to happen to us."[9]

The next two affirmations intensify the foundational promise to "turn to Jesus Christ and accept him as our Savior." If we thought that faith was just a matter of subscribing to a set of creedal propositions, we are here confronted with the challenge of a faith that is fully personal: "Do you put your whole trust in his grace and love?" Faith in anyone, and certainly in Jesus, means trusting him, but such confidence does not spring up instantly. We come to trust people over time, sensing their steadiness of character through all sorts of circumstances. People prove themselves trustworthy; there is no other way for trust to be instilled. The same process holds true in our relationship with God. Deep down, many of us wonder whether God really loves us, either because we have inherited harsh images of God, or because we doubt whether we are really loveable, or both. We will never be able to place our "whole trust in his grace and love" without a vibrant, ongoing relationship with Christ. By using all the means at our disposal, including prayer, meditation, sacrament, worship, and study, we can come to know Jesus in an altogether personal way. We can let him show us just how trustworthy he is. For baptismal life will be hard, that much we know; only the form that difficulty will take is unknown. We can assume that it will be arduous to die daily to sin, to "persevere in resisting evil," but what other sacrifices might be asked of us? We cannot know the full extent of them. At times we will be tempted to give up, wondering whether we have it in us to endure. Knowing full well our own weakness, we turn once again to Jesus, placing our "whole trust in his grace and love." Even if we falter, he will not fail us.

With the final affirmation we move from attitude to action: "Do you promise to follow and obey him as your Lord?" When

9. Sermon preached at Grace Episcopal Church, Kirkwood, Missouri, on May 6, 2014.

Jesus called his first disciples, he simply said, "Follow me." Responding to the call to follow Jesus sets us on the path of discipleship and connects us to a community of disciples. Jesus deliberately gathered a group of his followers around himself, forming them by teaching and example, and keeping company with them in everyday life. They travelled, prayed, and worked together. In the end, these first disciples witnessed his death and resurrection. Finally, the Risen One sent them out to make new disciples, and we are their heirs. St. Matthew's Gospel concludes with the risen Lord's issuing a resounding mandate and breathtaking promise: "Go therefore and make disciples of all nations, baptizing them in the name of the Father and of the Son and of the Holy Spirit, and teaching them to obey everything that I have commanded you. And remember, I am with you always, to the end of the age" (Matt. 28:19–20). This "Great Commission" is loaded with meaning. It defines discipleship actively: Jesus's followers are entrusted with bringing the gospel to every corner of the earth. Disciples are made, not born, through teaching and obedience, as one generation after another hands on what Jesus himself taught his apostles. Baptism "in the name of the Father and of the Son and of the Holy Spirit" is charged with divine power. To do anything "in the name of" a higher authority—whether of a king or of God—is to do it as a surrogate, as one representing that very regal or divine authority. And finally, the Lord's promise to be with us always assures us that his presence among us is real and palpable. God is not far off: Jesus remains Emmanuel, God-with-us. We know Jesus in the community of his disciples, the church. We continually experience him from the inside, as an abiding presence.

We may wonder how any of this can apply to the baptism of babies and children, who cannot understand the significance of what is taking place. Yet in the natural order of things children inherit all sorts of conditions which they will only understand later, if at all: their DNA, for instance, or a windfall bequest. God graciously gives all the baptized the fullness of life in Christ: sharing his death and resurrection; becoming members of his body, the church; the indwelling of the Holy Spirit; even the forgiveness of sins. Babies do not need forgiveness now for personal sins, but they will later. For all children are born into a world, society, and family warped by sin; and all children are born with a death warrant hanging over them. Baptism pushes our boundaries beyond these limitations into the freedom of forgiveness and the joy of resurrection. The baptismal renunciations and affirmations prepare us for the core commitments of the Baptismal Covenant. Here the candidate professes faith in God, who is Father, Son, and Holy Spirit. The question-and-answer form of the creed reflects ancient baptismal usage. The Apostles' Creed itself is based on an early Roman baptismal creed. Unlike the corporate confession of faith ("We believe") of the Nicene Creed used in the Eucharist, the Apostles' Creed exhibits its baptismal origins in the "I believe" format. In the liturgy of baptism the candidate must confess personal adherence to God, revealed as Father, Son, and Holy Spirit.

The creeds of the church are sometimes disparaged as a dry set of dogmas imposed from above. This charge, however, creates a false dichotomy between "creedal faith" and "heart faith," true to neither the baptismal liturgy nor Christian experience. The baptismal affirmations themselves, as we have seen, unify the believer's faith on several levels at once—mind, heart, and will—as the candidate confesses faith in Christ, affirms trust in Christ, and pledges obedience to Christ. Within the household of faith, the creeds serve as summary statements—a kind of distillation—of the church's lived experience of God. Most of their language is drawn from Scripture. Even when the Nicene Creed employs philosophical terminology, it does so to clarify, not obscure, what we know of God in Christ and the Spirit. When baptismal candidates profess faith in "God the Father . . . in Jesus Christ, the Son of God . . . in God the Holy Spirit," they are aligning themselves with generations of Christians before them. They are not joining a "Christian club," in the way one might join a political party or action group. Nor are they subscribing to a particular philosophy, in this case, a Christian one. They are making a confession of faith—a personal yet shared witness and testimony. The candidates will then be baptized in the name of the one God they have come to know as Father, Son, and Holy Spirit for Christian spiritual experience is radically Trinitarian. Thus the significance for Christian spirituality of baptism in the threefold name can scarcely be overestimated, as we shall see.

What immediately follows is a key commitment to a distinctive way of life: "Will you continue in the apostles' teaching and fellowship, in the breaking of bread, and in the prayers?" This, too, serves as a crucial framework for the practice of Christian spirituality. The four terms of this promise are identical to the patterns of living described in Acts 2:42, immediately after the first Pentecost baptisms: "They devoted themselves to the apostles' teaching and fellowship, to the breaking of bread and the prayers." These promises constitute a corporate Rule of Life—that is, a set of practices which Christians embrace so that the life of Christ, begun in baptism, can flourish in them.

It should be apparent by now that Christian spirituality is a fundamentally corporate exercise, not a solitary quest, though it contains individual dimensions. Such a corporate context makes the practice of Christian spirituality both easier and harder. Easier because we live out Christian discipleship not solely on our own but within a community to which we are accountable and which is accountable to us. The faith community is the Body of Christ of which we become members at baptism. As part of this Body we participate in the sacraments, and are built up by the teaching, preaching, guidance, and companionship we receive. The church, ideally at least, should be there to support us through the varied challenges we face with prayer, counsel, and fellowship. But as we all know from family life at least, "community" can be a mixed blessing. We can be disappointed in our local church, usually our parish, for any number of reasons. Or we may be disheartened by larger trends in the church. People invariably let us down sometime or other. We can find the faults, pettiness, limitations, or more monumental failings of our fellow Christians a hard pill to swallow. And certain personalities can be just plain irritating. Yet we promise to be part of the church—the "fellowship"—in a vital way for the rest of our lives. There is an arduous asceticism involved in belonging to the church's fellowship, just as in any form of family or community. It is a primary way we learn to "die to self" in order to live in Christ. It is among the most distinctive features of

Christian spirituality, and we must undertake the pledge to continue in the apostolic fellowship with our eyes open to its graces and its suffering.

When we promise to "continue in the apostles' teaching and fellowship, in the breaking of the bread, and in the prayers" we embark upon a way of life that has characterized Christians from the first. There are four somewhat overlapping elements to this corporate discipline: fidelity to apostolic teaching; involvement in the fellowship of the church; participation in the Eucharist (the "breaking of bread"); and observance of "the prayers." This last item probably refers to the round of Jewish devotion that punctuated the day at set intervals: evening, morning, and mid-afternoon. Whenever possible, devout Jews joined with others at the temple or synagogue for this service of psalms, prayers and, at least on the Sabbath, lessons from Scripture. Otherwise these daily devotions were performed at home, in a spirit of solidarity with other members of the Covenant community. As we learn from Acts, first-century Jewish Christians continued to join in these communal prayers. Over time, this devotional matrix developed into what we know as the Daily Office. The rule of life embedded in the Baptismal Covenant is so defining for Christian spirituality that later chapters will be devoted to discussing each of its elements. For now, it is sufficient to note that the baptismal life entails active participation in the community of the church as well as the performance of specific practices.

The final three promises of the Baptismal Covenant turn us beyond ourselves to evangelism and service. Since the liberating word of the gospel is not for ourselves alone, we will "proclaim by word and example the Good News of God in Christ." Naturally, we want to make the joy we have discovered in coming to know Jesus available to others. It takes generosity and courage to share something of our faith or to invite people to consider what the Christian church has on offer. It also requires us, as we do so, to honor the final promise of the Baptismal Covenant to "respect the dignity of every human being"—including someone's freedom to reject Christian faith or any faith at all. Without succumbing to timidity, we need considerable wisdom, tact, and discernment to know when and how to fulfill the command to "make disciples" in our own cultural context. Yet there will be opportunities to speak of Christ and his church to unbelieving or lapsed family members, colleagues, neighbors, or total strangers. We also effectively proclaim the gospel "by example." "Example" includes every aspect of faithful adherence to Christian belief and practice, including unstinting service. The second promise of this trio, to "seek and serve Christ in all persons, loving your neighbor as yourself," directs us to ongoing, sacrificial ministry. Nothing is more converting than love.

BY WATER AND THE HOLY SPIRIT

Most obviously, baptism involves *water*. Utterly commonplace, yet increasingly precious, water encompasses a wide range of disparate associations, many of which are captured in the baptismal rite. We begin to be born when our mother's amniotic sac breaks and we leave the aqueous environment of our first nine months. We need water for cleansing, and we delight in a good shower or a refreshing swim. For some who have suffered hurricanes and floods, water is a feared and destructive force. For all of us, water is essential. Plants and animals require water to survive and thrive. Astronomers scan near and distant planets for traces of water, a necessary condition for even the most primitive forms of life. Our own planet seems awash in water; but increasingly clean, available, and potable water is becoming scarcer, with climate change causing flooding in some areas and drought in others. We are beginning to realize just how valuable this substance is and how it must be conserved and protected.

Water imagery, drawing on these natural resonances, abounds in the Bible. Water is mentioned in the opening verses of the Book of Genesis when the Spirit activates creation (Gen. 1:2). The Holy Spirit appears again over water at the baptism of Jesus as a new creation is inaugurated. The story of the Great Flood dramatizes the destructive potential of water by cleansing the earth of sin, while the Crossing of the Red Sea involves both destruction (for the pursuing Egyptian army) and salvation (for the escaping Hebrews). Already in the New Testament some of these water events began to be understood allegorically as prototypes of baptism. Exodus itself, the foremost instance of salvation in the Old Testament, came to be seen as a foreshadowing of salvation through baptism. Just as the ancient Hebrews were delivered from the bondage of slavery by passing through the waters of the Red Sea, so new Christians are delivered from the bondage of sin by entering the waters of baptism. Several of these biblical allusions are woven together in the opening words of the Thanksgiving over the Water in the liturgy of Holy Baptism:

> We thank you, Almighty God, for the gift of water. Over it the Holy Spirit moved in the beginning of creation. Through it you led the children of Israel out of their bondage in Egypt into the land of promise. In it your Son Jesus received the baptism of John and was anointed by the Holy Spirit as the Messiah, the Christ, to lead us through his death and resurrection, from the bondage of sin into everlasting life.

This solemn prayer continues with nearly direct quotation from St. Paul's Epistle to the Romans, where he interprets baptism as effecting union with Christ in his death and resurrection. It also affirms the infusion of the Holy Spirit, promised in Acts 2:38. Hence "baptism in the Holy Spirit," characteristic of the messianic age, is not relegated to some future, post-baptismal event. It is not the result of a dramatic conversion experience. The Holy Spirit is given in sacramental baptism, a feature of rebirth in Christ. We are baptized by water and the Holy Spirit:

> We thank you, Father, for the water of Baptism. In it we are buried with Christ in his death. By it we share in his resurrection. Through it we are reborn by the Holy Spirit.[10]

And so, after plunging the candidate three times in the water of baptism, the bishop or priest marks the forehead with chrism— that is, olive oil that the bishop has previously blessed for this

---

10. *The Book of Common Prayer* (New York: Church Hymnal Corporation, 1979), 306. All future references to the BCP are given in the text.

purpose. "Chrism" and "Christ" are etymologically related words. "Christ" (*Christos* in Greek) means "Messiah" or the "Anointed One." Just as Jesus was anointed by the Holy Spirit as the Christ or Messiah at his baptism, so the newly-baptized are anointed with the Holy Spirit at theirs: "You are sealed by the Holy Spirit in Baptism and marked as Christ's own for ever." We are thus "christened." We belong to Christ; we become "another Christ" through the sanctifying and creative energy of the Holy Spirit.

Chrism is applied to our foreheads in "the sign of the cross" (BCP, 308). It is a terrible and glorious moment. Once again the death of Jesus is stamped on our flesh and thus into our souls. Then the newly baptized are usually given a small candle lit from the large paschal candle: we are led "through fire and water." Signifying the light of the Risen Lord, the paschal candle stands near the font. Its use at baptism is bound up with the other distinct occasions when it is employed in the liturgies of the church. Lit from the new fire kindled at the Great Vigil of Easter, the paschal candle is most plainly on display during the Great Fifty Days of the Easter season. It stands near the font at every baptism, and it stands next to the coffin at the burial liturgy. Thus the light of the Risen Christ frames baptismal life from font to grave.

For the baptized, Jesus's death and resurrection are not simply stupendous events, evoking our awe and gratitude. They do not stand outside us as something to admire—or even believe in—from the remote past. Baptism links us to them. It is how Jesus's death and resurrection get inside us. From the moment of our baptism, our very identities are shaped by these realities. The baptismal liturgy dramatizes and enacts the process of becoming one with Christ by sharing in his death and resurrection. It is a process that reverberates through every season of life. We never get to the bottom of it, and it becomes the lens through which we interpret the world and the events of our life.

PASCHAL MYSTERY

Suffering and death are everywhere, from roadkill to mass shootings to tsunamis: "We know that the whole creation has been groaning in labor pains until now, and not only the creation, but we ourselves . . ." (Rom. 8:22–23). Paul's metaphor of "labor pains" implies that suffering is woven into the process of creation from the very start, and it continues through the birth of the new creation. "Life is suffering" is the first of Buddhism's Four Noble Truths. All sentient beings suffer, and even what we might regard as the inanimate creation is in some sense in travail as stars explode, galaxies form, volcanoes erupt, and tectonic plates laboriously shift. Over the millennia the scale of human suffering alone from warfare, disease, and scarcity has been monumental. Even if we happen to be among those who enjoy relative security, our lives are riddled with both physical and mental suffering: disappointment, illness, pain, loss, bereavement, failure, dislocation, and shame.

Theologians often distinguish between horrendous evils (including natural disasters, exceptional losses, and heinous crimes) and the ordinary forms of suffering common to all.[11] But in no case does God *send* suffering our way. Jesus saves us from the manifold evils we have committed and liberates us from those which afflict us. We particularly need deliverance from horrendous evils and healing in their aftermath. Those who have endured appalling evil or outrageous pain are one with the Crucified. As with Jesus's own suffering, such afflictions cannot be rationalized. They never "make sense." Yet the other sort of sufferings—ones that come through the daily vicissitudes of life—can play an educative and purgative role. We can view them as sheer bad luck and so learn nothing from them, growing ever more bitter. Or we can notice how God might be effecting our deeper conversion through them. According to Robert Hughes, in most cases God uses the material closest to hand—our experience of life with its various developmental stages—to work the ongoing conversion we need:

---

11. It is the horrendous evils which usually constitute the "problem of evil." See Thomas G. Long, *What Shall We Say? Evil, Suffering, and the Crisis of Faith* (Grand Rapids, MI: Eerdmans, 2011) for a compelling treatment of the issue.

God provides ordinary life with all its ups and downs as the pedagogy, school, or discipline by which we are formed as persons for the fellowship and citizenship of God's reign, the dominion of love. As long as we remain unconverted and stuck in the mire, we will continually be offered by life a series of shocks inviting us to get unstuck, to give up our illusions and disillusions, resentments, judgments, and unwarranted expectations, to get in touch with reality, and unleash our co-creativity with God. This is not life as a "test," but a setting in which the Holy Spirit makes concrete offers for self-transcending growth. . . . One of the mysteries of the graciousness of ordinary life is that as long as we are stubbornly refusing to learn a particular lesson, we will be vouchsafed an endless series of annoying opportunities to learn it.[12]

There are also distinctive forms of spiritual suffering which many people assume separate them from God: a sense of the absence of God, for instance, or the silence of God. Yet a sense of abandonment by God actually unites us to Jesus in his own dereliction on the cross. This theme runs through Japanese novelist Shūsaku Endō's gripping novel *Silence*, set in seventeenth-century Japan. It is the story of an idealistic Portuguese missionary who secretly enters Japan after Christianity has been banned and terrible persecutions are underway. The situation rendered in the novel is historically accurate: during the period 1614–1640, five or six thousand Christians were martyred, most of them Japanese peasants.[13] The priest, who spends his brief ministry in hiding until his inevitable capture, repeatedly asks God why he permits his children to suffer as they do. But this, like nearly all of his prayers, is met with resounding silence. On only one night, as he "felt the face of Christ looking intently at him," did an answer seem to come: "I will not abandon you" (113). Another time, after the priest had witnessed the forced

---

12. Hughes, 106–107.

13. William Johnston, "Translator's Preface" to Shūsaku Endō, *Silence* (New York: Picador Modern Classics, 2016), xviii. Subsequent references given in the text are to this edition.

drowning of Japanese Christians who had befriended him along with the death of his sole missionary companion, he meditates on the face of Jesus in the Garden of Gethsemane. He then asks himself:

> On that night had that man, too, felt the silence of God? Had he, too, shuddered with fear? The priest did not want to think so. . . . The rainy sea into which Mokichi and Ichizo had sunk, fastened to stakes! The sea on which the black head of Garrpe, chasing after the little boat, had struggled wildly and then floated like a piece of drifting wood! The sea into which those bodies wrapped in straw matting had dropped straight down! This sea stretched out endlessly, sadly; and all the time, over the sea, God had simply maintained his unrelenting silence. "Eloi, Eloi, lama sabacthani!" With the memory of the leaden sea, these words suddenly burst into his consciousness. "Eloi, Eloi, lama sabacthani!" It is three o'clock on that Friday; and from the cross this voice rings out to a sky covered with darkness. The priest had always thought that these words were that man's prayer, not that they issued from terror at the silence of God. (147–148)

The priest is beginning to grasp the paradox of the cross. For the experience of abandonment by God is precisely a form of union with God. We can find ourselves in the same spiritual territory as Jesus, as he cries out in anguish, "My God, my God, why have you forsaken me?" A sense of the absence of God or the silence of God does not in fact separate us from God. It is one of the most real if painful ways by which we are "united with Christ in his death."

In the riveting conclusion of *Silence*, Endō dramatizes an almost unthinkable case of union with Christ in his passion: fidelity to Jesus through the act of apostasy. The priest at this point has been in prison for some time, interrogated by the authorities, and urged to commit the act Japanese officials have devised for indicating abandonment of the Christian faith: stepping upon an image of Jesus. In the case of this priest, such a step would be a singularly painful act of treason to his Lord. Despite the silence of

God that he has suffered in prayer, the beloved face of Jesus in his meditations has been a regular source of comfort and companionship. Yet the authorities are especially keen to have priests commit apostasy in order to demoralize the thousands of secret, lay Christians. Rather than subject the priest himself to physical torture, which might backfire as a heroic martyrdom, they instead force him to hear the groans of other Christians, suffering a horrendous, slow death, suspended headlong over a filthy pit containing corpses and excrement. The agony will cease and the prisoners be released only if the priest agrees to set his foot on a copper image of Jesus crowned with thorns. In this hell of moral ambiguity, the priest decides, "to perform the most painful act of love that has ever been performed":

> The priest raises his foot. In it he feels a dull, heavy pain. This is no mere formality. He will now trample on what he has considered the most beautiful thing in his life, on what he has believed most pure, on what is filled with the ideals and the dreams of man. How his foot aches! And then the Christ in bronze speaks to the priest: "Trample! Trample! I more than anyone know of the pain in your foot. Trample! It was to be trampled on by men that I was born into this world. It was to share men's pain that I carried my cross." (183)

In this act of love, the priest loses everything dear to him: his Christian identity, his priesthood, his self-respect. He can never return to his homeland. But in the self-emptying, kenotic act by which he "tramples" on Christ, he is profoundly united to him. He "dies in Christ" more completely in this act of apostasy than in any version of heroic martyrdom that was his early dream. Although to outward appearances he seems to save himself by a fatal compromise, in reality he has turned himself inside out in sheer self-giving love. He has become Christ, utterly one with Jesus in his passion and death—yet he does not know it.

Recent centuries, including our own, have also produced thousands of martyrs. Most readers of this book, however, will probably not be called to witness to Christ by that ultimate sacrifice nor be faced with anything like the ordeal of Endō's main character. Yet our own sufferings—whether physical, emotional, or spiritual—are real enough. We who have been "buried with Christ by baptism into death" experience his death every day in innumerable ways—some small, and some momentous. Many of these "death" experiences are common to everyone. Baptism into Christ's death frees us to face them. "Marked as Christ's own for ever" with the sign of the cross, we can stop pretending that we are not growing old, or that our bodies are not slowly wearing down, or that death is only a remote possibility—an accident befalling the unlucky. The cross liberates us from an oppressive culture that tells us that being young, beautiful, healthy, well-regarded, and if possible, rich, is all that matters. The cross allows us to walk into hospitals, nursing homes, and funeral homes without being overcome with revulsion. It permits us to experience losing our job, losing our health, or losing our spouse without losing Christ. For Christ is present in all our losses until, finally, we lose even life. Through all these divestments, we dive ever more deeply into the grace of baptism: union with Christ in his death and resurrection.

Every day we hear and see terrible events on the news: warfare and the hosts of refugees it produces; earthquakes and airline crashes; domestic violence and abused children; epidemic drug addiction, the human cost of economic downturns; and the public denigration of minorities. Obviously, baptism obliges us to work, as we have opportunity, for justice, human betterment, and the integrity of creation. But baptism gives us something more fundamental than an appropriate sense of moral responsibility: it gives us vision. St. Ambrose (339–397) referred to baptism as an "illumination." In baptism we begin to see things clearly: It is life with the lights on. Above all, the clarity of baptism sheds light on the suffering of the world. Jesus's passion and death become the interpretive key to tragedies that seem otherwise random, meaningless, or just plain evil. Evil may indeed be operative, as it was at Golgotha. But because suffering is of a piece with Christ's own cross, it is invested with immense, though often paradoxical, dignity. Union with Christ in his death, first forged in baptism, inevitably joins us in sympathy with all who suffer, even as it joins us spiritually with Christ. As we grow into baptismal grace, we find this other dimension lurking just under the surface of ordinary human suffering: We begin to notice the presence of Christ Crucified in our afflicted neighbor, and Christ's quiet companionship in our own trials. If we see the suffering Christ in the suffering "other," moral obligation is transposed into compassionate love: love for the Christ who is present though in disguise.

Suffering serves as a kind of connective tissue for the whole human race, and in his humanity, Jesus embraced every bit of it. As Rowan Williams writes,

> If we ask the question, "Where might you expect to find the baptized?" one answer is, "In the neighborhood of chaos." It means you might expect to find Christian people near to those places where humanity is most at risk, where humanity is most disordered, disfigured and needy. Christians will be found in the neighborhood of Jesus—but Jesus is found in the neighborhood of human suffering, defencelessly alongside those in need.[14]

We experience resurrection, as St. Paul did, embedded in travail itself: "We are afflicted in every way, but not crushed; perplexed, but not driven to despair; persecuted, but not forsaken; struck down, but not destroyed; always carrying in the body the death of Jesus, so that the life of Jesus may also be made visible in our bodies" (2 Cor. 4:8–10). Without the resurrection to enliven his experience of suffering, Paul would have been both afflicted and crushed, perplexed and driven to despair, persecuted and forsaken, struck down and destroyed. But he is not. The Risen Christ illumines everything. How else could Shūsaku Endō's afflicted Christ speak from the bronze icon? According to the gospel accounts, the risen Jesus repeatedly displays his wounds: they are not left behind. Christ is both crucified and risen, and baptism is immersion into both sides of this paschal mystery. The resurrection irradiates present affliction with hope streaming to us from the glory yet to be revealed.

---

14. Rowan Williams, *Being Christian: Baptism, Bible, Eucharist, Prayer* (Grand Rapids, MI: William B. Eerdmans, 2014), 4.

CHAPTER TWO

Communion with Christ

"Then they told . . . how he had been made known to them in the breaking of the bread." (Luke 24:35)

We would scarcely expect to encounter the One through whom "all things were made" in a bit of bread and a sip of wine. Yet if we consider the short but tantalizing resurrection narratives, we notice that the Risen Christ is typically unrecognized, at least at the start. The evangelists are unabashedly candid about the disciples' lack of perception when they first meet Jesus returned from the dead. Mary Magdalene mistakes him for a gardener—until he speaks her name. St. Matthew concludes his gospel with the eleven apostles going to an appointed mountain in Galilee: when they see the Risen Lord, "they worshipped him, but some doubted." The epilogue to St. John's Gospel relates how the risen Jesus once stood on the beach as the disciples concluded a night of unsuccessful fishing. Even after discussing their unproductive venture with him, they still failed to recognize Jesus. Only when they take his odd advice about casting their net off the other side of their boat—and then take in an enormous haul of fish—does the penny drop. "It is the Lord," cries the beloved disciple. Later, when they return to shore, Jesus cooks them breakfast—a meal that includes the fish they have just caught and bread which Jesus already had at hand, which he breaks and distributes among them. Nearly all the resurrection stories contain these elements of doubt or non-recognition of a Jesus who is now somehow strange and elusive. Yet the disciples eventually come to perceive him, often by doing something very familiar: eating with him. Nowhere in the gospels is this theme more dramatically presented than in the account of the disciples en route to Emmaus (Luke 24:13–35).

The story takes place on Easter Day. By now the women have been to the tomb, so some report of the resurrection is already out. But since their announcement to the Eleven of the empty tomb and the angelic message had been dismissed as an "idle tale," the disciples remain in grief and unbelief. The next episode picks up with two other disciples, not members of the inmost circle of the Eleven, traveling to the village of Emmaus seven miles from Jerusalem. Like all bereaved people, the two disciples need to take in their new situation. Talking things over with others who are grieving is one way people try to make sense of a life and a death, especially when circumstances defy all reckoning. The disciple named Cleopas and his companion are therefore reviewing "all these things that had happened," going over the extraordinary and tragic events of Jesus's final days in Jerusalem. A stranger falls in with them. It is "Jesus himself," Luke tells us, but "their eyes were kept from recognizing him." Jesus plays dumb and inquires about their topic of conversation. After expressing amazement that anyone in Jerusalem could be ignorant of the recent *cause célèbre*, they describe how their religious leaders had handed over Jesus, a "prophet mighty in deed and word before God and all the people," for crucifixion. Their wrenching disillusionment becomes apparent when they acknowledge that "we had hoped that he was the one to redeem Israel." Now, obviously, that hope is dashed. Grief, for them, is compounded with a sense of religious disorientation and bewilderment. Had they misread all the signs of grace at work in Jesus? The disciples round off their tale by mentioning the women's astonishing report from the tomb, but indicate that it came to nothing, even after further investigation.

Jesus does not mince words. "Oh, how foolish you are," he begins. He then explicates the two most revered sections of the Hebrew Scriptures—the Torah and the Prophets ("Moses and all the prophets")—elucidating passages "about himself" and pointing out that it was "necessary that the Messiah should suffer these things and then enter into his glory." We are not told precisely which Scriptures Jesus brought forward for interpretation nor *why* the Messiah had to suffer. That great theological question remains unanswered. Nevertheless, as we noticed in our

The Road to Emmaus. J. Kirk Richards, 2011. *Courtesy of the artist.*

consideration of baptism, Jesus, by associating inevitable suffering with the mission of the Messiah, invests that suffering with unexpected dignity. He removes the mark of sheer disgrace from crucifixion. As Jesus interprets his own suffering to the disciples, aligning it with God's saving purposes, implicitly he does something more: He shows the disciples how to understand their own experience of suffering, including their recent grief and sense of dislocation. So also for us. The suffering embedded in our creaturely condition is sanctified and transformed by union with Christ's affliction.

As the threesome approaches the village that is its destination, Jesus makes as if to continue on the road. But the two disciples point out that it is getting very late, and he goes in to stay with them. Then, during the meal, Jesus does what he had done so often for them in the past: "he took bread, blessed and broke it, and gave it to them." This characteristic gesture is immediately recognizable: "Then their eyes were opened, and they recognized him; and he vanished from their sight." This fourfold action—taking, breaking, blessing, and sharing the bread—is the setting for numinous encounter with the Risen Lord.

There are two significant sequels to this moment of electrifying insight. First, the disciples come to understand what had happened along the road. They begin to identify, although only in retrospect, their experience of Jesus as one who explicates Scripture with searing clarity: "Were not our hearts burning within us while he was talking to us on the road, while he was opening the scriptures to us?" they ask. In the course of that elucidation, Jesus had revealed to them a new dimension to Scripture, as sacred text revealing "the things about himself." Then, after the disciples have validated their discovery with each other, they instinctively return to the larger community of disciples for further confirmation and blessing. They go back to Jerusalem, find the Eleven, and learn that the Lord has also appeared to Simon Peter. The community is newly bound together in thanksgiving and wonder. The two disciples then report their own double revelation: how Jesus opened the meaning of Scripture along the road and later made himself known to them in the breaking of bread.

In the course of transmitting foundational accounts of the first encounters with the Risen Lord, the resurrection narratives offer crucial hints about how he *continues* to be present among us. The Emmaus story must have exploded within the church for whom Luke was writing. Those gathered for the Eucharist would have found themselves situated directly in that story. They would have grasped immediately how it illuminated what they were experiencing at that very moment: the opening of Scripture and the breaking of bread. For from the first Christians came together on the Day of Resurrection—what came to be known as the "Lord's Day"—for "the breaking of bread." Continuing a tradition going back to synagogue worship, they would have begun their service with psalms, hymns, and readings from Scripture. At first, these lessons would have been similar to those read in the synagogue—passages drawn from what we call the Old Testament. In time, the readings would be augmented by letters from Paul or other apostles and, eventually, written gospels would be read to the assembly. In other words, the service began with a "Liturgy of the Word" and then continued with the "Breaking of Bread"—the Liturgy of Holy Communion. The Emmaus story would have confirmed what these Christians knew from their weekly experience: that it is Christ who speaks to them through the Scriptures and who illumines their meaning. It is Christ to whom the Scriptures point, and from him they derive new, searching levels of significance.

Over the centuries, and despite wide variation in language and culture, the structure of the eucharistic liturgy has remained fundamentally the same: There is a Liturgy of the Word, followed by a Liturgy of the Sacrament. Christ's risen presence suffuses the entire rite. He is present in the gathered community, for the church is the Body of Christ. He speaks to us through the scriptural lessons and through the proclamation of the gospel. His Holy Spirit animates our intercessions. Above all, we offer the Eucharistic Prayer—the Great Thanksgiving—"by him and with him and in him." And like the disciples at Emmaus, we know him with compelling vividness in the breaking of bread, as Jesus takes, blesses, breaks, and gives us that bread which is his very self. In Holy Communion we are united with him and with one another, constituted once again as the Body of Christ.

And yet like the disciples en route to Emmaus we also can be blind to the company of Christ. Many things conspire to "keep our eyes from recognizing him." The Emmaus disciples were hindered by their presuppositions. Although they had heard rumors of Jesus's resurrection, they did not expect to meet him risen from the dead! They were, moreover, preoccupied with their grief: confused, downcast, and disillusioned. So their state of ignorance and unbelief, combined with an array of disconsolate emotions, turned them in upon themselves. They could not "see" Jesus. Because we are apt to suffer from the same incapacity, the collects for Easter Wednesday and the Third Sunday of Easter, when this gospel is read, begin: "O God, whose blessed Son made himself known to his disciples in the breaking of bread: Open the eyes of our faith, that we may behold him in all his redeeming work." The grace of spiritual illumination, conferred in baptism but always in need of deepening, sheds light on what is transpiring in the sacraments, enabling us to perceive Christ at work in them.

If we want to meet the Risen Jesus as we travel along the road of our lives, desperately trying to make sense of them, we can always meet him in the Eucharist. When we are with him there, we breathe in a new atmosphere: the air of resurrection. Christians have sensed this from the first, and for this reason the Day of Resurrection, the first day of the week, became the preeminent day of Christian worship. Although the Bible clearly mandates a Saturday Sabbath, and although the first Jewish Christians continued to observe this holy day (as did Jesus), the overwhelming significance of the Resurrection as the day for the "breaking of bread" gradually brought about the audacious transfer of the principal day of worship from Saturday to Sunday. The joy and thanksgiving that permeated the Sabbath was not left behind, however, but taken up into this new feast. Coming as it does at the conclusion of the "six days of creation," the Sabbath is a day of rest for the purpose of communal worship, over family meals and in the synagogue, to celebrate the wholly gratuitous divine act of creation. It is no accident that nearly all our Eucharistic Prayers begin with reference to the gift of creation. We therefore give thanks to God for setting in motion and sustaining this marvelously evolving universe, even as we give thanks for the "new creation" wrought by the resurrection of Christ.

The First Day of the Week is also, by another reckoning, the "Eighth Day." That day presses us beyond our ordinary reckoning of "seven days of the week" into another dimension of time: into time beyond time. The resurrection of Jesus confronts us with our own future: our eternal, resurrected life with Christ. In many places, church art and architecture seek to express this mind-stretching reality in diverse ways. Baptismal fonts are often designed in an octagonal shape, indicating that the newly baptized, who now participate in the resurrection life of Jesus, have crossed over to a new plane of existence. Upon entering an Eastern Orthodox church, one is immediately struck by the icons all around. The presence of saints and angels, and the beautiful depictions of Jesus and Mary, indicate that the worshipper has stepped into another reality: heaven. A similar intimation is conveyed very differently in many medieval European churches, which often depict the Last Judgment over the western door. The position of this scene carries various messages. As the usual door of entrance through which everyone—kings, bishops, nobles, scholars, craftspeople, peasants, and children—had to pass, it declared that all, no matter their station in this life, must come under the judgment of God. But even more, as the final action of God in history, the Last Judgment scene stands as a hinge, on the other side of which is eternity. To enter the church—as we do at baptism—is thus to pass under divine judgment and then find oneself in heaven. By distinct artistic strategies, then, both Eastern and Western traditions evoke the sense that entering the church building renews the sacramental "change of location" entailed in baptism; and as the locus of Christian worship, the church is the place where the eucharistic feast offers a foretaste of the heavenly banquet.

In his parables, Jesus often likened the kingdom of heaven to a great feast, and sometimes to a marriage feast, which, in the culture of the day, was a lavish social occasion, often lasting for days at a time. Such nuptial imagery had its roots in the Old Testament, where in prophets such as Hosea and Isaiah, the Lord is depicted as the bridegroom of Israel. It is worth observing that the marriage is not between God and the solitary soul but between God and his *people*. It is an image of covenant fidelity and tender affection.

This same imagery reaches forward to the final book of the Bible. The concluding chapters of the Book of Revelation celebrate a richly symbolic marriage of "the bride and the Lamb." The "bride" here is a composite figure: "the holy city, the new Jerusalem, coming down out of heaven from God, prepared as a bride adorned for her husband" (Rev. 21:2). Above all, she stands for a purified and perfected Church, whose "fine linen is the righteous deeds of the saints" (Rev. 19:8). As in the prophets, this final vision of union between Christ, the Lamb of God, and the Church employs corporate and social imagery, in fact *urban* imagery: "the holy city, the new Jerusalem." As in Jesus's parables, the Marriage of the Bride and the Lamb takes place at a great wedding banquet;

and as in the parables, we are invited to it. The angel speaking to the seer proclaims: "Blessed are those who are invited to the marriage supper of the Lamb" (Rev. 19:9). This is a marriage that could only be consummated by a supper, by eating together, by Communion. We are blessed indeed to share in it even now.

In the eucharistic liturgy, the words leading up to the Sanctus, and the Sanctus itself, convey this sense of participation in celestial worship. At the conclusion of the Preface, the celebrant prays: "Therefore we praise you, joining our voices with Angels and Archangels and with all the company of heaven, who for ever sing this hymn to proclaim the glory of your Name." Then follows the Sanctus, which begins with the chorus of "Holy, holy, holy"—a chant taken from the stupendous vision granted the prophet Isaiah. At the time of his call in the Jerusalem temple he apprehended seraphs, majestic and awesome angelic figures, calling out these words to one another, glorifying God (Is. 6:1–8). The ritual taking place in the temple in Jerusalem, like our own liturgy, drew worshippers into this higher praise, the earthly counterpart of what goes on eternally in heaven.

Because the presence of the Risen Lord suffuses the Eucharist, we have access through him to an intensified communion with both visible and invisible realities, including the "communion of saints." Baptism first initiates us into this vast community of all who are bound together in Christ. The communion of saints encompasses both the living and the dead, in all times and places, and it has some very practical consequences. It means we are never alone, even in situations of complete physical solitude. We always live enmeshed in a powerful spiritual network, and what we do or fail to do affects everyone else. Our membership in the communion of saints is also the ground of intercessory prayer; our union with one another in Christ makes prayer for one another effective, as we shall see. Our spiritual community is therefore the widest imaginable, making us contemporaries even with those who have lived before us: we are "citizens with the saints and also members of the household of God" (Eph. 2:19). Sometimes people wonder how they can be near to those they love, but who have died. Such yearnings can drive people to occult practices or, more typically, to salutary customs such as visiting the gravesite. But our beloved dead are nowhere closer to us than at the Eucharist, where we enjoy communion in the Risen Christ along with "all the company of heaven." Jesus binds us together by uniting us to himself. His risen presence makes us present to one another. He bridges the incalculable distance between the living and the dead.

At the conclusion of Alan Paton's classic novel *Cry, the Beloved Country*, the Reverend Stephen Kumalo seeks a communion with his estranged son Absalom, who is alive but will soon be dead. The story is set in South Africa in 1946. Kumalo has withdrawn to a mountaintop refuge not far from where he serves as the Anglican priest in a beautiful but remote village. He has come to this place of brief retreat before, in other times of personal crisis. Now he faces the wrenching loss of his only son Absalom, who will be executed in far-away Pretoria at dawn the next day for the murder of a white man. The scene is saturated with biblical and liturgical allusions.

Like Elijah fleeing to Mount Horeb, or like Jesus going up to a mountain to pray, Kumalo seeks the solitude and wide horizon afforded atop a mountain. He goes there, above all, to pray. Once he arrives at the summit, he inevitably begins thinking about Absalom: "His heart went out in a great compassion for the boy that must die." But then his thoughts quickly devolve into the self-flagellating "what if's" that torment many a parent whose child has gone astray. He soon realizes, however, that these ruminations are a distraction from the business before him: "He turned aside from such fruitless remembering, and set himself to the order of his vigil. He confessed his sins, remembering them as well as he could since the last time he had been in this mountain."[1] After a forthright confession of his particular sins, he "prayed for absolution." The next part in his order of service is thanksgiving mingled with intercession: "Then he turned to thanksgiving, and remembered, with profound awareness, that he had great cause for thanksgiving, and that for many things. He took them one by

---

1. Alan Paton, *Cry, the Beloved Country* (New York: Simon and Schuster: 1987), 308. All subsequent references are to this edition.

one, giving thanks for each, and praying for each person that he remembered" (309).

After midnight, Kumalo's thoughts turn to "all those that were suffering," and especially to his son. Echoing the words of the biblical King David upon learning of the death of *his* son Absalom, Kumalo cries out: "My son, my son, my son." He then prays at length for him (310). As the hour of execution draws closer, Kumalo ponders Absalom's spiritual and mental state as the young man moves towards death. After considering possible scenarios, Kumalo finally longs for God to intervene through a ministering angel, who could lead his child to heaven: "Is there not an angel that comes there and cries, This is for God not for man, come child, come with me?" (312). With his mind now fixed on heaven, Kumalo prepares himself for the dawn by engaging in a repast whose eucharistic resonance is unmistakable:

> He looked out of his clouded eyes at the faint steady lightening in the east. But he calmed himself, and took out the heavy maize cakes and the tea, and put them upon a stone. And he gave thanks, and broke the cakes and ate them, and drank the tea. Then he gave himself over to deep and earnest prayer, and after each petition he raised his eyes and looked to the east. And the east lightened and lightened, till he knew that the time was not far off. And when he expected it, he rose to his feet and took off his hat and laid it down on the earth, and clasped his hands before him. And while he stood there the sun rose in the east. (312)

The dawn is the hour of execution. It is also, as Kumalo knows, the hour of resurrection. He gazes towards the east, which "lightened and lightened." Did the old priest's heart also become lighter as he took part in the familiar, sacred ritual of giving thanks, breaking, eating, and drinking? Was not the stone upon which he placed his cakes his altar that day? As he gives himself over to "deep and earnest prayer," he enters into communion with the Risen One who was also executed as a criminal. And in Christ, he gains communion with his son, moving from life to death to the life of the world to come.

"For as often as you eat this bread and drink the cup, you proclaim the Lord's death until he comes." (I Corinthians 11:26)

At the Last Supper, Jesus looked forward to the future banquet of the kingdom of God. Concluding the meal with the blessing of the cup, he announced to the Twelve: "Truly I tell you, I will never again drink of the fruit of the vine until that day when I drink it new in the kingdom of God" (Mark 14:25). Although Jesus shared countless meals with his disciples, friends, and even the most socially-scorned sinners, it was at this Last Supper before his death that he gave definitive shape to a meal "in remembrance" of him. The gospels differ on the precise nature of this final supper: was it a Passover celebration or not? The synoptic gospels (Matthew, Mark, and Luke) all say that it was. The Gospel of John presents a different chronology. It places the crucifixion of Jesus on the Day of Preparation for the Passover (John 18:28). Paul may be in agreement (see 1 Cor. 5:7). The Last Supper, then, would have taken place on the evening *before* Passover. Students of the Scriptures have never agreed as to which tradition is the more historically accurate, with learned defenses of both positions continuing to be written. Be that as it may, we may safely say that thoughts of Passover were certainly in the air during Jesus's last days, and we may note that in other parts of the New Testament, the death and resurrection of Jesus—and the Supper that connects them both—are already interpreted through Passover motifs.

The Passover commemorates what for Jews is the greatest of all God's saving acts: their deliverance from slavery in Egypt. The specifications for this meal are described in Exodus 12, a portion of which is read as the first lesson for the Maundy Thursday Eucharist. The meal centered upon an unblemished lamb, a year-old male, which is roasted entire. What is not eaten by a family, perhaps combined with another household, had to be burned. The lamb is, in other words, completely immolated. Exodus 12 also specifies that the animal's blood, which Jews always drained before cooking, was in this case to be smeared on the doorposts and lintel of their houses. This was a signal for the Lord to "pass over" the homes of the Hebrews on that fateful night when he would strike down every first-born animal and human among the Egyptians. The Hebrews are thereby "saved by the blood of the lamb."

Unleavened bread and bitter herbs are eaten with the lamb. Later tradition connected the bitterness of the herbs with the sharpness of slavery. The unleavened bread carried multiple meanings. Bread made without yeast was linked with the haste with which the Hebrews had to consume this first Passover, the night before their tense early departure from Egypt. The Festival of Unleavened Bread, however, harkens back to an even older springtime agricultural celebration lasting seven days, which entailed ridding the house of yeast. A natural fermenting agent, yeast spoils over time, as it is passed from batch to batch. The annual ritual of discarding rancid yeast became, naturally enough, in Hebrew and other cultures, emblematic of personal and communal renewal: "turning over a new leaf" and getting a fresh start.

The traditional Passover is a festive liturgical meal usually celebrated at home. (The synoptic gospels portray Jesus and his disciples gathered in a pre-arranged banquet room, an understandable provision for a group of men separated from their families and bound together by their relation to Jesus.) It consists in telling the story of the Exodus; blessings over the foods, including the unleavened bread and cups of wine; the breaking of the bread by the host and its distribution by him to those gathered for the meal; prayers and the singing of psalms; and of course, eating together. As a sacred meal, the Passover is more than a *looking back*; it is also a *making present*. The ritual makes participants in the meal participants in the story: They become the people who took part in the Exodus along with their ancestors. A contemporary Passover Haggadah reflects this ancient sensibility when it declares: "In every generation one must look upon himself as if he personally had come out of Egypt." When Jesus says, "Do this in remembrance of me," he is employing this liturgically rich Jewish sense of "remembrance." By telling the story and eating the meal, we are engaged in far more than a mere reminiscence. The event of the Last Supper, and all that it implies, becomes present to us. We become participants in it.

At this final meal Jesus dramatically anticipates his death the following day by the words he says over the bread and the cup of wine. The earliest written account of that action comes from St. Paul, writing to the Corinthians around the year 55, decades before the gospels were committed to writing. Paul is clearly passing on an oral tradition preserved in the church. Its verbal resemblance to the gospel accounts is remarkable, and this similarity testifies to its importance in the ongoing life of the church:

> For I received from the Lord what I also handed on to you, that the Lord Jesus on the night when he was betrayed took a loaf of bread, and when he had given thanks, broke it and said, "This is my body that is for you. Do this in remembrance of me." In the same way he took the cup also, after supper, saying, "This cup is the new covenant in my blood. Do this, as often as you drink it, in remembrance of me." For as often as you eat this bread and drink the cup, you proclaim the Lord's death until he comes. (1 Cor. 11:23–26)

Paul interprets the ritual repetition of the eating and drinking enjoined by Christ at the Last Supper as tantamount to proclaiming "the Lord's death until he comes." This linkage to the Lord's death is bound up with the words Jesus pronounced at that critical moment: "This is my body." His body would be handed over that night to those who would abuse it, strip it, and crucify it. This is the body Jesus gives as bread to his disciples. "This is my blood" (as Mark and Matthew render Jesus's words) would have been even more shocking to a group of Jews, for Jews scrupulously avoided ingesting blood. Blood was considered the life, the "life blood," of the animal. Since all life came from God, the Torah mandated draining blood from an animal upon slaying it for sacrifice, food, or both (Gen. 9:4; Deut. 12:16). The life of the animal was in this way acknowledged as returning to God.

Blood was also a vital aspect of the sealing of the Covenant, temple sacrifice, and the expiation of sin. In the solemn ratification of the Sinai Covenant Moses took basins of blood from the sacrificed animals, dashing half upon the altar and half upon the people, saying, "See the blood of the covenant that the Lord has made with you" (Exod. 24:8). Blood thus becomes the connecting fluid binding God and the people in a covenantal relationship. On the annual Day of Atonement, the priest, himself consecrated with blood, would sprinkle blood upon the altar as an expiation for sin (Lev. 16). And in the daily animal sacrifices offered in the temple, dashing the blood against the sides of the altar or smearing it upon the altar's horns was essential to the ritual.

All these associations form the background to Jesus's words over the cup: "Drink from it, all of you; for this is my blood of the covenant, which is poured out for many for the forgiveness of sins" (Matt. 26:27–28). The blood of Jesus would be "poured out" the next day. Like a slain animal, he would have his blood separated from his body on the cross, the immolated Lamb of God. St. John makes much the same point by his variant chronology: Jesus dies in the late afternoon of the Day of Preparation, at the very hour when lambs were being slaughtered for Passover.

In his treatment of the Lord's Supper, Paul refers explicitly to Jesus as the paschal lamb (1 Cor. 5:7). Paul has been exhorting the Corinthian church to engage in suitable ethical conduct. They have been radically changed, he argues, by Christ, the Passover lamb. Since the celebration of the Passover meal commenced the seven days' Festival of Unleavened Bread, Paul joins the image of the paschal lamb to that of unleavened bread, underscoring the need for fresh yeast—that is, for renewed behavior:

> Do you not know that a little yeast leavens the whole batch of dough? Clean out the old yeast so that you may be a new batch, as you really are unleavened. For our paschal lamb, Christ, has been sacrificed. Therefore, let us celebrate the festival, not with the old yeast, the yeast of malice and evil, but with the unleavened bread of sincerity and truth. (1 Cor. 5:6–8)

After the solemn silence following the Breaking of the Bread or "Fraction," the liturgy echoes these words of Paul's to announce:

Christ our Passover is sacrificed for us.
Therefore let us keep the feast.

The liturgy, therefore, brings into our *present time* the saving events of the *past*. Whenever we celebrate the Lord's Supper "in remembrance" of Jesus, we proclaim all that he accomplished for us and the whole creation. In the Great Thanksgiving we rehearse the full sweep of these saving acts: Jesus's incarnation, ministry, death, resurrection, ascension, and sending of the Spirit. But in remembering these events, we are not just calling them to mind. By the power of the Holy Spirit, they become present to us. Our words in the Eucharist, as in all the sacraments, are *effective* signs. The Greek word *anamnesis*, usually translated as "remembrance," is the key term for this time-bending character of liturgy. It refers to the "making present," through the Holy Spirit, those events we recall and by which we are saved. These events, which took place at a certain time in history, are not repeated, but their grace is fully available to us. We participate in them; we are "there."

Not only are the *past* actions of Christ available to us, but we also touch our *future* with him. The "last things"—the consummation of the kingdom of God in the *eschaton*—breaks into the present, and we step into this eschatological time beyond time. The Eucharist is thus our foretaste of the heavenly banquet. Memory and anticipation, past and future, link together in a brief moment of eternal present. As one Greek Orthodox theologian has put it, "The Spirit changes linear historicity into *presence*. . . . the Church's *anamnesis* acquires the Eucharistic paradox which no historical consciousness can ever comprehend, i.e. the *memory of the future*."[2] This conjunction of past, present, and future is expressed succinctly in the "mystery of faith" proclaimed by celebrant and people alike during the Eucharistic Prayer: "Christ has died, Christ is risen, Christ will come again." The proclamation itself makes it so: we are simultaneously stretched towards the past and towards our future with Christ.

2. John D. Zizioulas, *Being as Communion* (Crestwood, NY: St. Vladimir's Seminary Press, 1985), 180.

"You are what you eat."
(Victor Lindlahr, Nutritionist, 1942)

The sacraments are grounded in nature. The need of every living thing for water transposes in baptism into the sacrament of new birth and cleansing: What water does in nature it does supernaturally in baptism. And just as every animal and plant must have water to live and thrive, so all animate creatures need some form of nourishment. Human beings, however, tend to make what is necessary for mere survival into something more. Eating becomes dining; food becomes cuisine. While we could stay alive by eating bland food all by ourselves, we would prefer whenever possible to make eating pleasurable: tasty food in company with others. By a very strong instinct, human beings across cultures recognize that eating together creates bonds of community. When we eat food, especially the same food, with other people, we experience a sense of unity with them. A process based on the physical metabolism of nutrients can serve as the means towards an emotional, social, and even spiritual enrichment. When the food that passes into our bodies and *becomes* our bodies is shared with another person or group, that same source of life now binds us to one another. Hence meals taken together often strengthen the core of family identity and harmony, especially when eating is combined with sociable conversation. And what families know from their experience is true also for colleagues, friends, and community groups. People get together for "a bite to eat" or just "a cup of coffee." Hospitality, even when impromptu, always entails offering food or at least something to drink.

Some meals, even in fast-paced and fast-food America, have symbolic significance. Thanksgiving dinner unites not only families but also the nation. It is infused with a common store of national mythology, taught from childhood, with youngsters drawing Pilgrims and turkeys from kindergarten on. It is the only meal in mainstream American culture whose menu, like Passover dinner, is "scripted." When people across the country partake of the same foods, more or less, out of the same adherence to tradition, a wholesome feeling of national unity is bolstered. The force of

Thanksgiving dinner for family bonding is so strong that airports and roads are clogged with travelers intent on getting home for this one dinner. Birthday celebrations are also laden with their own secular liturgies. Here the presentation of the birthday cake is the centerpiece, along with singing the requisite song, blowing out candles, and making a wish. If an invited guest to the birthday party is ill or otherwise away, what happens? A piece of the cake is sent home so that the absent friend can still participate by extension. Eating makes us one.

Such powerful intuitions underlie the communion meals common to many religions. Eating a sacred meal unites participants to "the gods" and to each other. Of the many sacrifices performed in ancient Israel, some involved consuming part of the animal or cereal offering by the worshippers. And while the Passover was not so much a temple as a domestic celebration, it entailed eating a ritual meal and drinking ritual cups of wine while retelling the sacred story. The Lord's command to eat and drink in remembrance of him, therefore, grew out of this rich religious context which, in turn, is founded upon instincts embedded in human nature itself.

Yet the particular words spoken by Jesus over the bread and the wine were utterly unprecedented. "This is my body" and "This is my blood" convey a graphic realism that heightens the sense of sacred meal inherited from Jewish tradition. Insisting that the Corinthians avoid eating in any social situation that could be construed as pagan worship, Paul recalls to them what the Lord's Supper really is: "The cup of blessing that we bless, is it not a sharing in the blood of Christ? The bread that we break, is it not a sharing in the body of Christ? Because there is one bread, we who are many are one body, for we all partake of the one bread" (1 Cor. 10:16–17). The Greek word here translated as "sharing" is *koinonia*. It is variously rendered in other parts of the New Testament as "participation," "fellowship," and "communion." *Koinonia* is the word patristic theologians would later use to describe the inner life of the Trinity. And when Paul speaks about our participation in that divine life, he says: "The grace of the Lord Jesus Christ, the love of God, and the *koinonia* of the Holy Spirit, be with all of you" (2 Cor. 13:14). To have *koinonia* in the body and blood of Christ is, therefore, to share sacramentally in the fullest possible way in Christ's own life. So powerful is this *koinonia* that it binds us to each other as "one body" because the bread and wine make us one with Christ.

Writing in the mid-second century, Justin Martyr offers a precious glimpse of early Christian worship. The continuity between the basic order of worship he describes and our own liturgical pattern is remarkable. The Eucharist, which takes place on Sunday, begins with a service of the word, in which "the memoirs of the apostles or the writings of the prophets are read," followed by an address delivered by the presider. Next come prayers, and then the kiss of peace.[3]

> Then there is brought to the president of the brothers bread and a cup of wine mixed with water, and the president takes them and sends up praise and glory to the Father of all through the name of his Son and of the holy Spirit, and he makes thanksgivings at length for being considered worthy of these things by him. And when he has finished the prayers and thanksgiving all the people present give their assent saying "Amen." . . . Those called deacons amongst us give to each of those present to partake of the Eucharistized bread and wine and water, and they carry it away to those who are not present. (65.3, 5; 253–55)

In his *Apology* Justin does more than recount the components of the service and its progression; at critical junctures he also interprets key aspects of the Eucharist for his non-Christian readership. It is telling that he attests to a vividly realistic view of the consecrated elements of bread and wine, comparing them to the physical body of Jesus the Incarnate Word. Justin also insists on the necessity of baptism for all those participating. Baptism prepares them for sharing in Christ's body and

---

3. *Justin's Apology on Behalf of Christians* in *Justin, Philosopher and Martyr*, ed. Denis Minns and Paul Parvis (Oxford: Oxford University Press: 2009), par. 67.3–4, 259; par. 65.2, 253. Subsequent references, which first give the paragraph and verse number corresponding to the Greek text and to the translation, and then the page, are to this edition.

blood by confessing faith in him, by a cleansing from sin, and by spiritual rebirth.

> This food is called among us "Eucharist," of which it is lawful for no one to partake except one believing the things that have been taught by us are true, and who has been washed in the washing which is for the forgiveness of sins and for rebirth, and who lives in just the way that Christ handed down. For we do not receive these things as common bread or common drink. But, just as Jesus Christ our Saviour was made flesh by means of a word of God, and had flesh and blood for our salvation, just so we have been taught that the food that has been Eucharistized through a word of prayer which comes from him is the flesh and blood of that Jesus who was made flesh—from which food our flesh and blood are nourished by metabolic process. For the apostles, in the memoirs which they caused to be made and which are called gospels, handed down in this what Jesus commanded them. Taking bread and giving thanks, he said: "Do this in memory of me, this is my body," and taking the cup and Eucharistizing it he said: "This is my blood," and he shared it with them. (66.1–3; 257)

As is evident from this fascinating account of second-century worship, the eucharistic elements were not regarded as "common food or common drink." They had been changed—"Eucharistized"—by a "word of prayer" made in faithful obedience to the Lord. Justin does not deny that the bread and wine are ingested by believers through ordinary "metabolic process." They are eaten like any other food. But they are in fact not like any other food, not "common food or drink." By adherence to Jesus's command to "Do this in memory of me," they become "the flesh and blood of him who was made flesh." Justin, like theologians after him, is attempting to express the mysterious truth of Christ's exceptional eucharistic presence. In declaring that the bread and wine become "the flesh and blood of him who was made flesh," Justin is advancing a vigorously incarnational theology of the sacrament. Bread and wine are earthy things, he seems to be saying, just as the human Jesus is earthy, fleshly. The two realities are intimately connected; the sacraments are an aspect of the mystery of the Incarnation. Christian worship requires embracing this earthiness, the Word made flesh now present to us in the bread and wine. Subsequent theology would speak of Christ's eucharistic presence "in" the bread and wine or "under" the elements of bread and wine. Words fail us, as indeed they must. Yet in every age the church still tries to articulate this aspect of our faith as best she can.

In the high Middle Ages the term "transubstantiation" began to be used to describe the change in the elements of ordinary bread and wine during the course of the Eucharist. Medieval Western theologians were applying categories they had learned from Aristotelian philosophy to the eucharistic mystery. According to Aristotle, a "substance" was what something really was; and an "accident" was a property incidental to the substance. For instance, "human being" would be a "substance"; "brown eyes" would be an "accident." Applied to Holy Communion, this meant that the "substance" of the bread and wine was "transubstantiated" during the Eucharistic Prayer: What they really became were the body and blood of Christ. The "accidents" (what we might call their physical properties—appearance, taste, touch, and smell) remained the same. Some Lutheran theologians later used the expression "consubstantiation" to convey much the same idea: the body and blood of Christ were the "substance" together with ("con") bread and wine.

These efforts to articulate the transforming grace of the eucharistic prayer should not be scorned. Theologians of this period were seeking to express what happens during the Eucharist by drawing on the best scientific categories available to them, just as we seek to integrate and probe what we learn from scientific inquiry with our faith. The limitations of this endeavor when dealing with the unfathomable mystery of Christ's unique presence in the eucharistic elements, however, are obvious. When in time a particular scientific worldview is superseded, the categories of that science become dated, and theological language based upon those categories becomes obsolete. The Roman Catholic Church, which inherited the word "transubstantiation," today recognizes the problems associated with the term as a way of

explaining how Christ becomes present. The 1971 Agreed State-
ment between Anglicans and Roman Catholics on *Eucharistic
Doctrine* contains this helpful note:

> The word *transubstantiation* is commonly used in the Roman
> Catholic Church to indicate that God acting in the Eucharist
> effects a change in the inner reality of the elements. The term
> should be seen as affirming the *fact* of Christ's presence and of
> the mysterious and radical change which takes place. In con-
> temporary Roman Catholic theology it is not understood as
> explaining *how* this change takes place.[4]

The faith-affirming use of this traditional term by Roman
Catholics and others is therefore congruent with an Anglican
approach. For Anglicans have generally refrained from trying to
explain *how* Christ is present in the consecrated bread and wine.
Our Eucharistic Prayers simply state that holy presence. The
transformation of the bread and wine comes about through offering the entire prayer of Thanksgiving. The invocation of the Holy
Spirit (*epiclesis*) upon the elements makes this explicit: "Sanctify
them by your Holy Spirit to be for your people the Body and
Blood of your Son, the holy food and drink of new and unending life in him" (BCP, 363). Other ecumenical statements have
similarly testified to the extraordinary gift of Christ's eucharistic presence. The so-called "Lima Document" (*Baptism, Eucharist
and Ministry*), the fruit of more than fifty years of ecumenical
dialogue among a wide range of church traditions, attests to the
hopeful and growing consensus about the presence of Christ in
the Eucharist. Such statements add clarity to our common witness. Correcting some notions that Christ's eucharistic presence
depends upon the spiritual state of the believer, thus making
Christ's presence wholly subjective, this document instead stresses
something objective—Jesus's fidelity to his promises:

> Christ fulfills in a variety of ways his promise to be always with
> his own even to the end of the world. But Christ's mode of

---

4. *Eucharistic Doctrine* in *The Three Agreed Statements* (London: CTS/SPCK, 1978),
10, note 1.

presence in the Eucharist is unique. Jesus said over the bread
and wine of the Eucharist "This is my body . . . this is my
blood. . . ." What Christ declared is true, and this truth is fulfilled every time the Eucharist is celebrated. The church confesses Christ's real, living and active presence in the Eucharist.
While Christ's real presence does not depend upon the faith of
the individual, all agree that to discern the body and blood of
Christ, faith is required.[5]

DISCERNING THE BODY

Faith, indeed, is necessary to discern the body and blood of
Christ in the Eucharist. St Paul warns against partaking of the
supper without such discernment. He maintains that those who
"eat and drink without discerning the body, eat and drink judgment against themselves" (1 Cor. 11:29). He even goes so far
as to suggest that those who share in the Lord's Supper "in an
unworthy manner" will be "answerable for the body and blood of
the Lord." Why such vehemence? Here as elsewhere in his letters Paul brings theological insight to bear on pastoral matters.
He is alert to the power of holy things. If you touch a high volt-
age electrical wire, the effect will be the same whether you were
aware of the danger or not. In our casual ethos, where churches
take pains to make everyone feel "comfortable" (although there
is much in the gospels to discomfort), it takes some mental
readjustment to appreciate Paul's argument. Paul is sounding
a theme that will later appear throughout the New Testament,
including the gospels, but he is applying it to our eucharistic
situation: contact with the Lord brings judgment. "Judgment"
sounds like a harsh word to us, and our therapeutic culture urges
us to be "non-judgmental"—an admonition often taken to mean
setting aside any sort of ethical standards. But in the Bible divine
judgment confronts us with truth—something people of faith
welcome, even yearn for. It brings to light the sham, duplicity, lies,

---

5. "Eucharist" in *Baptism, Eucharist and Ministry*, Faith and Order Paper no. 111
(Geneva: World Council of Churches, 1982), paragraph 13.

and injustice that riddle nations and wreck them. It exposes the secrets of our hearts so they can be purified. To be in the presence of Christ is to encounter that light.

Paul therefore urges preparation for the Eucharist: "Examine yourselves, and only then eat of the bread and drink of the cup" (1 Cor. 11:28). Because we "proclaim the Lord's death" at every celebration, sharing in the supper indicates our readiness to lay down our lives in union with Christ, once again, in faith and love. It also bespeaks our desire to meet our risen Lord and be renewed by him. In other words, every Eucharist brings us into that paschal mystery of Christ's death and resurrection into which we were baptized. It deepens baptismal grace while requiring us, at least implicitly, to reaffirm our commitment to it. What we are "examining," then, is our willingness to live the grace-filled, sacrificial lives of the baptized, approaching the holy table with faith. For this reason in the first few centuries of the church's life, those preparing for holy baptism—the catechumens—were dismissed from the assembly before the Liturgy of the Table. It simply did not apply to them. While today anyone may stay through the entire liturgy, only the baptized may receive Holy Communion. This discipline of the church, which goes back to the first century, protects us. It prevents us from approaching the sacrament without faith in the risen Lord, whom we encounter whether we know it or not. It asks all parties to be honest about where they are, to "examine" themselves. Perhaps in time faith will grow, and then one can then look forward to sharing in the sacrament with holy anticipation. It also asks the baptized, as Paul did, to refrain from receiving Holy Communion thoughtlessly. If we are in fact resisting commitment to Christ on some level, our sacramental encounter with him functions as a denial of him and reinforces our blindness and lack of integrity. As Paul explains, in that case we "eat and drink judgment" upon ourselves (1 Cor. 11:29). The presence of Judas in all gospel accounts of the Last Supper serves as a chilling reminder that the betrayal of the Lord is ever a possibility among his disciples.

The Book of Common Prayer contains these pastoral guidelines, but they are embedded in parts of the prayer book that are, unfortunately, seldom used. "An Exhortation" stands right at the beginning of the eucharistic liturgies. Based on liturgical exhortations that go back to the earliest Books of Common Prayer, it begins with succinct but weighty teaching about the Lord's Supper and its abundant graces. It then calls upon us to "remember the dignity of that holy Sacrament" and cites St. Paul's admonitions in this regard. It urges self-examination in light of "God's commandments," presumably those of both the old and new covenants. It further counsels repentance and amendment of life including, when necessary, restitution of wrongs. It stresses the need for mutual forgiveness and reconciliation. All this reiterates Jesus's own teaching about the relationship between forgiving and being forgiven, and the interior dispositions necessary for right worship, scattered throughout the gospels. Our worship is hollow and self-deceiving if we stubbornly withhold love from anyone. How then could we meet Love incarnate?

The longer, traditional invitation to the Confession of Sin in Rite I presents a similar set of conditions for authentic repentance prior to Holy Communion:

> Ye who do truly and earnestly repent you of your sins, and are in love and charity with your neighbors, and intend to lead a new life, following the commandments of God, and walking from henceforth in his holy ways: Draw near with faith, and make your humble confession to Almighty God. . . . (BCP, 330)

It is easy to slip into rote participation in the Holy Eucharist. The specificity of these words can wake us up. They require a reorientation; they focus on our intention. What do we want? How shall we live? Baptism immersed us in a "new life." Sinlessness is not the issue here. Were that the case, no one except very young children could receive the Sacrament. The baptismal life is instead characterized by a daily death to sin and ongoing repentance, since we all fail repeatedly. Above all, the insistence here on being "in love and charity" with our neighbors brings us back to St. Paul's worries about the Corinthian church. The breakdown of this community into factions revolving around competing loyalties had prompted his letter to them in the first place. But things got worse. Because a common meal was the setting in which the Lord's Supper was celebrated, the situation lent itself to an accentuated divisiveness based on social stratification. The two aspects of the supper—community meal and Eucharist—were later separated in Christian practice, but at this time they were merged. The setting was ripe for abuse, and in Corinth they stemmed from a disastrous mix of gluttony with social insensitivity. Those who arrived early indulged themselves, leaving little food for latecomers—most likely poor people and slaves, who were required to work longer hours. Hence Paul's words about "discerning the body" are double-edged. They refer to Christ's body and blood in the bread and wine, but they also press home the necessity of "discerning the body" of Christ in the church, in one's fellow Christians. The wealthier Corinthians were starving out their humbler members, and humiliating them to boot. Paul insists that our relations to one another reflect the eucharistic identity Christ imparts to us: "We who are many are one body, for we all partake of the one bread" (1 Cor. 10:17). Just as the material earthiness of consuming sacramental bread and wine is a facet of the Incarnation, so are the flesh-and-blood relationships we have with others. We are to be "in love and charity" with our neighbors.

"One day in your courts is better than a thousand in my own room." (Psalm 84:9)

The Eucharist confronts us with community. While we know that baptism initiates us into the church, the Eucharist literally "fleshes out" that reality week after week. We might prefer a more solitary path of spirituality, but Christ comes with his body, the church. Baptism commits us, like the first believers recorded in Acts, to "continue in the apostles' teaching and fellowship, in the breaking of bread, and in the prayers" (Acts 2:42; BCP, 304). For some people it is the "fellowship" that poses the biggest hurdle in the practice of Christian spirituality. Human beings with all their limitations, foibles, and quirks can be such a challenge to us! Yet we cannot celebrate the Eucharist all on our own; it requires the community of faith. Every time the Eucharist is celebrated, the church becomes once again the body of Christ. The breaking of bread and the fellowship go together. For most people, the local community of faith is the parish.

Sometimes it is hard to go to church. We may be tired from the workweek and look forward to sleeping in. Our attendance may have become haphazard, not because we consciously decided to forgo church, but out of sheer habit. If that is the case for us, we should not underestimate the difficulty of forming a new pattern of church attendance. Studies have shown that it takes a long time to undo an old habit and establish a new one, as anyone who has embarked on an exercise program knows. Good intentions and willpower are not enough. Steady perseverance and, in this case, prayer are required.

Because society no longer encourages churchgoing, considered in some locales to be decidedly odd, civic groups and schools now schedule events for Sunday morning hours that used to be considered sacrosanct. Parents may feel genuinely torn when team practice, intervarsity games, or theater rehearsals for their children conflict with church school and the Eucharist. We might also let church attendance slip because we harbor some complaints, perhaps quite legitimate, about our local congregation or clergy and find it difficult to accept what we consider their inadequacies. We may tell ourselves that we can meet God during a walk in the woods or sitting quietly on our back porch, and of course we can. But this outlook misses the point, for the Eucharist offers a distinct, unparalleled grace. The Catechism of the Book of Common Prayer therefore maintains that "The duty of all Christians is . . . to come together week by week for corporate worship" (856). While we may chafe at the suggestion that we come to church out of sheer duty (a resistance that would not serve us well in other spheres of life), it is often true that we must practice a discipline for some time before we grasp the inner logic of it.

Among Americans, a consumer mentality promotes "church shopping" for a "place that fits my needs." Unlike the situation of the early church, where one city/one bishop/one Eucharist would have been the state of affairs, most people today have some choice about their place of Christian worship. For good or ill, we have options, and we will inevitably consult our preferences about theological tilt, quality of preaching, liturgical style, musical taste, educational opportunities, congregational demographics, or even the attractiveness of the building before settling into a particular parish. The spiritual dangers inherent in this circumstance of ours—the fostering of rampant subjectivity, and the disintegration of the church into exclusive enclaves of the like-minded—is surely apparent.

It is not that we should try to find the parish most disagreeable to ourselves in order to avoid these pitfalls. There is a wealth of wholesome diversity in style and emphasis that marks the church catholic, comprising, as it does, "every family, language, people, and nation." Over the course of church history, various spiritualities have taken shape in diverse monastic and religious communities or the several church traditions, each of which has its own distinctive character. Some self-knowledge can be useful here, and it can add a touch of humility to our deliberations. For instance, is having a warm and friendly church community really crucial for us, or do we hunger for theologically penetrating preaching, if we have to choose between them? To some extent our decision will be governed as much by our growing edges as by our gifts.

Once we have become part of a community of faith, though, we need to settle in. The household of faith is like other households, only more so. Jesus himself applied the metaphor of family relations to those who belong to him: "Whoever does the will of God is my brother and sister and mother" (Mark 3:35). We want to think of our families as havens of comfort, security, mutual support, growth, and love, and well-functioning families often provide these blessings. All families, however, have occasional quarrels, points of disagreement, and some aggravating personalities. Healthy families accept these difficulties in stride and grow through them. In the family of the church as in ordinary family life, God can work on our impatience, pride, and selfishness precisely through these irritating frictions if we are open to this grace. It has been said of community members in religious life that "like stones in a bag, they rub each other to smoothness."

We come together on Sunday not to "recharge our batteries" or in the hope of personal spiritual uplift. We come because we're part of the family: we need them and they need us. Showing up is a vital discipline; it is an essential practice that we never outgrow, like the five-finger exercises of a beginning or accomplished musician. Eventually we may discover that we simply cannot live without the Eucharist. It is the place of our death and resurrection in Christ; every liturgy is potentially transformative. We need to enter it as wholeheartedly as we can and let Christ carry us through its varied movements.

THE LITURGY OF THE WORD

"Your word is a lantern to my feet and a light upon my path." (Psalm 119:105)

ENTERING

We should strive to be on time and, if at all possible, early for the liturgy. Our minds, hearts, and bodies have to transition from the concerns that occupied us before church to the new reality we are entering. We are stepping into heaven, remember? It takes a while to settle ourselves, breathe deeply, and relax the tension stored in our bodies. If particular concerns weigh upon us, we may wish to bring them before God in prayer. It could be that we are seated beside visitors or newcomers to the church, whom we might assist in finding the hymn or page for the service. We want to welcome them, of course, but part of the welcome involves drawing them, by our calm demeanor, into the prayer of the church. The Quakers speak of cultivating "holy expectancy." We do not know in advance what particular grace God may give us during the Eucharist, but we should expect divine generosity and look forward to it. In other words, we want to enter the liturgy "recollected"—a traditional term denoting a gathering together or "collecting" our scattered thoughts to focus our attention on *where we are*. And just where are we? We want to be fully present to the moment: fully present to ourselves, fully present to the congregation with whom we are joined in worship, and fully present to the presence of God. It is a stance of unpretentious, loving openness. We will be immeasurably helped if our parish maintains a corporate discipline of quiet before the start of the liturgy. There is a time and place for friendly conversation, but it is not now.

PRAISING

"Enter his gates with thanksgiving; go into his courts with praise," cries the psalmist (Ps. 100:3). The first words of the eucharistic liturgy are an acclamation of praise to God: "Blessed be God: Father, Son, and Holy Spirit" or in the Easter season, "Alleluia. Christ is risen." Even in Lent we begin with praise, "Bless the Lord who forgives all our sins." The people respond to these opening words of the celebrant with a corresponding word of praise of their own. Then, after the penetrating "Collect for Purity"—a brief but incisive preparatory prayer that dates from the eleventh century—we continue in the mode of praise with an ancient hymn such as the Gloria, Kyrie, or Trisagion or with another "song of praise." No matter how heavy our hearts or low our spirits when we crossed the threshold of the church, we are immediately caught up in something much bigger than ourselves: the praise of God. Other parts of creation—plants and animals, rocks and soil, stars and galaxies—no doubt praise God by their sheer existence. Human beings, however, are uniquely endowed with the capacity for conscious praise of their Creator. Because it pulls us out of ourselves towards adoration, praise is the beginning of ecstasy—literally, a "standing outside" of ourselves. All our thought is upon God: "We praise thee, we bless thee, we worship thee, we glorify thee, we give thanks to thee for thy great glory." The words tumble out, cascading in torrents, never adequate to the divine Reality, but still pouring forth in joyful chorus. Such prayer is *doxological*; that is, it offers a "word of glory" (Greek *doxa*, glory). The liturgy thus begins doxologically, as pure worship. At this point, we are asking nothing for ourselves; our delight consists solely in giving glory to God. The very being of God is supremely attractive and attracting. What we know of Christ and the Holy Spirit overwhelms us. Like a magnet, God's love draws our loving praise Godward: "You only are the Holy One."

Before the Collect of the Day, celebrant and people greet each other for the first time in a mutual benediction: "The Lord be with you . . . And also with you." Whatever their relationship outside the liturgy, priest and people here acknowledge that they are bound together in the holy work of worship. They offer each other a blessing as they come together to pray. The Collect of the Day is said or sung, ideally after a significant pause for silent prayer. The Collect then "collects" our scattered thoughts and prayers in a unified vocalized prayer. Many of these prayers are centuries old, the product of the praying community over generations. They change with every Sunday and feast day. The collects that are offered during special liturgical seasons such as Advent or Easter embody the particular spirit of those seasons. The collects during the long Season after Pentecost have a more general character. Many collects in any of these seasons are of such beauty and insight that they easily adapt themselves to personal prayer as well. There are some we may want to learn by heart.

LISTENING

The Liturgy of the Word at a typical Sunday Eucharist includes three lessons from Scripture and a psalm. This is a very rich offering; it is also quite demanding. The lessons are read aloud, and this in itself is significant. We could, after all, simply distribute printed copies of the lessons and ask everyone to read them silently. But this would undermine the public reading of Scripture as an *event*. It would disconnect us from each other and from the experience of our ancestors, who for millennia heard stories around the tribal campfire or from a poet reciting long epics from memory. It would distance us from generations of Christians, including the very first, who *listened* to the Scriptures. In that act of listening together, the Scriptures *came alive* and melded them as one. As New Testament scholar Christopher Bryan has observed:

> Our forebears in antiquity took it for granted that most people would experience most words, including sacred words, by hearing them. . . . When the New Testament texts were collected

and recognized as sacred, their role within the communities that assembled them was already established: they were performed, and such performance was understood to affect the ethos of both performer and community. . . . Orality, then, is communal, and bonding.[6]

We sometimes experience this communal bonding in other venues—hearing exceptional music at a concert or seeing stirring drama at the theatre. Great art changes us, and it is particularly powerful when the experience is shared. The liturgy is a form of sacred drama, but in this case we are not witnessing a fictionalized version of the human condition. It is the real thing: God speaking to us or acting on our behalf. Even though the Scriptures employ a variety of literary genres, including poetry and myth, they remain God's word to us. How else could God address us except through language and literary forms that we can understand?

The dynamic of *anamnesis* underlies the Liturgy of the Word and not just the Liturgy of Holy Communion. As in the case of the Passover recitation of the sacred story, so in the Spirit-charged reading of the Scriptures, the events they narrate become present to us. Bryan describes the initial readings of the Gospel of Mark, which probably took place within the liturgy, as explosive:

> As with any effective dramatic performance, the tension between past and present would to a considerable extent be collapsed. The audience would feel themselves to be at once hearing what had happened and yet experiencing it and living in it *now*. They would hear how Jesus addressed their predecessors, and they would hear Jesus addressing *them*. Sometimes they would hear both at once, and sometimes one rather than the other.[7]

---

6. Christopher Bryan, *Listening to the Bible: The Art of Faithful Biblical Interpretation* (New York: Oxford University Press: 2014), 114, 115, 116. The chapter here cited, "The Drama of the Word," deals with the necessity of discerning and training those with gifts for public reading in our churches, a crucial matter for those in positions of leadership to consider.

7. Christopher Bryan, *The Resurrection of the Messiah* (New York: Oxford University Press: 2011), 66.

To hear God addressing us through the public reading of Scripture requires focused attention. Obviously, well-executed reading holds our attention. Poor reading may be either dull or overly theatrical: the one is boring and the other irritating. If we cannot do anything about the quality of readers at our church, we can at least cultivate in ourselves the art of paying attention.

Attention is rooted in love. When we give others our full attention, we honor them. Careful listening is a sign of respect. It indicates that we hold the other worthy of our entire consideration. Each day brings numerous contacts with people and opportunities to practice attention. In various ways, children ask us to "pay attention" to them. We meet and greet neighbors and colleagues. We rub shoulders with clients or those we serve, and those who serve us. Not every encounter will be profound, but every encounter can be focused and deliberate: there is another human being at the end of my "thank you" as I drive through the tollbooth. Multi-tasking tends to erode attention. When people attend meetings, one eye on the speaker, the other on e-mail, attention, respect, and courtesy are all compromised. Even friends allow conversation to be distracted by the omnipresent iPhone.

But it is not only people who merit our attention; so do our tasks. Our work requires attentiveness, whether we are employed at our job, preparing a meal, or balancing our checkbook. Even activities that do not demand much concentration can be engaged with "mindfulness": a straightforward, open awareness of where I am and what I am doing. "Hands to work and hearts to God" is how the Shakers put it. A simple "letting be" can increase the pleasure of eating an orange or decrease the pain of sitting in the dentist's chair.

In 1942 French philosopher and mystic Simone Weil wrote a remarkable essay, "Reflections on the Right Use of School Studies with a View to the Love of God." Weil had occasionally worked as a teacher herself and pondered the spiritual possibilities latent in academic study. What she write about "school studies" applies to other areas of endeavor:

> Prayer consists of attention. It is the orientation of all the attention of which the soul is capable towards God. The quality of

attention counts for much in the quality of the prayer. Warmth of heart cannot make up for it. . . .

Of course school exercises only develop a lower kind of attention. Nevertheless they are extremely effective in increasing the power of attention which will be available at the time of prayer, on condition that they be carried out with a view to this purpose and this purpose alone.

Weil distinguishes this kind of attention from "muscular effort" or "contracting the brows" that only leads to fatigue. She counsels, "Above all our thought should be empty waiting, not seeking anything, but ready to receive in its naked truth the object which it is to penetrate."[8] Such an empty, waiting, expectant openness to God's word should characterize our listening to Scripture and the sermon that follows. All our activities and encounters can conspire to prepare us for such attentiveness if we let them.

Our bodies can help or hinder us. Weil realized that the sort of strained concentration that triggers tense muscles and shallow breathing worked against the attentiveness she advocated. But even when we are not consciously on edge, most of us carry a fair amount of tension in our bodies all the time. For centuries, practitioners of meditation, both East and West, have realized that something as simple as breathing deeply and deliberately allows the body to shed this strain. It fosters an awareness of where we are and what we are doing. Although we might think that assuming a casual posture—crossing our legs or flinging an arm over the chair—might help, in this case it does not. In liturgy as in personal prayer, having both feet solidly on the floor with the back straight but not stiff, hands relaxed in one's lap, serves as an alert and peaceful posture. If we are unaccustomed to engaging our body in the service of prayer, it may seem artificial at first. But we ignore our bodies to the detriment of our souls. As practitioners of yoga have recognized for millennia, sound posture and deep breathing can engender calm, open awareness. Why not bring such an accessible practice to bear on our participation in

---

8. Simone Weil, "Reflections on the Right Use of School Studies with a View to the Love of God" in *Waiting On God* (London: Routledge and Kegan Paul, 1951), 51, 56.

the liturgy? We want, after all, to be fully present to Christ as he "opens the Scriptures to us." Some saints, such as Anthony of Egypt and Francis of Assisi, had their lives turned upside-down by careful listening to the gospel read in church. Especially when proclaimed in the context of the liturgy, "the word of God is living and active, sharper than any two-edged sword" and "able to judge the thoughts and intentions of the heart" (Heb. 4:12).

RESPONDING

According to Acts, those who first heard the gospel preached were "cut to the heart" by it. If we have "ears to hear," we allow the scriptural word to work on us, changing us, however slightly. It may be that we will want to ponder the lessons or sermon later, at greater leisure, to take in more fully their implications for us. For now, on Sundays and major feast days the community responds in unison with a profession of faith summarized in the Nicene Creed. This creed is generally more developed than the Apostles' Creed used at baptisms and in the Daily Office. To fathom its ancient, beautiful, and sophisticated language requires study, not because anyone set out to make the Christian creed impenetrable, but because it is not superficially grasped. The creeds are not so much statements *that* we believe such-and-so *about* God. They rather describe briefly the God we believe in: *how* God is towards us. What we affirm about God affects everything: how we view the world, how we understand ourselves, and above all how we relate to God. To say "we believe in" God takes us back to the Baptismal Covenant. We are saying that we "trust in" God, that we have "faith" in this God. And, significantly, we make this profession of faith, this response to the God revealed in the Scriptures, together. As Rowan Williams writes:

> "I believe in God the Father almighty" isn't the first in a set of answers to the question, "How many ideas or pictures have I inside my head?" as if God were the name of one more doubtful thing like UFOs and ghosts to add to the list of the furniture of my imagination. It is the beginning of a series of statements about where I find the anchorage of my life, where I find solid ground, home. . . .

It won't really do to say that "we believe" is a general formula that allows individuals more latitude in what they individually sign up to: it sets out what Christians can expect each other to take for granted. You can say that it tells us why we can trust each other in the Christian community. We're looking in the same direction, working with the same hopes and assumptions. So both "I" and "we" have their place, and not a great deal hangs on which of them we use at any moment.[9]

The Prayers of the People encompass a wide range of concerns. While our own intercessions rightly focus on those people and circumstances that are of particular concern to us, the intercessions of the church fling open our hearts to an even greater expansiveness. Engaging in the prayer of the church, then, counters any narrowness of spirit into which we might fall. The rubrics governing the intercessions (BCP, 383) indicate that prayer is to be offered for:

The Universal Church, its members, and its mission

The Nation and all in authority

The welfare of the world

The concerns of the local community

Those who suffer and those in any trouble

The departed (with commemoration of a saint when appropriate)

While our personal prayers might not embrace all these situations, repeated exposure to the Prayers of the People shapes us to a more comprehensive compassion. A later chapter in this book deals at greater length with the theology and practice of intercessory prayer. For the present, suffice it to say that to engage in intercession requires entering to some degree into the needs and suffering of others. We take that immensity of pain to heart. It is something we can only do "in Christ," in union with the crucified and risen One.

---

9. Rowan Williams, *Tokens of Trust: An Introduction to Christian Belief* (Norwich, UK: Canterbury Press, 2007), 6, 7. For those wishing to delve more deeply into what the creeds say about God, this fine short book would be an excellent place to start.

Finally, the Confession of Sin serves both as a response to the Word of God and a preparation for Holy Communion. The Scriptures have the capacity to "judge the thoughts and intentions of the heart." They illumine and expose us. Under grace, our conversion from sin and towards Christ can go deeper. In most eucharistic liturgies, the community will at this point join in the General Confession. But what are we confessing? The time to think about that is not during the brief silence (if it is even honored) between the invitation to confession and the confession itself. If the Confession of Sin is not to dissolve into an empty exercise, we must prepare for it well beforehand. We need to follow St. Paul's advice to "examine ourselves." We look over the past week or whatever interval since we last took stock of our state before God, noticing where we have fallen short. Some sins may be immediately apparent; others may take longer to surface into our conscious memory or for us to acknowledge them.

The General Confession is deliberately, well, general: "We have not loved you with our whole heart; we have not loved our neighbors as ourselves"(BCP, 360). Its terms have to be sufficiently broad if all members of the community are to say it as one. Sin, however, is never generic; it is always specific. One danger in using the General Confession is that we can hide behind it, avoiding confrontation with our particular sins. While this does not have to be the case, the practice does require vigilance. The General Confession demands preparation if it is going to function authentically as a vehicle for bringing our sins before the throne of divine mercy.

The General Confession, however, serves another, even more primary purpose in the church than the confession and absolution of our personal sins. It offers the occasion for the community of faith to confess its sins *as a community*. The notion of "social sin" is not a recent invention of liberal church people. The awareness that the community itself commits sin, and is guilty of hardness of heart and all manner of blindness, is rooted in the teachings of the prophets and of Jesus. It runs through the pages of the Old and New Testaments. It is the subject of the second baptismal renunciation that deals with "the evil powers of this world which corrupt and destroy the creatures of God." We are all complicit in social, economic, and political structures that ruin lives and undermine whole cultures. This has always been the case, but our collusion with evil is even more pervasive in the age of globalization. We take many of our privileges and products for granted, often unaware of their impact on other people, animals, or the earth. Serious energy conservation is still a minority practice. Slavery, now at an all-time high, is almost everywhere, but mostly covert. We do not know, and often do not want to know, where our food comes from or how it is produced. We use medications and cosmetics tested on live animals, causing them horrendous pain and finally, death. When our political policies fail to align with the gospel, or even basic justice, our taxes still support them. And then the church, including our own local congregation, has its own store of sin to confess. The General Confession offers the opportunity, not to engage in false posturing or to be thinking about other people's sins, but to lay before God our corporate entanglement in things that cry out for mercy. It places upon us the obligation of amendment of life: to remedy our willed ignorance and change our ways, insofar as that is possible.

Having confessed our sins and received absolution, we exchange the Peace, an ancient ceremony. It is not a merely casual, friendly intermission in an otherwise serious liturgy. We are offering each other nothing less than the Peace of Christ—a peace that is our Lord's own gift to us. Although in some small communities every person present may exchange the Peace with everyone else, it remains an essentially symbolic gesture. We do not, and cannot, exchange the Peace with everyone in the world! Yet the act betokens just such a universal love. We have been reconciled to God and with each other. We forgive others as we have been forgiven. And so, we are now ready to "offer [our] gift at the altar" (Matt. 5: 23–24).

THE LITURGY OF HOLY COMMUNION

"While they were eating, he took a loaf of bread,
and after blessing it he broke it, gave it to them, and
said, 'Take; this is my body.' Then he took a cup, and
after giving thanks he gave it to them, and all of them
drank from it. He said to them, 'This is my blood of
the covenant, which is poured out for many.'"
(Mark 14:22–24)

TOOK

The Liturgy of Holy Communion begins with the Offertory. Here
Jesus, in the person of the deacon or celebrant, "takes" the offerings of bread and wine that the people bring forward. Sometimes
monetary gifts are presented as well. In our economy, money sub-
stitutes for the food offerings the congregation once proffered to
support the clergy and assist the poor. Our financial gifts likewise
underwrite the mission of the church. All these offerings—bread,
wine, and money—serve practical purposes but they are also laden
with symbolic meaning. Today, when our relation to the natural
world has become seriously distorted, it is worth pondering the
significance of offering bread and wine.

Humans began making bread in the Neolithic period. Leav-
ened bread dates from about 4000 BCE, and winemaking from
the same period. Bread and wine made from grapes, mixed with
water to dilute it, were staples of the Mediterranean diet in the
time of Christ; and bread in some form remains the "staff of
life" in many parts of the world today. Bread and wine carry
diverse associations for us. Bread is wholesome, nutritious, and
commonplace; wine is festive, celebratory, and a bit dangerous.
The psalmist speaks of "bread to strengthen the heart" and
"wine to gladden our hearts" (Ps. 104:16, 15). These foods are a
source of both sustenance and pleasure, and the psalmist thanks
God for both.

Neither bread nor wine, however, are naturally occurring
foods. They require human skill and labor to produce them. What
we bring to the altar, then, are complex gifts: fruits of the earth,

to be sure, yet in every case shaped by human craft. They carry in them the giftedness of creation but also the vigor and pain of human toil. In this sense, too, the monetary gifts that we present (typically at a Sunday celebration) represent time, energy, and work. Both the glory and suffering of creation, including that of human endeavor, find expression in *The Mass on the World* by French Jesuit and paleontologist Pierre Teilhard de Chardin. Composed in 1923 on the steppes of Asia on the Feast of the Transfiguration, this extended prose-prayer conveys his sense of the transfiguration of creation through the Mass. Longing to celebrate the Eucharist but without an altar or altar vessels, Teilhard was moved to "make the whole earth my altar" in order at daybreak to offer God "all the sufferings and labours of the world." He begins, naturally enough, with "The Offering":

> I will place on my paten, O God, the harvest to be won by this renewal of labour. Into my chalice I will pour all the sap which is to be pressed out this day from the earth's fruits. . . .
>
> All the things in the world to which this day will bring increase; all those that will diminish; all those too that will die: all of them, Lord, I try to gather into my arms so as to hold them out to you in offering.[10]

The creation in all its intricacy and ambiguity is placed on the altar. We place ourselves there, too, even though we can scarcely fathom the mystery of ourselves any more than the wildness of creation. We present the totality of our lives with the bread and wine. We may be eating the "bread of adversity and the water of affliction" (Is. 30:20); we may be content and thankful; we may be confused or exhausted. We have daily work, cares, and relationships to bring to the altar. To present these things at God's altar is to present ourselves. We offer them so the bread and wine will be transformed into Christ, and that we ourselves will become Christ anew. Jesus "takes" the bread and the cup from us. We await transformation.

---

10. Pierre Teilhard de Chardin, "The Mass on the World," in *Hymn of the Universe* (New York: Harper & Row, 1969), 19, 20.

The earthiness of bread and wine connect us to the soil, sun, rain, and seasons; to the labor of farmers and vintners and everyone who, one way or another, brings food to our tables. Because the principal act of Christian worship is a communal *meal*, the way we approach food is, or ought to be, changed by it. Every meal is sacred. Giving thanks before eating—an almost universal custom among believers of all sorts—witnesses to this holy intuition. Our daily dependence upon food is both an instance of, and an emblem of, our dependence upon the life-sustaining goodness of creation, and the Creator whose love upholds it all. "Saying grace" before meals is more than a pious habit. It is a practice that brings us back, again and again, "to the good earth which God has given us."

But over what sorts of foods can we give thanks with integrity? We cannot give thanks if our food represents self-indulgence at the expense of our hungry neighbor. Could the rich man in Jesus's parable offer thanks to God while starving Lazarus hoped for some of his crumbs? We cannot give thanks if we prepare more food than we can eat, and throw away the rest. Today our relation to food is further complicated by the unnatural methods by which much food is produced: Petroleum-based fertilizers offer short-term productivity but long-term soil depletion, and their run-off destroys the health of lakes and streams and the animals that inhabit them. Feedlot cattle are forced to live in filthy, confined conditions, fed with an unnatural diet (for them) of corn, supplemented with antibiotics. Monoculture food production, encouraged by developed nations to satisfy our appetites, destroys biodiversity in many parts of the world. If we cannot give thanks over such food, participation in the Eucharist challenges us to change our ways, to conversion of life.

BLESSED

After presenting the bread and wine with all that they signify, we join "all the company of heaven" in the seraphic hymn, the Sanctus. The whole communion of saints surrounds us as we begin to give thanks. In the Great Thanksgiving we bless God—that is, we give thanks to God (in the Aramaic that Jesus spoke, the same word meant both "give thanks for" and "bless"). In the course of this blessing the food is blessed, too. It is the "blessing before eating" to a superlative degree because here we thank God for everything God has done for us. The scope of the Great Thanksgiving stretches from the beginning of creation to its culmination "at the last day," as we rehearse the sweep of God's saving actions toward us. The various forms of the Great Thanksgiving begin by acknowledging, at least implicitly, our need for salvation. Eucharistic Prayer A, for instance, describes a human situation marked by mortality and sin: "when we had fallen into sin and become subject to evil and death" (BCP, 362). Prayer B speaks of our desperate condition while rendering thanks for deliverance from this plight. It thanks God for having "brought us out of error into truth, out of sin into righteousness, out of death into life" (BCP, 368). Rite One moves immediately to bless God for giving us his Son, as it recalls the price of our salvation: "for that thou, of thy tender mercy, didst give thine only Son Jesus Christ to suffer death upon the cross for our redemption" (BCP, 334).

Although differing among themselves in their precise rendition of God's gracious deeds, all the eucharistic prayers recount the gift of our savior, Jesus, in his incarnation. God responds to the oppressive weight of sin and the fearful power of death by sending his Son to undo these crushing forms of bondage. The role of the Virgin Mary in the taking-flesh of Jesus, mentioned in several prayers, underscores its anchorage in history. The Great Thanksgiving always remembers Christ's self-offering in the narrative of the Last Supper on the "night before he died for us." The "words of institution," during which the celebrant is charged to hold or at least touch the bread and wine, dramatizes the words and actions of our Lord. We recall Christ's death, resurrection, gift of the Spirit, and return at the end of time, giving thanks for these saving events. Past, present, and future come together in this charged liturgical moment.

Compared with the Liturgy of the Word, the Great Thanksgiving is relatively brief. It therefore requires our utmost attention. If we are not listening with engaged devotion, before we know it the words will simply wash over us. But we do not want to miss them. For the stupendous events of salvation—Jesus's incarnation, death, resurrection, ascension, sending of the Spirit, and return at the *parousia*—all become present to us in the straightforward act of recalling them (*anamnesis*), and through them we are exposed to their saving power. We are also here engaged in the priestly work of oblation, a work we share through the priesthood of Christ.

What priests do is offer sacrifice and make intercession for the people. The Epistle to the Hebrews offers a remarkable, extended argument that Jesus is our "great high priest." The originality of the author's insight might escape our attention until we recall that, according to the New Testament, Jesus was descended from David, not the priestly tribe of Aaron. For the author of Hebrews, though, Jesus brings to stunning fulfillment the complete expiation of sin, which the sacrificing priesthood of the first covenant could only foreshadow: "But when Christ came as a high priest of the good things that have come . . . he entered once for all into the Holy Place, not with the blood of goats and calves, but with his own blood, thus obtaining eternal redemption" (Heb. 9:11–12). Although the sacrifice of the cross is not repeated in the Eucharist, its grace is present to us through anamnesis, and united to Christ we now "offer our sacrifice of praise and thanksgiving." Through our union with Christ we are now a "priestly people"—a term the New Testament applies to the Christian people in various places. First Peter refers to the baptized as a "royal priesthood," combining priestly with regal imagery, as does the Book of Revelation, where the saints are dubbed a "kingdom of priests" (Rev. 5:10). These titles are more than honorific: they indicate the work of the priestly people. We are, according to this same passage in 1 Peter, "to offer spiritual sacrifices acceptable to God through Jesus Christ" (1 Pet. 2:5).

It is worth noticing that in all these cases the priestly people are understood as a *body*. The "priesthood of all believers," as it is sometimes called, does not make each Christian a priest or presbyter, nor does it do away with our need for an ordained priesthood. It refers rather to the dignity and vocation of the Christian *people* (the words are always plural), united to Christ in his sacrificial self-oblation. It is telling that we welcome the newly baptized with the words "share with us in his eternal priesthood" just as we are about to begin the Liturgy of Holy Communion (BCP, 308). We are about to offer ourselves, in union with Christ and the gifts on the altar, in a "sacrifice of praise and thanksgiving"—but a sacrifice nonetheless.

"Are you able to drink the cup that I drink, or be baptized with the baptism that I am baptized with?" Jesus asks his ambitious disciples (Mark 10:38). Jesus would drink that cup in Gethsemane, and his baptism would be one of fire. Sacrifice is costly, but it is usually undramatic, and often hidden. It is transacted, for the most part, in the mundane details and circumstances of daily life: "And here we offer and present unto thee, O Lord, our selves, our souls and bodies, to be a reasonable, holy, and living sacrifice unto thee" (BCP, 336). Nothing is held back; the sacrifice is, at least in intention, total. It is life in and with the Crucified One. It begins at baptism with the renunciation of sin in all its manifestations and disguises. Life under the cross is the taking up of our daily work, and cares, and worries. It means responding with discernment and courage to the particular historical moment in which we happen to live, which we do not get to choose. It takes to heart the wrongs and barbarities of the world, praying for them in union with Christ, the high priest who "always lives to make intercession" for us (Heb. 7:25). Yet precisely because we can—and must—offer everything up in union with Christ, both the littleness of our lives and the magnitude of suffering are invested with surpassing dignity. These are our "spiritual sacrifices acceptable to God through our Lord Jesus Christ."

Everything we offer is sanctified by the Holy Spirit, who is explicitly invoked upon the bread and wine and upon the people in the *epiclesis* (Greek, "calling down"). For Eastern Orthodox churches, this is the climax of the Eucharistic Prayer, the transforming word. The epiclesis gives voice to the Spirit's agency throughout the whole prayer of Thanksgiving. We pray "that in your goodness and mercy your Holy Spirit may descend upon us, and upon these gifts, sanctifying them" (Prayer D). This is the Pentecostal moment for the people of God, as we pray that the

Spirit will transform us, along with the bread and wine, into the body of Christ.

The Eucharistic Prayer ends with an eschatological thrust. Having "proclaimed the death of the Lord until he comes," having offered thanks for the fullness of salvation now made present to us through anamnesis, we find ourselves on the very edge of the heavenly kingdom. The future approaches us with the risen, living Christ: "In the fullness of time, put all things in subjection under your Christ, and bring us to that heavenly country where, with all your saints, we may enter the everlasting heritage of your sons and daughters" (Prayer B). This is the destiny of the entire created order; this is who we are. Our life is with and in Christ. The power of the holy Trinity infuses our prayer, offered to the Father, in union with the Son, animated by the Spirit. And so this great prayer of thanksgiving concludes with a glorious Trinitarian doxology: "Through Christ, and with Christ, and in Christ, all honor and glory are yours, Almighty God and Father, in the unity of the Holy Spirit, for ever and ever." To this the people give their exultant "Amen."

BROKE AND GAVE

Having just prayed "through Christ, and with Christ, and in Christ" in the Great Thanksgiving, our prayer continues emphatically "in Christ" by using "the words our Savior Christ has taught us": the Lord's Prayer. Somewhat different wordings of this prayer are found in the gospels of Matthew and Luke. But a version nearly identical to the one traditionally recited by Christians is found in a late first-century document, the *Didache*, which directs Christians to pray "just as the Lord commanded in his gospel," and to do so three times a day. Even though Christians frequently pray the Lord's Prayer privately, it remains essentially a communal prayer, even when we say it alone: "*Our* Father . . . Give *us* this day *our* daily bread." The various petitions take on a strong eschatological coloration when prayed in the context of the Eucharist. "Thy kingdom come" seems to announce its very arrival in this foretaste of the messianic banquet. And there seems no better way to prepare to meet Jesus in the Sacrament than to pray with him in his own words. Especially apt is the petition, "Forgive us our trespasses, as we forgive those who trespass against us," for we cannot come to the altar holding grudges or in a state of hatred. This petition puts into words what the exchange of the Peace put into gesture. We are a community of the reconciled and the reconciling.

The consecrated bread is then broken. St. Paul had written, "Because there is one bread, we who are many are one body, for we all partake of the one bread" (1 Cor. 10:17). By consuming the "one bread" together (ideally, a single loaf) we become one in Christ, for our union with him is the basis of our unity with each other. Yet, paradoxically, this one loaf must be divided many times over for unity to occur on any level. From one point of view, the breaking of the bread serves a purely practical purpose. The Fraction, as it is called, is a necessary action, like cutting up a cake or a pie, for everyone to receive a piece. But from another point of view, it is a profoundly symbolic action: To be united in the one loaf, the bread must be torn to pieces. This is how Christ makes himself available to us, broken in sacrificial love. It is how we love one another as he has loved us. The Fraction bespeaks the paradoxes of the paschal mystery: life from death, unity from brokenness.

All that we have offered now returns to us transformed into Christ, whom we receive as food. It is the only food that satisfies our bottomless hunger for God: "I am the bread of life. Whoever comes to me will never be hungry, and whoever believes in me will never be thirsty" (John 6:35). We receive our future hope and present joy in the "Body of Christ, the bread of Heaven" and the "Blood of Christ, the cup of salvation." Receiving Holy Communion is an occasion of intense sacramental union with our Lord, experienced with piercing personal intimacy, yet shared with all: a communal mystical union. The long "Bread of Life" discourse in John 6 illumines the experience of generations of Christians who have found in this climactic moment a palpable sense of the inflow of divine presence: "Those who eat my flesh and drink my blood abide in me, and I in them" (John 6:56). The promise of mutual indwelling that Jesus offers in this gospel—"Abide in me as I abide in you" (John 15:4)—is here sacramentally realized. Yet the sweetness of this communion is no mere passing consolation.

It is always *viaticum*, "provision for the journey," not just for the dying (as viaticum is usually understood), but for the living as well. It is pilgrim food, bread to sustain us along the way of this life, while preparing us for the age to come. It creates Christ's risen life in us, a life that breaks the barrier of death and thrusts us into the unimaginable kingdom of God: "Those who eat my flesh and drink my blood have eternal life, and I will raise them up on the last day" (John 6:54). The first-century bishop and martyr Ignatius of Antioch (d. 107) called the Eucharist the "medicine of immortality, and the sovereign remedy by which we escape death and live in Jesus Christ for evermore" (Eph. 20).

The power of the Eucharist to transfer us, here and now, into the heavenly banquet is captured in the homely, concluding scene of the film *Places in the Heart* (1984). Set in a small town in Texas during the 1930s at the depths of the Great Depression, the opening and closing scenes bracket the film with images of sacred meals. Opening shots show people gathered after church for Sunday dinner: a couple in a restaurant, a homeless man receiving a plate of food at a door, white families and black families in their respective homes. All heads are bowed in giving thanks while "Blessed Assurance" is sung in the background. The ending of the film, however, brings a surprising conclusion to this riveting drama. It is Sunday again, and we see some of the main characters gathered in their little church at what has been called the country's most segregated hour: the hour of worship. Again "Blessed Assurance" is sung, harkening back to the beginning. Because it is a Communion Sunday, the pastor begins by reading from 1 Corinthians, chapter 13. The camera focuses first on a couple sitting uneasily in the front of the church. Their marriage has been wounded by infidelity, and real reconciliation seems to escape them. But the words, "And though I have the gift of prophecy, and understand all mysteries . . . and have not charity, I am nothing," hit home. The wife quietly places her hand on her husband's, taking him back into her love. The word of God proclaimed in the assembly is effective.

Next we see the bits of bread and small cups passed from congregant to congregant. Suddenly we glimpse characters from disparate scenes participating in the Communion: the homeless woman who was living in her car when a tornado struck and killed her; the black man who has been driven out of town by the Ku Klux Klan; the town sheriff sits next to the young black man who accidently shot him, both now dead. As they pass Communion to each other, each person offers it with the words, "the peace of God." All are reconciled, all are gathered in: black and white, living and dead. We see before us the peace that the world cannot give. Communion creates the community of the kingdom of God. It is made up of the ingredients of everyday life, its sin purged and its tragedy transformed by the living Christ.

LIVING EUCHARISTICALLY

"So if I, your Lord and Teacher, have washed your feet, you also ought to wash one another's feet." (John 13:14)

St. John's Gospel does not relate the story of the institution of the Eucharist, possibly because, as the last of the four gospels to be written, that narrative was already well known. Instead the evangelist tells how Jesus found another way to shock his disciples

Jesus Washing the Disciples' Feet. Coptic painting on goatskin. *Courtesy of photographer Betsy Porter.*

during his last meal with them the night before he died. In a culture acutely sensitive to social stratification, Jesus left the table where he had been reclining for dinner, removed his outer robe, tied a towel around himself, and began washing his disciples' feet. This was work only slaves would do. In fact, it was considered so demeaning that a Jewish master could not demand this service of his Jewish slave. Under ordinary circumstances, upon entering a house guests would be provided with water to bathe their own feet, since sandaled feet would quickly become dirty on unpaved roads. But Jesus is not washing feet for the sake of hygiene. He interrupts the meal to perform a prophetic action. No one was expecting this to happen, any more than the disciples were expecting Jesus to say, "This is my body" in the synoptic accounts of the Last Supper. But why did he do it?

The evangelist offers an interpretation. He tells us that Jesus, "knowing that the Father had given all things into his hands, and that he had come from God and was going to God, got up from the table . . ." (John 13:3–4). In other words, the foot-washing springs from Jesus's awareness of his impending death. In this scandalously self-abasing service, he acts out the degradation of the cross. In the institution narratives, the violent separation of body and blood was anticipated in the distinct, even disjointed, words over the bread and cup, "This is my body" and "This is my blood." In St. John's Gospel, the love impelling Jesus's imminent death is enacted prophetically in a shockingly humble action.

Given St. John's keen eye for symbolic density, this washing may carry an intimation of baptismal cleansing. In any case, Jesus makes it clear that this washing is not optional. Its necessity comes out in his exchange with Peter, who initially opposed having Jesus wash his feet, just as Peter protested the first prediction of Jesus's suffering and death (Mark 8:32). Jesus brushes Peter's reservations aside: "Unless I wash you, you have no share with me" (John 13:8). It must be all or nothing. This washing constitutes alignment with Jesus: either life with him or life without him. Whether or not the evangelist viewed the foot-washing through a baptismal lens, having a "share" or "part" in Jesus means sharing in his death and resurrection. And death-and-resurrection is enacted, practically, by performing the most humble service imaginable. After washing his disciples' feet, Jesus reframes his action for them: "Do you know what I have done to you? You call me Teacher and Lord—and you are right, for that is what I am. So if I, your Lord and Teacher, have washed your feet, you also ought to wash one another's feet" (John 13:12–14).

This is no bland summons to do-goodism. Loving one another in the Christian community is costly in the extreme. Slightly later in St. John's account of the Last Supper, Jesus presents his disciples with a "new commandment": "Love one another as I have loved you. No one has greater love than this, to lay down one's life for one's friends" (John 15:12–13). As Jesus is about to offer his life for us—the ones he now calls his "friends" (John 15:15)—he insists that his community embody the same sacrificial love as his. On our own, this would be impossible for us, self-protective and self-serving as we are. But baptism opened a new set of possibilities as we moved into life-in-Christ; and the Eucharist repeatedly nourishes and enlarges that identity. "Abide in me as I abide in you": loving one another as Jesus loves us means letting Jesus's loving presence dwell in us, creating in us a wellspring of love not of our own making. The paschal mystery is plumbed to its furthest reach in this work of love; it is death-and-resurrection.

Jesus's charge "to wash one another's feet" can seem simple and straightforward, and sometimes it is. The unfolding of Christlike compassion in our homes and communities, and among the "least of Christ's brethren," can be a powerful witness to the risen Christ. However, in the course of Christian history, appeals to "Christian service" or "Christian humility" have sometimes been twisted to justify a false asceticism in which one's own legitimate needs or desires must always give way to the wishes or whims of others. It is worth noticing that Jesus's service is free of these distortions. Throughout his ministry, he gave himself unstintingly to rich and poor, the sick, and those eager to hear his teaching. But he also refused to be co-opted into other people's plans and projects for him. The Fourth Evangelist prefaces the foot-washing scene by grounding it in Jesus's intimacy with the Father, whose mission he shares: "knowing that the Father had given all things into his hands, and that he had come from God and was going to God, got up from table . . ." (John 13:3–4). Jesus knows who he is: He lives in relation to his Father. The Eucharist grounds our identity-in-Christ. From that place we freely offer ourselves, as the Spirit directs, in service to others.

We do not leave the Eucharist in order to begin ministry, although the liturgy is sometimes misconstrued as a mere filling station for grace to empower ministry. On the contrary, in the Eucharist we participate in the most redemptive action conceivable on behalf of the world. In the intercessions we offer for all people, "Christ unites the faithful to himself and includes their prayers within his own intercession so that the faithful are transfigured and their prayers accepted. . . . The Eucharist thus signifies what the world is to become."[11] It is the supreme instance of the church's mission "to restore all people to unity with God and each other in Christ" (BCP, 855). Rather than begin mission as we leave the liturgy, our focus changes. Now we endeavor to live eucharistically: in prayer, in self-offering service, ever mindful of the death and resurrection of Jesus. The eucharistic community is called to be a microcosm of what God desires for all his children, a sign of the coming kingdom of God. We long for that day when "people will come from east and west, from north and south, and will eat in the kingdom of God" (Luke 13:29).

---

11. "Eucharist," paragraph 4, in *Baptism, Eucharist and Ministry*.

CHAPTER THREE

Sanctifying Time through the Liturgical Round

"My times are in your hand." (Psalm 31:15)

We seem to have a problem with time. We want it to pass more slowly or more quickly, seldom satisfied with its appointed pace. Children, for whom experienced time passes slowly, would usually like to speed things up: They can scarcely wait for Christmas or their birthday or summer vacation to arrive. Adults, too, can find the passage of time tedious: prisoners, family members awaiting the return of a loved one, passengers stuck in an airport, those afflicted with burdensome illness, and residents of convalescent homes. We devise ways to "pass the time" or, worse, "kill time." At least by middle age, however, most adults would like time to slow down. After all, we know where it is heading. And if we fear a future that inevitably spells death, backward reflection is often no better, either because the past holds painful memories or because the irretrievable loss of beloved people, places, and occasions triggers aching nostalgia.

Toward the end of *Macbeth*, Shakespeare's protagonist anguishes over the ruthless course of time:

To-morrow, and to-morrow, and to-morrow,
Creeps in this petty pace from day to day
To the last syllable of recorded time;
And all our yesterdays have lighted fools
The way to dusty death. Out, out, brief candle!
Life's but a walking shadow, a poor player
That struts and frets his hour upon the stage

And then is heard no more. It is a tale
Told by an idiot, full of sound and fury,
Signifying nothing. (Act V, Scene V, 19–28)

Even if we do not share Macbeth's final nihilism, his speech poignantly expresses our useless protest against time's gradual but inexorable march: "To-morrow, and to-morrow, and to-morrow/ Creeps in this petty pace from day to day." Little by little time eats away at our lives, and we can do nothing to stop it. We enjoy, perhaps, our "hour upon the stage" of life, but then we must make our exit, leaving room for other actors to take our place until they, too, must depart.

In itself, of course, time is neither threatening nor benign, although just what time is has puzzled many a philosopher or scientist. It is only as it affects conscious creatures, who move from birth to growth to maturation to decay and finally death, that time seems like an enemy. And as creatures uniquely endowed with the capacity to reflect on time, we are left wondering why we yearn for longevity—if not immortality—when it is beyond our grasp. Several voices within Scripture lament the brevity of life, but perhaps none more eloquently than Psalm 90:

You turn us back to the dust and say,
"Go back, O child of earth."
For a thousand years in your sight are like yesterday when it
    is past
and like a watch in the night.
You sweep us away like a dream;
we fade away suddenly like the grass.
In the morning it is green and flourishes;
In the evening it is dried up and withered . . .
The span of our life is seventy years,
perhaps in strength even eighty;
yet the sum of them is but labor and sorrow,
for they pass away quickly and we are gone. (3–6, 10)

Yet meditation upon the transience of life does not drive the psalmist to despair, as it does for Macbeth, but to faith. Given the brief span of life, the psalmist prays for wisdom to use the remaining days well: "So teach us to number our days /that we may apply our hearts to wisdom" (v.12) and "prosper the work of our hands; /prosper our handiwork" (v.17). Trust in God enlivens the daily round, even though it must come to an end: "so shall we rejoice and be glad all the days of our life" (v.14). We can accept the life we have as gift, rendering thanks for it with joy. Only for God are "a thousand years . . . like yesterday."

God resolves our problem with time by entering it: "when the fullness of time had come, God sent his Son, born of a woman, born under the law, in order to redeem those who were under the law, so that we might receive adoption as children" (Gal. 4:4–5). If the limitations of time frustrate our longings, writing an absolute "the end" upon the final chapter of our life, God breaks into these very constrictions through the Word made flesh. Jesus enters into the finitude of our lot. Like all of us, he is born of a particular human mother, and he dies a human death, tossed about by social and political forces he does not control. At his baptism Jesus stands in complete solidarity with human beings even in their sinfulness. Yet as he passes through his life, finally embracing his horrific death, he undoes the tragedy of time, the finality of death, and the prison of sin. The Orthodox icon of the "Anastasis" (Resurrection), displayed on the book cover, shows the risen Lord not emerging from the tomb but entering the abode of the dead, breaking down the "gates of Hades." It depicts what the Apostles' Creed calls his descent to the dead. Christ takes by hand Adam and Eve—and the whole human race represented in them—and pulls them into his risen glory. In him, our time-bound human life moves with him into eternal life. This is the transformation we begin with baptism, to which Paul refers when he speaks of our "adoption as children." There is not a speck of sentimentality undergirding this designation of his. Paul means that those baptized into Christ now by grace stand in the same relation to God as does the Son by nature. That is why, as Paul goes on to explain,

we call upon God just as Jesus did, "crying, 'Abba! Father!'" We
share in Jesus's prayer, his relationship, his Spirit, and his life.

The Christian liturgical year marks by its annual cycle key
phases in this "fullness of time." It traces Jesus's earthly movement through time and beyond time, starting with the coming
of Christ into the world and ending with his ascension and gift
of the Spirit. In its early stages, the church calendar began with
observance of the great festivals of the Christian Pascha (Easter
and Pentecost) as well as Epiphany. It then grew to encompass
the whole spectrum of events from Jesus's birth to his glorification. The grace of anamnesis is at work in the celebration of these
days and seasons; for we recall these events in order to participate in them through liturgy. As we pass through the days of our
life, then, both individually and collectively we become ever more
immersed in Christ's life. Our brief time on earth is thus sanctified and charged with eternity.

The church calendar carries us through an annual cycle that
starts with Advent and concludes with the long, six-month "Time
after Pentecost." But time is sanctified—that is, our lives, which
are only lived "in time," are sanctified—each day from morning
to night by the church's round of daily prayer, the Office. The
church received from Judaism this pattern of prayer punctuating
the hours of the day. Indeed, other religions have evolved similar arrangements for daily devotion. The regular calls to prayer
in Islam are well known. Such a widely practiced form of piety
has for centuries sustained the souls of its members, while today
this consistent, ordered form of prayer continues to attract converts to Islam. By contrast, the Christian counterpart—the Daily
Office—seems to be a well-kept secret.

Jewish piety evolved a round of prayer for the temple, the synagogue, and personal use. Temple sacrifice occurred each morning
and evening, and local synagogues arranged systematic readings
of Scripture, together with psalmody and prayers. If unable to be
present at the temple or synagogue service, devout Jews prayed on
their own three times a day: "in the evening, in the morning, and
at noonday" (Ps. 55:18). When the Acts of the Apostles describes
how the first Christians "devoted themselves to the apostles'

teaching and fellowship, to the breaking of bread and the prayers" (Acts 2:42), "the prayers" in this case probably refer to these practices inherited from Judaism. In the first centuries of the church, cathedrals and monastic communities devised their own schemes of Scripture reading, psalmody, hymns, and prayers based on these precedents: the origins of our Daily Office (Latin *officium*, duty). In his Rule for monasteries, St. Benedict calls the Office the "opus Dei," the "work of God." This monastic office enacts the psalmist's claim, "Seven times a day do I praise you" (Ps. 119:164), with a seven-fold office consisting of Lauds, Prime, Terce, Sext, None, Vespers, and Compline. The office begins around three o'clock in the morning with Lauds and is completed the following evening with Compline at twilight. Over the course of the Middle Ages, the Divine Office underwent considerable elaboration. While these embellishments produced music of surpassing beauty, the complexity of the Divine Office had the effect of removing it from ordinary parishes, rendering it inaccessible to the laity. At the time of the English Reformation, Thomas Cranmer simplified these offices for early editions of the Book of Common Prayer, making them the daily prayer of the parish church.

Ideally, the Daily Office is said each morning and evening in the parish church; this expectation undergirds various versions of the Book of Common Prayer. Since these offices may be lay-led, some parishes have a regular rotation of lay officiants who carry the leadership of the Office through the week. A full congregation is not essential for "where two or three are gathered in my name, I am there among them" (Matt. 18:20). For many of us, the demands of family or work will prevent us from praying the Office with the gathered community. But even when we pray the Office on our own, we are still praying with the church. It is the church's daily prayer, offered day in and day out for the glory of God.

If the Daily Office is not offered locally or if other obligations keep us from joining the community, the Office lends itself to recitation by Christian couples or households. If young children are present or a shorter form of the Office is desired, the Book of Common Prayer provides brief "Daily Devotions for Individuals and Families" for morning, noonday, and evening. These Daily Devotions might also help those new to this ordered way of praying take a first step towards praying the full Office. Since they follow the basic structure of the Daily Office and can be augmented by the psalms and readings in the Daily Office Lectionary, using the Daily Devotions could ease our way into praying at set intervals during the day. The newly revised edition of *St. Augustine's Prayer Book*, a classic of Anglican devotion, also provides simplified versions of the Daily Office conducive to personal piety.[1]

To commence praying the Daily Office we may need instruction about how to find each day's readings and psalms, how to interpret the rubrics (that is, the instructions before, after, and within the service), and how major feasts alter the usual pattern. Once we have located the service in the front of the Book of Common Prayer, we turn to the Daily Office Lectionary in the back of the prayer book. A careful reading of "Concerning the Daily Office Lectionary" (BCP, 934) explains how to use the readings and psalms for the two-year lectionary, and it shows us how to determine whether we are in Year One or Year Two. To find the correct set of lessons, we first have to locate our place in the church calendar. For instance: Was last Sunday the Third Sunday of Advent or the Fifth Sunday in Lent? The lectionary grid for the Time after Pentecost, by contrast, simply follows the secular calendar date. After determining the specific week, we then find the appropriate Sunday or weekday in that week. Major feast days have their own special psalms and readings, which enhance our celebration of those days. The lectionary for these festivals is placed at the very end of the lectionary schedule. These "red letter days" (so-called because they used to be printed in red ink) are now printed in bold type in "The Calendar of the Church Year" at the beginning of the Book of Common Prayer. While the task of locating the church's liturgical position amid these various coordinates may seem daunting at first, it is worth the effort. Eventually it will become second nature. Learning "where we are"

---

1. *St. Augustine's Prayer Book*, rev., eds. David Cobb and Derek Olsen (Forward Movement: 2014). This "Book of Devotions," as it is subtitled, contains valuable material drawn from the longer, catholic tradition of the church.

in the church year immensely enriches our liturgical life and prepares us for fuller participation in the mystery of Christ that is the focus of that particular season.

There are many benefits to praying the Office. Like all liturgical prayer, it is objective; its faithful performance does not depend upon our mood or creativity. The Office is available as an instrument of prayer even when we do not feel like praying or when we find ourselves utterly uninspired. It can carry us through long stretches of spiritual dryness. It can serve as an anchor when other aspects of our life are falling apart. It has held communities together during periods of divisiveness and strain. It puts words around the mere desire to pray, our simple need to connect with God. Above all, it unites us to the daily prayer of the church. We just have to do it.

"Yours is the day, O God, yours also the night; you established the moon and the sun." (Psalm 74:15; BCP, 115)

The Milky Way. *iStock.com/stock_colors, #592025468.*

The Office places us in harmony with the cosmic rhythms of day and night, light and dark, as the earth turns on its axis and rotates around the sun in an annual cycle. This is how we measure the passage of days and years, and praying the Office sanctifies this journey through time. Moreover, in this mechanized world we have constructed for ourselves, where we suffer alienation from the rest of creation, the Office helps join us to the wholesome cycles of nature, beginning with day and night. Morning Prayer is suitable only for the morning hours; and Evening Prayer is likewise geared solely to the mood and outlook of the evening. Several of the opening sentences for Evening Prayer celebrate these cosmic oscillations: "Yours is the day, O God, yours also the night; you established the moon and the sun. You fixed all the boundaries of the earth; you made both summer and winter" (Ps. 74:15, 16). Others turn our attention to the constellations of stars and to their Creator: "Seek him who made the Pleiades and Orion, and turns deep darkness into the morning, and darkens the day into night . . ." (Amos 5:8).

For people of faith, morning brings a sense of anticipation and hope for a fresh start. It is the hour associated with the Resurrection. Yet it takes courage to begin anew. Among the renowned desert ascetics of the fourth century, one monk was forcibly struck by the faith of his brother at the dawn of each day: "Abba Poemen said concerning Abba Pior that every day he made a new beginning." The invitation to renewal of life comes with each day. The morning office therefore provides apt prayers for the day that is about to unfold, a day that holds both promise and challenge. Consider "A Collect for the Renewal of Life":

> O God, the King eternal, whose light divides the day from the night and turns the shadow of death into the morning: Drive far from us all wrong desires, incline our hearts to keep your law, and guide our feet into the way of peace; that, having done your will with cheerfulness during the day, we may, when night comes, rejoice to give you thanks; through Jesus Christ our Lord. Amen. (BCP, 99)

The prayers for the evening, by contrast, offer thanksgiving for a day now past and ask for divine protection during the coming night. Even modern people can find the night hours somewhat threatening. Although our bright lights and electricity keep us from experiencing the all-enveloping darkness our pre-modern ancestors knew, nighttime still brings some dangers. Crime is often committed "under the cover of darkness," and we are more prone to certain temptations and sins at night than at other times. One of the evening prayers for mission expresses something of our spectrum of need as night sets in:

> Keep watch, dear Lord, with those who work, or watch, or weep this night, and give your angels charge over those who sleep. Tend the sick, Lord Christ; give rest to the weary, bless the dying, soothe the suffering, pity the afflicted, shield the joyous; and all for your love's sake. Amen. (BCP, 124)

One of the loveliest additions to the 1979 Book of Common Prayer comes from the Eastern Orthodox tradition: the hymn, *Phos Hilaron* (O Gracious Light). Based upon the ritual lighting of lamps at sunset, it bursts with joy, recalling how Christ is the "pure brightness of the everliving Father in heaven" (BCP, 118). As evening sets in, we celebrate the true light that "shines in the darkness" (John 1:5). Here, as in several other places in Evening Prayer, there is lively interplay between the onset of nightfall and reliance upon Christ, the Light of the world.

The Office further sanctifies our sense of time by directing us to the great mysteries of the faith associated with particular days of the week: Sunday as the day of resurrection, Friday as the day of Jesus's passion and death, and Saturday as the Sabbath day of rest and joy in creation. "A Collect for Sundays" in both Morning and Evening Prayer links our Sunday worship to thanksgiving for our Lord's resurrection. While the morning collect prays for continuing blessing through the coming weekdays, as Sunday draws to a close, the evening collect, appropriately enough, sets our sight more eschatologically. It looks forward to the unending day in which we will offer God praise in the "new Jerusalem," the "City of which he is the light."

The Collects for Friday focus on the cross and death of Jesus and underscore our participation in that cross. As we might expect in the morning office, "A Collect for Fridays" takes an active tone at the start of the day, asking as it concludes, "that we, walking in the way of the cross, may find it none other than the way of life and peace" (BCP, 99). Among the prayers for mission in the morning office is one particularly suited for Friday:

> Lord Jesus Christ, you stretched out your arms of love on the hard wood of the cross that everyone might come within the reach of your saving embrace: So clothe us in your Spirit that we, reaching forth our hands in love, may bring those who do not know you to the knowledge and love of you, for the honor of your Name. Amen. (BCP, 101)

In Evening Prayer, however, the outlook becomes both retrospective and anticipatory. By Friday evening, we are meditating on Jesus's already accomplished death; his body lies in the tomb at this hour on Good Friday: "Lord Jesus Christ, by your death you took away the sting of death." The collect goes on to recall the inevitability of death, imploring a safe passage from death to life in Christ: "Grant to us your servants so to follow in faith where you have led the way, that we may at length fall asleep peacefully in you and wake up in your likeness." Such a prospect of coming to a peaceful and holy end does indeed lessen the "sting of death."

"A Collect for Saturdays" in Morning Prayer masterfully weaves together the traditional theme of Sabbath as a day of rest and thanksgiving for creation—thus forging a bond with our Jewish brothers and sisters—with readiness for Sunday worship. Like the Epistle to the Hebrews (4:8–10), it regards present Sabbath rest as a portent of eternal Sabbath rest in God:

> Almighty God, who after the creation of the world rested from all your works and sanctified a day of rest for all your creatures: Grant that we, putting away all earthly anxieties, may be duly prepared for the service of your sanctuary, that our rest here upon earth may be a preparation for the eternal rest promised to your people in heaven; through Jesus Christ our Lord. Amen. (BCP, 99)

Saturday is the only day of the week with a particular collect designated for use in Compline. Its presence there underlines the significance of preparation for Sunday worship, a theme also echoed in Evening Prayer.

Beyond the main morning and evening services, the monastic office had provided for the "little offices" of Terce, None, and Sext, which correspond to the hours of nine, noon, and three o'clock in the afternoon. Besides offering praise to God at key junctures of the day, these offices would regularly reorient the monks' minds and hearts towards God. It is easy amid the press of work to lose sight of God, even in a monastery. In the course of streamlining the offices at the time of the Reformation, however, these little offices were eliminated, along with Compline, the night prayer of the church. For centuries, the offices of the Book of Common Prayer consisted solely of Morning and Evening Prayer, and these remain the core of the Daily Office. But with the 1979 Book of Common Prayer, Compline was restored to its traditional place, and "An Order of Service for Noonday" drew on elements from the three little offices of Benedictine monasticism. Noonday Prayer and Compline, like their monastic precedents, are brief and straightforward. Although one may use psalms and Scripture readings other than those appointed, one customarily prays these short offices straight through, perhaps selecting from among the three or four psalms, short readings, and collects provided.

The Noonday Office provides respite in the midst of our labors. It is a time to pray for strengthening grace in the heat of the day. The collects that recall Christ's crucifixion or the noonday call of St. Paul conclude with prayer for the universal mission of the church. There is space for meditation and spontaneous intercession, if desired. The Lord's Prayer is said, as in all the other offices.

In some parishes and other communities Compline has become a much-beloved office, especially when parts of it are chanted to traditional melodies and the space is illumined by candlelight. Some families have adopted it for their domestic night prayers. The appointed psalms pray for protection and repeatedly call upon God as our "refuge." Compline is a gentle and comforting office. The tender antiphon, "Guide us waking, O Lord, and guard us sleeping; that awake we may watch with Christ, and asleep we may rest in peace," frames the canticle *Nunc Dimittis*. This "Song of Simeon," which also appears in Evening Prayer, ushers us into the repose of sleep. As we pray it, we recall its setting in St. Luke's Gospel (2:29–32), when the aged Simeon takes the Christ Child in his arms, declaring him to be a "Light to enlighten the nations, and the glory of your people Israel." Simeon waited his entire life for that moment. Having at last seen the Messiah, he announces that he is ready to die: "Lord, you now have set your servant free to go in peace as you have promised." Sleep is our rehearsal for death. We cannot sleep, but will endure the misery of insomnia, if we cannot let go of anxieties, worries, and restless thoughts. For centuries, the church could think of no better way to put her children to bed than with Simeon's prayer on their lips—a prayer full of thanksgiving, trust, and surrender into God's hands.

"Come, let us sing to the Lord." (*Venite* in Morning Prayer; Psalm 95:1)

Both Morning and Evening Prayer begin with optional "Opening Sentences"—a selection of brief verses from Scripture that call us to prayer. Those appointed for the morning office are organized according to liturgical season, thereby enriching our participation in those seasons. These sentences may be brought forward for use in Evening Prayer, but the sentences listed specifically for that office have to do, as we have already noticed, with nocturnal themes of light and darkness. At all the offices except Noonday Prayer, a Confession of Sin is provided for those who wish to use it.

After these preliminaries, the office begins with a versicle and response. In all the offices except Morning Prayer, the office opens with the prayer: "O God, make speed to save us." This psalm verse (70:1) is prescribed in the Rule of St. Benedict, but it is based, in turn, on traditions going back to the desert ascetics. The response mirrors it: "O Lord, make haste to help us." In the morning office, the opening versicle and response ensure that the first words of our day glorify God: "Lord, open our lips" / "And our mouth shall proclaim your praise" (Ps. 51:16). We then move into joyful praise of God with the Invitatory Psalms, the *Venite* or *Jubilate* or, in the Easter season, the canticle *Pascha Nostrum*. The *Phos Hilaron*, also a jubilant outburst of praise, occupies the same position in Evening Prayer. Just as the Eucharist opens doxologically, so does the office. We are lifted out of our narrow concerns into the wide, expansive venture of glorifying God.

The praise of God continues in the appointed psalmody. While St. Benedict had his monks pray the entire psalter over the course of a week, our lectionary covers most of it in six weeks. The psalms, which almost always conclude by expressing trust in God or rendering thanks, nevertheless cover a broad range of moods and situations. Some psalms ring with ecstatic joy: "Bless the Lord, O my soul, and all that is within me, bless his holy Name" (Ps. 103:1). Some yearn for God: "As the deer longs for the water-brooks, so longs my soul for you, O God" (Ps. 42:1). Others howl in grief: "Out of the depths have I called to you, O Lord" (Ps. 130:1). "You have noted my lamentation; put my tears into your bottle; are they not recorded in your book?" (Ps. 56:8). Some anguish over hurt and betrayal: "Even my best friend, whom I trusted, who broke bread with me, has lifted up his heel and turned against me" (Ps. 41:9). Many are distraught by the success of arrogant evildoers: "How long shall the wicked, O Lord, how long shall the wicked triumph? / They bluster in their insolence; all evildoers are full of boasting. / They crush your people, O Lord, and afflict your chosen nation" (Ps. 94:3–5).

Some psalms, however, go beyond lamenting evil to invoking God's vengeance on its perpetrators: "Make an end of them in your wrath; make an end of them, and they shall be no more" (Ps. 59:14), or "Let them vanish like water that runs off; let them wither like trodden grass. / Let them be like the snail that melts away, like a stillborn child that never sees the sun" (Ps. 58:7–8). Just as troubling in another way are those psalms which boldly claim personal innocence: "For I have been blameless with him and have kept myself from iniquity" (Ps. 18:24). What are we to make of these psalms, which express sentiments that may not be our own? Or curse their enemies or seem to pretend to a false, or at least naïve, innocence? How can we pray these psalms with integrity or without damaging our souls? It may be some consolation to realize that this problem—which is really an aspect of a larger question of faithful biblical interpretation—has engaged the church from the first. Within the New Testament itself, we can notice the beginnings of a solution. The first generation of Jewish Christians naturally turned to their Scriptures to interpret what God had done in Jesus. They read the "Servant Songs" in Isaiah, among many other texts, in a new light: the light of Christ. Without denying the original, historical context and authorial intention of any text, we come to see that many of the Scriptures contain a "surplus of meaning." There is more on the page than meets the eye. Recall how St. Luke tells us that en route to Emmaus the Risen Christ "interpreted to them the things about himself in all the scriptures" (Luke 24:27). The Scriptures are not self-explanatory; they demand interpretation. Robert MacSwain observes:

> The church does not read the Bible in what Wordsworth memorably called "the light of common day," but rather in the brighter light of Christ's resurrection.
>
> As we all know, the light in which you read determines what you can see. The text changes its texture according to the light that you shine upon it. Like the existence of God, the various and sundry meanings of the Bible are not immediately available or obvious or recognizable to the casual observer, but require a shift in perspective to appreciate fully. This is not an individual but a communal enterprise, and not just a secular reading but also a spiritual one.

Jesus, the Word of God, stands at the center of the Bible. This does not mean that the authors of the Hebrew Bible, including the psalmist, were thinking of the coming Christ as they wrote. Of course they were not. As MacSwain goes on to say:

> Textual meaning . . . is not simply inherent in the intention of the original author, but rather emerges from imaginative and prayerful engagement with the wide but still limited range of

semantic possibilities provided by the given words and sentences of Holy Scripture. The Bible, you might say, is a hypertext, each word and sentence of which is linked to another. When the curser of your mind hovers over a word or sentence, it takes you to another, and another, and another.[2]

Praying the psalms from a Christological axis opens wide horizons. Because we are enmeshed in the context of the praying church, we realize as we recite the psalms that we are engaging in prayer precisely as *Christ's body*. There is another voice we can hear as we pray the psalms. This resolves the dilemma of purely subjective mood: While I may not be feeling joyful today, someone else in the body of Christ is. I therefore join my prayer to that member's joy. Indeed, through the psalms I can offer the prayer some prisoner, hostage, or other endangered or despised person cannot pray; I pray out their lament, grief, or questioning. With Christ at the center, I can pray the psalms of innocence *in him*.

In times of political or social turmoil, psalms that fulminate against "the lying lips . . . which speak against the righteous, haughtily, disdainfully, and with contempt" (Ps. 31:18) may provide just the words we need—or someone else may need—to pray our outrage at the injustice of a "post-truth" society. Most disturbing of all, of course, are the imprecatory or curse psalms. We cannot pray these with malicious intent, and the lectionary has made some of the most offensive verses optional. Yet even these psalms can work for our benefit. They reveal us to ourselves: they exhibit our most hateful thoughts and sinister motives, which we usually keep under wraps. One way or another Scripture tells the truth. Here it holds a mirror up to us, unmasking the ugly side of human nature. We pray the imprecatory psalms with humility, convicted of sin personally and as a species. Finally, because the psalms articulate an extensive range of human emotions—joy and sorrow, grief and indignation, praise and wonder—they school us in honest prayer. We do not have to hold anything back from God: what cannot be blessed needs to come under judgment. Without

---

2. Robert MacSwain, "The Hermeneutics of Easter," *Sewanee Theological Review* 56:2 (Easter 2013), 163–64.

repeated exposure to God in prayer, our thoughts and feelings remain hidden, perhaps even from ourselves, and unsanctified.

"Give me life according to your word." (Psalm 119:25)

When the English Reformation restored the Office to the parish church, it recovered the practice of reading substantial, consecutive lessons from Scripture. Our present lectionary provides for most of the Old Testament (including much of the Apocrypha) to be read over the two-year cycle; and the New Testament will be read twice. Exposure to such a sizable expanse of Scripture has several advantages. Clearly, it helps inculcate a measure of biblical literacy, an urgent need in every generation. Regular listening to, or reading of, the Bible instills acquaintance with its contents. And because the lessons are read *in course*, one chapter succeeding upon another, each book can begin to be grasped *as a whole*. This is very different from hearing passages, however inspiring, lifted out of context. With consecutive readings one can follow the movement of a narrative or take in the direction of an author's argument or teaching. So aside from whatever "word of the Lord" one might hear on any given day, one can over time be further enriched by assimilating a gospel, epistle, or other biblical book as an integral whole.

Yet the advantage of comprehensive reading of Scripture goes beyond our enhanced appreciation of its individual books. Those who pray the Office over time, thus hearing the course of Scripture year in and year out, come to appreciate the Bible itself as a living whole. This is all the more remarkable since the books of the Bible were written over centuries. They come from different periods of history, varied social contexts, and a range of authors. They embrace a wide spectrum of literary genres: history, myth, poetry, laws, letters, gospels, and apocalyptic, among others. Attentive readers notice that the books of the Bible seem to be in dialogue with each other, sometimes affirming and sometimes challenging the received tradition. The Book of Job, for instance, with its eloquent protest against undeserved suffering, presses against a Deuteronomic perspective in which the good are always rewarded and evildoers, punished. The New Testament is saturated with the Old, endorsing, interpreting, and occasionally overturning this heritage.

Our first duty in reading the Bible is to try to understand what the text is actually saying. Since the most recent parts of the New Testament were written nearly two thousand years ago, we are bound to find some passages obscure or puzzling. All ancient texts require some scholarly elucidation, including their historical, religious, and cultural matrix. Fortunately, we need not, and indeed should not, attempt to comprehend the Bible all on our own. As Robert MacSwain reminds us, "This is not an individual but a communal enterprise." The fruits of the scholarly community, at least, can be at our fingertips. Simply by using a sound translation in a reputable annotated version of the Bible, we have access to centuries of scholarly labor, including the most recent. These editions are equipped with ample explanatory footnotes and brief introductions to each of the biblical books.

Because the lectionary encompasses the breadth of Scripture with few omissions, from time to time we will encounter distasteful and even shocking material. It is hard to march through the books of Joshua and Judges, for example, and learn in graphic detail about the slaughter of indigenous Canaanite inhabitants— men, women, children, and animals—in the conquest of that region. That the authors interpret such genocide as the will of God strikes us, rightly, as all the more horrendous. Patristic and medieval commentators relied on allegorical interpretations to navigate such passages, usually seeing "the enemy" as sinful proclivities in ourselves that God must conquer. Such approaches are also available to us, but we will still be troubled by whatever history underlies such texts. Even if the conquest was not as extensive as the writers triumphantly assert, it remains true that these authors looked back on what they thought was history through a very different moral lens from our own. This is an aspect of the biblical heritage which, like the curse psalms, shows how religion can be twisted to violent, self-serving ends. This distressing material is part of the family history of the household of faith, and as such it is *our* history and not some other group's. In these cases we must acknowledge that the past was what it was, repent of it, and learn from it.

If we find ourselves wondering how something in the Bible can possibly be God's revealed word, we must return to the most ancient Christian hermeneutic or principle of interpretation. Jesus, the Word made flesh, is God's definitive word to us. He alone can "open the scriptures" for us. We read the texts by the light of the resurrection under the guidance of the Holy Spirit. Addressing the demanding task of coming to terms with the Bible's dizzying array of genres and the fact of unsettling passages, Rowan Williams maintains that there is something even in these texts that God wants us to hear:

> How can all of this be addressed by God to us? The simplest way in which we can understand this is the one I have already hinted at: this is what God wants you to hear. He wants you to hear law and poetry and history. He wants you to hear the polemic and the visions. He wants you to listen to the letters and to think about the chronicles. And from the earliest days, Christians, like Jews before them and like Jews now, wrestle with exactly how you can say, "This is the word of the Lord," the communication of God. You cannot go by just surface meanings because surface meanings do not immediately help you with understanding why God wants you to hear it. This may be the word of God, but why exactly is it important to God that you know it? . . .
>
> If in that story we find accounts of the responses of Israel that are shocking or hard to accept, we do not have to work on the assumption that God *likes* those responses. . . . The point is to look at God, look at yourself, and ask where you are in the story. Are you capable—*in the light of the Bible itself as a whole*—of responding more lovingly or faithfully than ancient Israel?[3]

As Williams advises, we take our cues from "the Bible itself as a whole" when we attempt a faithful response to any given passage.

---

3. Williams, "Bible" in *Being Christian*, 25–28. The entire chapter is well worth reading. See also Christopher Bryan, *Listening to the Bible: The Art of Faithful Biblical Interpretation*, 76–84 for discussion of these thorny issues.

Since God speaks to us through the whole of it, we must listen to the Scriptures in their fullness, allowing ourselves to be shaped by them. Otherwise our response is liable to be conditioned solely by our surrounding culture or by bits and pieces of our favorite biblical stories and verses.

Williams asks us to "look at God, look at yourself, and ask where you are in the story." For we are, one way or another, implicated in the story. The dynamic of anamnesis is at work whenever the Scripture is proclaimed in the liturgy, whether in the Eucharist or the Daily Office; it is also present when we read Scripture privately in a spirit of prayerful availability to God's word. We are part of the story. In *Life Together*, written in 1938 in the shadow of the Third Reich, Dietrich Bonhoeffer speaks of this anamnestic vitality, when he recommends to Christian communities seeking a shared spiritual practice the consecutive reading of Scripture:

> Because the Scripture is a corpus, a living whole, the so-called *lectio continua*, or consecutive reading, will above all be worth considering for the Scripture reading of the house church. . . . The community of believers is drawn into the Christmas story, the baptism, the miracles and discourses, the suffering, dying, and rising of Jesus Christ. It participates in the events that once occurred on earth for the salvation of the whole world. In so doing, it receives salvation in Jesus Christ here in all these events. . . . Forgetting and losing ourselves, we too pass through the Red Sea, through the desert, across the Jordan into the promised land. With Israel we fall into doubt and unbelief and through punishment and repentance experience again God's help and faithfulness. All this is not mere reverie, but holy, divine reality. . . . What is important is not that God is a spectator and participant in our life today, but that we are attentive listeners and participants in God's action in the sacred story, the story of Christ on earth.[4]

The Holy Spirit, whom Jesus calls the "Spirit of truth," is stirring in us as we read or listen to the text as members of the

---

4. Dietrich Bonhoeffer, *Life Together*, vol. 5 of *Dietrich Bonhoeffer Works*, English ed. Geffrey B. Kelly, trans. Daniel W. Bloesch (Minneapolis: Fortress Press: 2005), 61–62.

community of faith. The Spirit who first guided the biblical writers now engrafts us into the saving events to which the Bible offers witness.

"We praise thee, O God."
(Canticle 7: *Te Deum laudamus*)

The response to the Scripture lessons is doxological: the praise of God. Joy in God is a keynote of worship in the Daily Office as in the Holy Eucharist. With the exception of the ancient hymns *Gloria in excelsis* and the *Te Deum*, the canticles themselves are Scriptural texts, including poetry and prayers from the Apocrypha. Two New Testament Canticles, the *Magnificat* and the *Nunc dimittis,* are traditional for Evening Prayer, although the rubrics allow for the use of the other canticles. In penitential seasons, the *Gloria in excelsis* and the *Te Deum* are suppressed; the poignant *Kyrie Pantokrator* (Song of Penitence) would be employed more frequently, especially in Lent. As we say or sing the canticles, we join with millions throughout the world, and those who have lived centuries before us, who have prayed these texts uplifted in praise to God.

Every day we then confess our faith anew in the Apostles' Creed, the baptismal creed of the church. We pray the Lord's Prayer and become grounded, once again, in the prayer of Jesus. Through the suffrages we engage in wide-ranging intercession, for as in the Eucharist, the prayer of the church expands the boundaries of our concern. Collects "of the Day" situate us in the liturgical season or feast day that is being celebrated. Other collects, as we have noted, connect to the mysteries of the faith marked on Sunday, Friday, and Saturday. A prayer for the mission of the church is always part of the Office, unless the Eucharist is to follow. Hymns, additional intercessions, and other prayers may be included.

With all this richness, the Office with psalms, two lessons, canticles, and prayers can nonetheless be prayed in about twenty minutes. Its effect upon our lives, however, is felt over the long haul. The Daily Office is designed to be said daily, as its name indicates. The lectionary with its chart of readings and psalms creates depth by first offering breadth. We have to give it time to do its work, shaping in us the mind of Christ and his prayer. Since the readings are "in course," just dropping in on the Office now and then will probably be frustrating— like coming into the middle of a movie and wondering what is going on. When we are ready to move beyond the "Daily Devotions," beginning with one of the regular Offices makes sense. Even if we do not read all three lessons each day, staying with one or two of the same readings "in course" will bear the most fruit. Skipping around and dabbling will keep us on the surface. If we are fortunate enough to be part of a community that prays the Office, whether in our church or in our household, commitment to it will bolster our motivation. Yet even when we pray the Office in private, we are always praying with the praying church—and that, finally, constitutes our deep community. We slowly become immersed in the full mystery of Christ as we pray with the church over the course of the liturgical year, to which we now turn.

LIVING THE WHOLE MYSTERY OF CHRIST: THE LITURGICAL YEAR

"In him all things hold together." (Colossians 1:17)

While baptism initiates us into Christ's own life, a crucial means by which we continue growing into that life is through the annual observance of its pivotal moments, especially those marking Jesus's birth, baptism, death, rising, and glorification. These events, while belonging on one plane to the realm of history, are considered "mysteries"—not because they are an inscrutable enigma, but because they have eternal significance and infinite depth. In the New Testament, the word "*mystērion*" signifies something that human beings could not know except by divine revelation: Once hidden, it is now revealed in Christ, though we can never fully probe its inexhaustible meaning. Precisely because the whole mystery of Christ is so vast and multifaceted, the major feasts and seasonal celebration of the particular events of Christ's life are spread across the year.

It is through the liturgies of the Daily Office and the Holy Eucharist, above all, that we experience the distinct flavor of each liturgical season. The lessons appointed for both office and Eucharist change markedly in tone from one season to the next, inviting us to ponder the particular mystery of Christ commemorated in that season. Seasonal or festal antiphons in the office, hymns suitable to the day or season, and alterations in the color of vestments and decor all contribute to the usually subtle but sometimes dramatic shift from one liturgical season to the next. Like the change of seasons in the natural world, these variations are psychologically satisfying. In the northern hemisphere, where the liturgical year developed, the variations in sunlight over the course of the year reinforce the drama of the church's unfolding liturgical seasons. As in the natural world much remains the same: the structure of the liturgy is little altered. But the small differences add up, lending a distinctive coloration to each church season. The liturgical year allows us to move interiorly not so much in a cycle as in a spiral, every year plunging deeper into the mystery of Christ.

Woven into this annual round are the commemorations of particular saints. These are our spiritual friends who, across the threshold of time and death, offer us encouragement by their example: They lived into the mystery of Christ, each in his or her unique way, to an extraordinary degree. Some—the martyrs— witnessed to Christ in the face of death. Others lay down their lives in loving service, from care for the poor to missionary zeal to theological scholarship. Saints are found in every generation and in every walk of life. Some saints have left their writings to teach and inspire us; others are known through the legends and stories that grew up around them. Although the saints in our calendar lived in the past, they really belong to the future, for they illustrate the horizons of holiness and wisdom to which we are called in Christ.

ADVENT

As in ordinary English usage, Advent refers to a "coming." But which one? It turns out that the brief season of Advent is exceptionally thick with meaning. While most people, both in the church and outside it, think of Advent as a time of preparation for Christmas—the first "coming" of Christ into the world—the liturgies for Advent focus more on our Lord's final coming at the end of time. This eschatological orientation in the appointed collects and readings gets underway about a month before Advent even begins, officially at least, which is usually on the last Sunday of November. Advent, then, has a long run up to it.

The month of November comes late in autumn. In the temperate zones, early fall days are typically colorful and crisp, but by late autumn trees are largely stripped of leaves and dampness sets in. The days become shorter, darker, and colder. Ancient peoples responded to these natural occurrences, resulting as we know now from the earth's rotation around the sun, by enacting rituals to coax the sun god's return or to appease the spirits of the dead. Contemporary customs around Halloween seem to enact a modern-day version of the attempt to scare death to death. Reveling in the macabre and gruesome, in witches, ghosts, and things that go bump in the night, bespeaks a need to face the universal fear of death. It is no accident that this occurs as the cycle of nature, and even the sunlight, seems to fail, undergoing a kind of death. Late autumn is *memento mori* writ large.

Halloween, of course, is "All Hallows Eve," the night before All Saints' Day, November 1. The saints who have completed their course bear testimony to Christ's final victory: deliverance from death and the defeat of evil. The grace of Jesus's resurrection shines through them. Originally a feast of all the martyrs—the witnesses to Christ par excellence—All Saints' Day later came to celebrate other Christians of exemplary virtue. Since everyone needs models to inspire and emulate, All Saints' Day holds before us this "great cloud of witnesses." Its celebration might prompt us to delve still deeper: to become acquainted with the saints by reading some of their works or the writings about them, drawing wisdom and encouragement for our spiritual journey.

November 2 serves as something of an extension of the Feast of All Saints as the church commemorates All Faithful Departed—All Souls' Day, as it is popularly known. Unlike All Saints, this day has a domestic feel about it, as we hold in prayer, often with a twinge of sadness, our beloved dead: family members and friends passed from this world to the next. The Mexican "Day of the Dead," itself built upon Aztec foundations, embraces all three days in a unified remembrance of friends and ancestors.

With this eschatological horizon now before us, the readings for the last weeks of Pentecost sharpen the vision of the end of time by turning to "last things." The Scripture lessons for both Eucharist and Office have a somber tone. Predictions of the destruction of the temple, and parables about the return of Christ and the last judgment, dominate this season. While many in the church today shrink from contemplating the theme of judgment, assuming that it only spells condemnation, the insistence in both the Old and New Testaments on a final reckoning is actually an assurance that divine justice and truth will prevail in the end. In a world riddled by lies and cruelties, where the cries of the powerless often go unheard, the conviction that Christ will come again is grounds for hope. The lessons for the Last Sunday after Pentecost bring the season to a close with the climactic image of Christ the King, treated from various angles over the three-year Sunday lectionary.

The First Sunday of Advent seamlessly continues these themes, now adding the further dimension of apocalyptic. Here the birth pangs of the new creation are described in terms of cosmic catastrophe, with the sun becoming dark and stars falling from heaven. This dramatic imagery augurs the coming reign of God. The watchword here, and indeed throughout Advent, is vigilance: "Keep awake!" The stern figure of John the Baptist appears in gospels for the Second and Third Sundays of Advent, calling us, as he did his contemporaries, to repentance. His preaching prepared Israel for the advent of Jesus; his summons to renewal prepares us for the second advent of Christ as well as for the celebration of Christmas. It is only with the Fourth Sunday of Advent that the church turns our attention to that festival with pre-Nativity gospels, focused on the figures of Mary and Joseph.

As is the case with every liturgical season, Advent under-scores aspects of our life in Christ that are true throughout the year. Yet each season brings them into sharper focus. Vigilance, for instance, is a crucial spiritual practice. It demands that we pay attention to what is going on inside us and around us, dis-cerning what is of God and what is not. Naturally this leads—as John the Baptist would tell us—to ongoing repentance. Vigilance also embraces the holy expectation of meeting Christ, sometimes when we least anticipate it. The Collect for the Fourth Sunday of Advent speaks of God's "daily visitation":

> Purify our conscience, Almighty God, by your daily visitation, that your Son Jesus Christ, at his coming, may find in us a mansion prepared for himself . . . (BCP, 212)

Here, as in many of the Advent prayers, the "comings" of Christ are intertwined: the first coming in his incarnation, his final com-ing at the end of history, and his coming at the intersection with the everyday. This last sense, issuing in constant vigilance for the appearing of Christ, has sometimes been called the "sacrament of the present moment."

The spirituality of Advent is marked by urgent longing: "O that you would tear open the heavens and come down" (Is. 64:1) begins one of its lessons. Advent allows us to acknowledge the incompleteness of things, since the world as we know it is plainly far from perfect. Those who "hunger and thirst for righteous-ness" embody Advent spirituality as they yearn for the coming of Christ to establish his kingdom forever. In much the same way, Advent gives scope to our dreams. The extraordinary picture of the "Peaceable Kingdom" in Isaiah 11:1–10 combines hope of a messianic ruler with perfect harmony in the animal world, where "the wolf shall live with the lamb, the leopard shall lie down with the kid, the calf and the lion and the fatling together." The Amer-ican Quaker and folk artist Edward Hicks (1780–1849) was so taken with this vision—quite impossible in the present order of nature—that he painted over sixty versions of it.

Peaceable Kingdom, Edward Hicks, 1830–1835. Fenimore Art Museum, Cooperstown, New York. Gift of Stephen C. Clark. Photograph by Richard C. Walker. *Used by permission.*

Closer to our time, Martin Luther King Jr. also famously had a "dream" of justice in his land. When our dreams coincide with God's, when we are dissatisfied with present violence, when we can imagine the shape of justice, we live in an Advent spirit, no matter the time of year. The invocation, "Our Lord, come!" was ever the prayer of the early church.

CHRISTMAS

"At midnight there was a cry, 'Behold, the bridegroom! Come out to meet him'" (Matt. 25:6). At Christmas there is a turn, in nature and in the church. Since the New Testament does not indicate when Jesus was born, in the fourth century the church settled the Feast of the Nativity of our Lord to coincide with the winter solstice. No doubt a pastoral strategy lay behind this liturgical date, intended to counter prevailing pagan festivities. But there was a more compelling reason, too: The occasion of the solstice illustrated how "the true light, which enlightens everyone, was coming into the world" (John 1:9). Christmas Midnight Mass is celebrated in the darkest hours of the night. Yet the light of Christ pierces and illumines the darkness of the world, and turns it around. The Prologue of St. John's Gospel, always read on the First Sunday after Christmas, supplies this cosmic background to the Christmas story, as does the hymn "Of the Father's Love Begotten," whose opening stanza echoes this gospel:

> Of the Father's love begotten, ere the worlds began to be,
>
> he is Alpha and Omega, he the source, the ending he,
>
> of the things that are, that have been,
>
> and that future years shall see, evermore and evermore!

The tender domesticity of the Nativity story brings home the nearness of God as Emmanuel, "God-with-us." Because people often fear that God is distant, perhaps uncaring, the gift of the Incarnation is something to be savored, pondered long in meditation. God comes to us in the flesh, as vulnerable and unthreatening as a baby. Moreover, the naked helplessness of the newborn child, the hardships of Mary and Joseph, and the menacing cruelty of Herod, all link the Nativity narratives to the Passion narratives. Christmas points ahead to its culmination in the Paschal mystery. Christ was born to save us.

Precisely because many of the traditional Christmas hymns are familiar to us from years of repetition, we can easily overlook the theological strength that informs several of them. Consider, for example, the third stanza of Charles Wesley's "Hark! the herald angels sing":

> Mild he lays his glory by,
>
> born that we no more may die,
>
> born to raise us from the earth,
>
> born to give us second birth.[5]

---

5. All citations and references to hymns are from *The Hymnal 1982* of the Episcopal Church USA (New York: The Church Hymnal Corporation, 1985). Some texts, such as this one of Wesley's, have undergone slight alteration from the original.

These well-known lines skillfully juxtapose birth and death: Christ's birth to extinguish death. Following the Philippians' hymn (2:5–11), Wesley invites meditation on Christ's self-abasement for the sake of our salvation. He also plays with birth imagery as he writes of Jesus's human birth for our spiritual rebirth: "born to give us second birth." In much the same vein, the lessons during Christmastide press us to realize Christ's birth within ourselves: "But when the fullness of time had come, God sent his Son, born of a woman, born under the law, in order to redeem those who were under the law, so that we might receive adoption as children" (Gal. 4:4–5). Entering into the Christmas mystery, then, includes the ardent desire that Christ be born in us, his life constantly shaping our own. Phillips Brooks captures this prayer in the final stanza of "O little town of Bethlehem": "O holy Child of Bethlehem, descend to us, we pray; cast out our sin and enter in, *be born in us today*."

In a culture such as ours that understands Christmas very little and Advent not at all, the observance of these discrete seasons can be awkward for Christians to negotiate. But there is much to be lost in blurring their distinction in an amorphous "holiday season" that kicks off at Thanksgiving, if not at Halloween. We need to hear the Advent stress upon vigilance, a vigilance nurtured by quiet and silence. When a great deal of contemporary religion is artificially sunny, Advent's sober acceptance of darkness, waiting, incompleteness, and contemplative longing offers a unique perspective and grace. It grounds us in reality.

When Advent is observed in its integrity, the Twelve Days of Christmas can be celebrated as the festive season it is. This is the time for Christmas decoration and parties at home and at church. There are also major feast days scattered in the Christmastide season. We can let the joy of the Incarnation seep in. Theologians and poets have reveled in the paradoxes of Christmas: the Creator becoming a creature, the Infinite inhabiting the finite—in Mary's body, in the church, and in the world. The paradox of Christmas can take hold of us, too, as we continually invite Christ to be born in us, to grow in us and, as we turn to Epiphany, to be manifest in us.

EPIPHANY

The Feast of the Epiphany, observed on January 6, is one of the most ancient solemnities in the church. Originally, it celebrated the baptism of our Lord, and in the Eastern Orthodox Church, it still does. In the Western church, Epiphany marks the visit of the magi to the infant Jesus (Matt. 2:1–12). Both these events are rightly considered "epiphanies" or "manifestations" of Christ (Greek *epiphania*, manifestation). With his baptism Jesus emerged from obscurity to begin his public ministry. At that very moment, he is manifested as the Son of God and the Messiah. The Orthodox also refer to the baptism as a "theophany" of the triune God. Here the Trinity is explicitly revealed as the Spirit descends upon Jesus, anointing him as the Christ, while the Father's voice claims him as his beloved.

In its calendar, the Episcopal Church joins with Western observance in commemorating the visit of the magi on January 6. As "wise men from the East," the magi represent the Gentile world. Christ's manifestation to these seekers of truth prefigures the later apostolic mission to the non-Jewish world; embedded in the birth narrative is this hint of the universality of the gospel. Still, the Feast of the Baptism of our Lord is not by any means overlooked: Our church calendar significantly places it on the First Sunday after the Epiphany, thus yoking Eastern and Western church traditions. As we have already seen in chapter 1, the baptism of our Lord is of immense import for all who have been baptized into Christ. It is therefore one of the four feast days recommended for Holy Baptism (BCP, 312).

Having passed the winter solstice, the days gradually grow longer in the months of January and February. The Epiphany season builds on the impression of "light coming into the world" as the Sunday gospels proclaim the calling of the apostles, the early teaching and healing ministry of Jesus, or the Sermon on the Mount. The manifestation of Jesus presses forward; the kingdom of God is breaking in. That light now must penetrate and illumine our minds, hearts, and actions. A seasonal blessing sums up the grace of Epiphany: "May Christ, the Son of God, be manifest in you, that your lives may be a light to the world" (*The Book of Occasional Services*, 24).

Transfiguration of Christ. Theophanes the Greek, early fifteenth century. Tretyakov Gallery, Moscow. *Photo credit Scala/Art Resource, New York. Used by permission.*

The Epiphany season ends with the climactic epiphany of the Transfiguration. While the Feast of the Transfiguration of our Lord occurs in the summer (August 6), the gospels for the Last Sunday after the Epiphany bring forward this radiant moment of glory just as we are about to embark upon Lent. The Baptism of our Lord and his Transfiguration thus frame the Epiphany season. In the gospel accounts, the heavenly voice owns Jesus as "My Son, the Beloved" or "My Son, my Chosen." Here on the holy mountain Jesus, shining with unearthly light, is revealed in his divine glory. This dazzling epiphany comes towards the conclusion of Jesus's Galilean ministry. He is about to "set his face" towards Jerusalem, where he will suffer and die. The story of the Transfiguration signals a crucial turning point in the gospel narratives, and its placement at the end of the Epiphany season signals a decisive turning point for the church, too. With his chosen disciples, we are graced to apprehend Jesus transfigured with divine light before we see him disfigured in the darkness of his passion. At this juncture, we briefly glimpse the resurrection glory awaiting Jesus—and us—at the end of Lent.

LENT

"Remember that you are dust, and to dust you shall return." Lent begins with the somber recognition of our mortality. We celebrate the Resurrection at Easter only after facing squarely the inevitability of death. What we make of death determines what we make of life. In our death-denying culture, in which youth is extolled and getting old is considered a misfortune, Ash Wednesday is strangely liberating. The ashes are smeared upon our foreheads in the sign of the cross—the same sign with which chrism anoints our foreheads at baptism. All of Lent is moving towards the passion and resurrection of Jesus, culminating at Easter with baptisms or the renewal of baptism. Lent prepares us for this grace by taking us into the mystery of the cross, our bridge from death to life. It is the season to probe sources of bondage and diminishment: What feels like death just now? What is holding us back from fullness of life in Christ? Our renewing of baptism entails searching self-examination and repentance. We must undergo a death to sin and all forms of resistance to God.

The forty days of Lent have several biblical antecedents: Jesus's forty days fast after his baptism; the Israelites' forty years sojourn in the wilderness; even the forty days and nights of torrential rain in the Great Flood. These stories are connected: temptation, sin, and renewal are threads running through them in various configurations. Jesus's victory over the Tempter prefigures his final victory over evil on the cross. That Jesus was "tempted in every way as we are, yet did not sin" (BCP, 379; Heb. 4:15) is a consoling and heartening Lenten motif. Our weakness is buttressed by his strength.

The traditional disciplines of Lent—prayer, fasting, and almsgiving—are salutary habits inherited from Jewish piety, although the last two practices require some interpretation. Prayer, of course, is a fundamental discipline for Christians. Without it, we do not know God or live in Christ. Baptism commits us to corporate and private prayer: "the breaking of bread and the prayers." So if we have been negligent in eucharistic worship, in the prayer of the church (traditionally the Daily Office), or in setting aside time for personal prayer, resuming or enhancing these practices will be the obvious place for our Lenten discipline to begin.

The Episcopal Church designates only two days as "fasts": Ash Wednesday and Good Friday. In the Bible and in early centuries of the church, fasting meant refraining from food and drink until sundown, when a simple meatless meal would be taken. Over time, the Western church has greatly mitigated the discipline of fasting to entail two small meals and one meatless meal. By contrast, Muslims today engage in a complete fast, abstaining even from water, every day of Ramadan. Since there are now different traditions of fasting in the church, just how we practice it will depend upon our work and state of health, as we weigh the spiritual benefits of a more or less rigorous fast.

Abstinence refers to omitting certain foods or pleasures for the purpose of self-denial. Since all the weekdays of Lent and Holy Week and all Fridays throughout the year, except in the seasons of Christmas and Easter, are deemed "Days of Special Devotion" (BCP, 17), many Christians practice some form of abstinence on these days. Traditional forms of abstinence involve refraining from meat or alcohol. The Eastern Orthodox continue to require eliminating meat and all animal products throughout the Great Lent.

But what is the purpose of denying ourselves legitimate pleasures? At one level it trains the will. By occasionally denying ourselves innocent gratifications, we become more spiritually fit to deny ourselves the illicit ones. But on another level bodily self-denial constitutes a form of praying with the body. It expresses penitence and desire for conversion of life. We feel our weakness in cravings for pleasures to which we have become accustomed. We may grow more compassionate towards those who must "do without" every day of their lives. We sense in our very bodies utter dependence upon God, the giver of all gifts, and we realize anew our overwhelming need for grace to uphold us in our frailty.

Since alienation from our bodies is, oddly enough, an upshot of the sedentary and soft lifestyle of the affluent, it is worth asking ourselves as Lent approaches: What "fullness of life" might God wish for me? Contrary to the popular stereotype, St. Paul teaches that the body bears immense dignity because of our union with Christ in the resurrection—something that conditions our bodies even now. He further reminds us: "Do you not know that your body is a temple of the Holy Spirit within you, which you have from God, and that you are not your own? For you were bought with a price; therefore glorify God in your body" (1 Cor. 6:20). If we are to "glorify God in the body," what would that look like? Clearly, it would call us to relinquish habits that damage the body such as smoking, excessive or unhealthful eating and drinking, and failure to exercise. St. Paul is not here advocating the cultus of beautiful bodies so prevalent in today's advertising. He is rather pleading for honoring the body, offering a persuasive theological rationale for treating it with respect: The resurrection of the body governs how we regard the body. Nowadays, too, we need to consider the body of the earth so as to take into account the environmental impact of our food choices. Lent, then, can initiate a recovery of balance that leads to Easter joy. It could begin the hard process of undoing injurious habits that would continue the rest of the year.

"Almsgiving" sounds quaint to our ears, but in traditional religious cultures it is a pillar of practical piety. While at first glance it might seem to smack of *noblesse oblige*, the obligation laid upon the rich to give alms binds them tangibly to the poor. Sharing wealth enacts how we belong to each other in community. While acknowledging the unequal distribution of material goods among people, the Scriptures seek to lessen the burden on the poor by various provisions. Or as the prophet Micah summarizes the core of Old Testament teaching: "What does the Lord require of you but to do justice, and to love kindness, and to walk humbly with your God?" (6:8). Jesus further developed this tradition by frequently teaching about wealth, warning about its danger to ensnare: "For where your treasure is, there your heart will be also" (Matt. 6:21). In other words, if you want an accurate gauge of your values, "follow the money." Just how Christians should practice economic justice persists as a vexing issue. But our duty to seek some measure of fairness in this crucial aspect of our common life remains. The social fabric of community demands it. When writing to the Corinthians about a collection he is organizing for the poor in Jerusalem, Paul sets sensible limits to giving: Members of the church, he assures them, are under no obligation to impoverish themselves in order to assist others. Rather, he says, "it is a question of a fair balance between your present abundance and their need" (2 Cor. 8:13–14). What that "fair balance" might mean in our own circumstances is a hard question with which we must wrestle. But cultivating the habit of generosity—"almsgiving"—is a way to begin.

HOLY WEEK

By the end of Lent our eyes are fixed on Jesus. Everything in Lent, our personal observances and the liturgies of the church, has been preparing us for its culmination in Holy Week. Through the solemn liturgies of Holy Week, we participate in those events by which we and the entire world are saved. At times, these services can seem emotionally and physically exhausting, and rightly so. We will not easily be remade in Christ. The week begins with the gripping drama of The Sunday of the Passion: Palm Sunday. Here we feel our vacillation as we shift from "Hosanna" to "Crucify him!" Yet the faithfulness of Jesus, who "loved us to the end," reveals itself at every point in the passion narrative. Each day of this week is termed "holy," but none more so than the final three days: the Triduum. The observances on Maundy Thursday, Good Friday, and the Great Vigil of Easter really amount to one continuous liturgy. Unless some urgent obligation prevents us from attending, we should be present at this momentous liturgy in all three parts. For here, more than anywhere else, we "pass over" with Christ from death to life. We become again people of the Resurrection.

EASTER

The Easter gospels begin with the astonished women at the tomb. We remain thunderstruck at the Easter proclamation: "Alleluia. Christ is risen." We hear it, but find it hard to take in. Like the apostles listening to the women's report, deep down we may suspect this gospel to be too good to be true.

The risen Lord is a mysterious figure. As we observed earlier, even those closest to him fail, at first, to realize who he is. There seems to be both continuity and discontinuity with the Jesus of Nazareth they once knew. Now risen, Jesus comes and goes as he pleases. He can be in more than one place at the same time. He accompanies two disciples en route to Emmaus, yet on the same day appears to Simon Peter back in Jerusalem (Luke 24:33–35). Locked doors are no obstacle to him: he passes right through them (John 20:19). In the garden where she first encounters the risen Lord, Mary Magdalene wants, literally, to hold on to Jesus, but cannot (John 20:17). Yet in his risen state Jesus still maintains an intimacy with his disciples. He speaks with them and, most significantly, eats with them.

The resurrection narratives offer tantalizing glimpses of what the resurrection might mean, both for Jesus and for us. The resurrection of Jesus is altogether different from the raising of Lazarus (John 11:1–44), which serves in the Gospel of John as a "sign" pointing to the resurrection of Jesus. But that miracle, though astounding, is still not an instance of resurrection itself. Lazarus, after all, was raised to ordinary mortal life, and he would eventually die again. In the resurrection, Jesus is no resuscitated corpse. The resurrection does not simply put back him back together again like Humpty Dumpty in the nursery rhyme. His humanity has changed. In the risen Christ, we witness the beginning of the new creation. Jesus is no longer bound by death or, for that matter, the limitations of space and time. He is recognizably human and bodily, but his humanity is transfigured.

Other Christians before us have wondered just what the resurrection might mean. Evidently even in the first century, Christians in Corinth struggled with this issue. Fortunately for us, Paul devotes considerable thought to drawing out the implications of the resurrection in his first letter to them. Like many of us, the Corinthians were asking, "How are the dead raised? With what kind of body do they come?" (1 Cor. 15:35). In his reply, Paul employs an agricultural metaphor, comparing a corpse to a seed that is sown, which must first disintegrate: "What you sow does not come to life unless it dies. And as for what you sow, you do not sow the body that is to be, but a bare seed, perhaps of wheat or of some other grain" (1 Cor. 15:36–37). What springs to life at harvest time is so vastly different from the simple seed that was planted that it appears to us as something altogether different:

> So it is with the resurrection of the dead. What is sown is perishable, what is raised is imperishable. It is sown in dishonor, it is raised in glory. It is sown in weakness, it is raised in power. It is sown a physical body, it is raised a spiritual body. If there is a physical body, there is also a spiritual body. (1 Cor. 15:42–44)

Jesus uses much the same metaphor to speak of his impending death in St. John's Gospel—a gospel written decades after Paul's first letter to the Corinthians: "The hour has come for the Son of Man to be glorified. Very truly, I tell you, unless a grain of wheat falls into the earth and dies, it remains just a single grain; but if it dies, it bears much fruit" (John 12:23–24). The similarity to Paul may just be coincidental, or perhaps Paul is drawing on an oral tradition going back to Jesus himself.

In any case, the metaphor of the dying seed in both instances suggests both continuity and radical change. There is continuity: the risen Jesus is, finally, recognizable as the man Jesus of Nazareth. They are not two different people. Yet Jesus is profoundly altered. He is no longer constrained by the ordinary limitations of this world. He has what Paul calls a "spiritual body" (*sōma pneumatikon*). By this unusual term, Paul does not intend to evoke some sort of insubstantial, diaphanous body—the kind of "body" with which ghosts are usually portrayed. He means that the resurrection body is a real body shot through and through with the Spirit. Now liberated from mortality, it is no longer bound by any earthly restriction.

Because Jesus is risen and ascended, many things become possible. We can encounter him anywhere and anytime. He is present in the members of his body, the church, of which he is the head (Eph. 4:15). He dwells in the least of his brothers and sisters. He meets us in the sacraments and in prayer. Indeed, he "fills all things" (Eph. 4:10). The resurrection of Jesus affects everything and everyone. The whole universe is changed by the one who defeated death, a creation that has always been "groaning in travail" because it is subject to the "futility" of eventual decay and death:

> For the creation waits with eager longing for the revealing of the children of God; for the creation was subjected to futility, not of its own will, but by the will of the one who subjected it, in hope that the creation itself will be set free from its bondage to decay and will obtain the freedom of the glory of the children of God. We know that the whole creation has been groaning in labor pains until now; and not only the creation, but we ourselves, who have the first fruits of the Spirit, groan inwardly while we wait for adoption, the redemption of our bodies. (Rom. 8:19–23)

Paul's cosmic vision here anticipates what contemporary thinkers call the "web of nature." As John Muir famously said, "When we try to pick out anything by itself, we find it hitched to everything else in the universe." Since humans are part of creation, we stand in solidarity with the rest of nature, whether plants, animals, stars, or galaxies. Together we suffer from "bondage to decay," awaiting the full redemption of our bodies. So we are connected to creation, but we are also connected to Christ. What we have now received of resurrection grace is the "first fruits of the Spirit," and that is enough to anchor our hope. Hope is not wishful thinking, but rather a dimension of faith that is continually nurtured by contact with the risen Lord.

Throughout Easter Week and the Great Fifty Days of this season, the lessons help us identify *how* the risen Lord is present with us so that we, too, can recognize him and believe. The first gift of the risen Lord is forgiveness. Since Jesus's resurrection overcomes evil, even the most dire situations can be made new. The possibility of forgiveness is released into the world. So when Jesus appears to his fearful and guilty disciples—their locked doors are no barrier to him—he bears a message of peace and forgiveness: "Peace be with you" and "Receive the Holy Spirit. If you forgive the sins of any, they are forgiven them" (John 20:21–23; Gospel for Easter 2). Jesus then eats with his disciples when they gather, or by the seashore, or at Emmaus. We know him in the breaking of bread. For many, regular encounter with Christ in the Eucharist is the very ground of their faith in him. On the Fourth Sunday of Easter, we listen over the three years to different portions of John 10. Jesus is our Good Shepherd, who knows each of us by name. We recognize his voice, and follow where he leads.

Gospels for the last Sundays of the Easter season are taken from the "Farewell Discourses" of St. John's Gospel. These speak of ongoing communion between Jesus and his disciples: "I am the vine, you are the branches." Several speak of the promised Spirit: "The Advocate, the Holy Spirit . . . will teach you everything, and remind you of all that I have said to you." All these gospels, and the other Easter lessons in the Daily Office and in the eucharistic lectionary, offer ample material for our meditation. The risen Lord lives in us, "abides" in us, and in the church.

Forty days after Easter, following Lukan chronology, the church celebrates the Feast of the Ascension. For many people the Ascension is problematic, if they think about it at all. Some dismiss the pre-modern cosmology by which the event is described (Acts 1:9); others wonder what there is to celebrate. Yet the Ascension of our Lord is a crucial aspect of the Easter mystery. It portrays Jesus's glorification in his return to the Father. The New Testament indicates that the resurrection appearances eventually ceased, but Jesus did not go away. "And remember, I am with you always, to the end of the age" are our Lord's final words in St. Matthew's Gospel (28:20). Indeed, the whole Easter season has been revealing just how we encounter him now.

In the Ascension, Jesus's glorification is completed; and in that glorification, we have a share. As in the vision on the Mount of Transfiguration, we apprehend in Jesus our own eschatological destiny. For the Epistle to the Ephesians, this future glory catches us up even now: "But God, who is rich in mercy, out of the great love with which he loved us even when we were dead in our trespasses, made us alive together with Christ—by grace you have been saved—*and raised us up with him and seated us with him in the heavenly places in Christ Jesus*" (2:4–6). The Ascension of our Lord therefore celebrates our glory in Christ: where Jesus is, there we are. In his hymn for this feast day, "See the Conqueror mounts in triumph," Christopher Wordsworth notes this twofold glorification in the final stanza:

> Thou hast raised our human nature on the clouds to God's
>   right hand:
> there we sit in heavenly places, there with thee in glory stand.
> Jesus reigns, adored by angels, Man with God is on the throne;
> mighty Lord, in thine ascension, we by faith behold our own.

Pentecost brings the Easter season to a climactic close. With Mary and the disciples we receive anew the gift of the Holy Spirit. In the Acts of the Apostles, as we observed in chapter 1, the immediate effect of the Spirit upon the gathered community is a vigorous proclamation of Christ's resurrection. The apostolic mission begins with a newfound fearlessness in the face of persecution and death. For the resurrection of Jesus dispels our ultimate fear: fear of death. The Spirit brings the resurrection home, transforming disciples into apostles. Following a somewhat different tradition, St. John's Gospel also explicitly links Jesus's glorification with the outpouring of the Spirit (John 7:39). After the resurrection and as a consequence of it, the mission of God in sending Jesus is perpetuated in Jesus's commissioning of disciples: "As the Father has sent me, so I send you. . . . Receive the Holy Spirit." The risen Lord then breathes on them, effecting a new creation (John 20:21–22; cf. Gen. 2:7).

Yet before any of this happens, the Risen Lord first shows his disciples "his hands and his side." A week later he invites Thomas to place his finger in his wounded hands and his hand into his pierced side. Even in resurrection glory, the wounds remain. History inflicts scars. The tradition of placing five incense grains in the paschal candle, representing the five wounds of Jesus, witnesses to this insight. The grace of the resurrection, then, imparts no instant cheery optimism. Such an expectation can be burdensome. People sometimes doubt the sincerity of their faith if, as believers in the resurrection, they still experience anxiety, fear, or discouragement. The resurrection is our final horizon; it places suffering in perspective. But suffering persists. As Julian of Norwich testifies of Christ near the end of her revelations: "He said not, 'Thou shalt not be tempted; thou shalt not be troubled; thou shalt not be distressed,' but He said, 'Thou shalt not be overcome.'"[6] The resurrection instills strength and courage. It grounds us in hope to persevere, as Jesus did, to the end.

TIME AFTER PENTECOST

With the Christmas cycle and the Easter cycle now completed, the first Sunday after Pentecost is Trinity Sunday. Our contemplation moves towards the triune God: the One from whom and towards whom the events of salvation, just now celebrated, have their origin and goal. When everything is finally subjected to God, "God may be all in all" (1 Cor. 15:28).

For roughly the next six months, we will be in the "green" season of church décor and slow, organic growth. Our readings, in both Office and Eucharist, will resume "in course." Except for the major and minor feast days sprinkled throughout these months, there will be no great drama. In other words, the "Time after Pentecost" is like ordinary Christian life. It is time to get on with everyday faithfulness in prayer, study, work, hospitality, and recreation. The agricultural parables Jesus told about the coming kingdom, of its slow but often surprising growth, characterize this time:

> Jesus also said, "The kingdom of God is as if someone would scatter seed on the ground, and would sleep and rise day and night, and the seed would sprout and grow, he does not know how. (Mark 4:26–27)

---

6. *The Complete Julian of Norwich*, ed. and trans. Father John-Julian, OJN (Brewster, MA: Paraclete Press, 2009), chapter 68, 319.

We go about our daily tasks, sleeping and rising, working and praying, and God gives the growth—often secretly, we "do not know how." And so, our days are sanctified. It happens quietly, day in and day out, year in and year out, through the round of the liturgical year. The sanctification of time transpires through the regular pattern of Daily Office and Eucharist. As we live into these rhythms, we are bought into harmony with cycles of nature, while the mysteries of the Incarnation take flesh in our own. Evelyn Underhill gracefully sums up how the ordinary phases of human life are transformed through contact with the mysteries of Christ, enacted through the liturgical year:

> Since everyone, whatever his vocation, is obliged to repro-
> duce the common curve of human life in its passage through
> time—to be born, to grow, to make choices and accept respon-
> sibilities, form some human relationships, take some place in
> the social order, to meet hardship, difficulty, and disillusion, to
> suffer, and at last to die—it follows that all have in this inev-
> itable sequence of experiences something that can be trans-
> formed and directed Godwards. . . . So that, in the devout
> commemoration of the successive Mysteries of the life of
> Jesus, from Christmas to Easter and to their consummation in
> Pentecost, on which the liturgical year of the Church is based,
> all the phases of human experience are lit up by the radiance of
> eternity and brought into relation with the inexhaustible reve-
> lation of God in the flesh.[7]

---

7. Evelyn Underhill, *Worship* (New York: Harper & Brothers, 1937), 76–77.

CHAPTER FOUR

Prayer in Solitude

"In the morning, while it was still very dark, Jesus got up and went out to a deserted place, and there he prayed." (Mark 1:35)

The regular pattern of Christian prayer is liturgical, founded upon participation in Eucharist and Daily Office within the larger rhythms of the church year. Liturgical prayer situates us tangibly within the community of the baptized, reinforcing our corporate identity as the body of Christ and sanctifying each member of it. But a sole diet of liturgical prayer can become rote and, in time, exhausting. Sometimes we blame the liturgy for the feelings of flatness that set in: "I don't get anything out of it." We are bound to become bored and impatient with liturgical prayer if we fail to balance prayer in community with prayer in solitude. Communal forms of prayer start to lose depth if they do not alternate with another sort of prayer: personal engagement with God apart from the liturgy and our ordinary activities. Liturgy risks turning into empty formalism, superficial and bland, if it is not supported by periods of vital, individual encounter with God. A vigorous life of prayer moves between these two poles, each leading back to the other. For these two basic expressions of prayer, liturgical and personal, are refreshingly distinct. While prayer with others requires fixed liturgies to structure "common prayer," prayer in solitude allows breadth of freedom and elasticity.

The gospels indicate that Jesus regularly withdrew from his busy, active ministry for solitary communion with his Father. He recommends that his followers do the same: "Whenever you pray, go to your room and shut the door and pray to your Father who is in secret; and your Father who sees in secret will reward you" (Matt. 6:6). As Jesus teaches here, such prayer requires privacy: we must "shut the door." This is prayer at its most intimate. For deeper feelings to emerge we need uninterrupted space and a measure of quiet. Sometimes prayer releases strong emotions, and we will usually feel inhibited about expressing them—or even feeling them—if we are publically observable. Creating a sacred space for ourselves, even if it consists in a corner of our room, or habitually returning to the same location, generates an atmosphere conducive to prayer. Returning to this hallowed place sets in motion, at subliminal levels of our consciousness, a readiness for prayer.

We also need silence to become capable of hearing God's voice. In most cases, the place where we can most readily secure such quiet and privacy will be, literally, in our own rooms. It may take some courage and humility to ask family or other members of our household to allow us to withdraw for a spell. We may be embarrassed by displaying our piety even to this extent (the opposite problem from the one Jesus envisioned in his counsel), but the Lord assures us that it is worth the effort: There is a "reward" of closeness to God in such "secret" prayer. In other situations, though, the best place to obtain protected quiet may be in a church or chapel, if we are fortunate enough to find one open for prayer during the week. The presence of a few other people similarly engaged in prayer should not ordinarily compromise our sense of solitude. At other times, we might discover the seclusion we need in natural settings, whether sitting on our porch or in a park or during a walk in the woods. While some forms of walking meditation can be valuable, physical stillness usually allows the spirit to reach greater stillness as well. Jesus periodically invited his disciples to share his times of personal retreat. "Come away . . . and rest a while," he urges them after a particularly hectic stint of ministry (Mark 6:31). He sometimes sought refreshment for himself in the company of his closest friends, thus extending the same opportunity for renewal to them. Sometimes his invitation is taken up, but at other times, it is overlooked. The well-known story of Jesus's visit to his friends Mary and Martha of Bethany is a case in point (Luke 10:38–42). Unfortunately, this episode has suffered from a kind of allegorization that can obscure its rather straightforward message. While the story is certainly laden with symbolic undertones, patristic commentators tended to freeze the two sisters in their respective roles, with Mary representing the "contemplative life," and Martha, the "active life." Noting Jesus's patent rebuke of Martha, and reflecting their own culture's philosophical bias favoring the contemplative life, these theologians took the incident to demonstrate the inherent superiority of a life of contemplative withdrawal over active engagement in ministry. So powerful a hold has this allegory had on the Christian imagination that even today people sometimes categorize themselves as "Marthas" or "Marys." Yet contemporary treatments, while remaining allegorical, tend to turn the story on its head. In this case, Martha becomes the heroine of the tale—a reading that reflects our opposite cultural bias, one that privileges active service. It further ignores Jesus's gentle but clear rebuke of Martha: "Martha, Martha, you are worried and distracted by many things." Other modern interpretations blandly assert the common-sense notion that we all should strive to be "both Marthas and Marys." And while the story does have a decidedly feminist edge, it offers no ground to lament that women are always left to do the work. That comes close to Martha's complaint against her sister, but Jesus will not support her grievance. He has something better on offer.

We cannot suppose that this story denigrates active service or hospitality. St. Luke situates it in his gospel immediately after the story of the Good Samaritan, the consummate example of gracious care for others. But service can sometimes go awry, and in the case of Martha of Bethany it does. Like all of us, she probably began her ministry to Jesus with the best of intentions and with a cheerful heart. But before long, her service becomes stressful and compulsive, and she turns on her sister for not pulling her weight. Unlike Martha, Mary has seized the freedom of true discipleship. She will not allow herself to be defined by the socially scripted role of "women's work," and instead takes her place in the rabbinical circle of disciples listening to the Teacher. Jesus defends Mary's choice. The desire to listen to Jesus, learn from him, and deepen friendship with him, is always "the better part."

Jesus and St. Mary of Bethany. Courtesy of the Order of Julian of Norwich.

Without resorting to wooden allegory, we can still recognize ourselves in these two sisters. It is easy to move from being a generous servant of the Lord to a frenzied, self-pitying, blaming Martha. We also are familiar with our "inner Mary," who yearns for some time with Jesus and intimacy with him. It can be hard for this Mary of ours to get a hearing, because the Martha within always has something else for her to do. Indeed, telling ourselves that we are "doing the Lord's work" can become the perfect excuse for avoiding the Lord. We can fall prey to our culture's activist bias, which regards "holy leisure" with incomprehension, disdain, and suspicion. As in the first century, choosing the "one thing needful" can be decidedly counter-cultural.

So even before we endeavor to find a space for solitary prayer, or decide how we will use this time apart, we can expect to encounter considerable resistance both within and outside of ourselves. Our culture is afraid of silence and bombards us with stimuli at every turn. Almost every public space forces television or noise of some sort upon us. Medical offices and hospitals, where we might wish to ponder our existential situation, make such reflection nearly impossible. Even more seriously, our addiction to electronic devices impairs our capacity for sustained thought and attention. All this distracting stimulation serves, ironically, as an anesthetic. It dulls the pain we carry within us, but at the cost of dulling our sensibilities and awareness. Yet an interlude of quiet solitude often restores our sense of perspective, clears our minds, and cleanses our words. Never has such solitude been more needed—or resisted.

The avoidance of silence or even quietness in our society reflects an uneasiness that starts within ourselves. Blaise Pascal once observed that "most of man's troubles come from his inability to sit quietly in his chamber." Why this restlessness? Is it not because solitude involves confrontation with ourselves and, if we pray "in secret," with God? Our dreams, if nothing else, tell us there is a riot of passions and memories churning within us. Our waking consciousness, if we are honest, confirms the same. Who would want to spend time with the likes of us? Surely not ourselves! So the prospect of undistracted time alone provokes anxiety, and anxiety can find a thousand strategies to evade encounter with self. Yet those unwilling to confront their own inner turmoil invariably project it elsewhere. Like carriers of an undiagnosed contagion, they unwittingly infect others with it. It is apt to contaminate friendships, workplaces, families, parishes, and other communities by slow seepage or by volatile outbursts, causing injury to the community one way or another.

"Whoever cannot be alone should beware of community," wrote Dietrich Bonhoeffer.[1] As a pastor and director of a small residential seminary, Bonhoeffer saw what happened when individual members resist regular periods of solitude. He observed how people are apt to throw themselves into community in a futile attempt

---

1. Dietrich Bonhoeffer, *Life Together*, 82.

to escape their aching loneliness. Such strategies of avoidance are doomed to fail. Rather than alleviate a sense of inner isolation they end up compounding it. And the community always suffers as a result. Without the silence of solitude, speech—so essential for genuine interaction—becomes hollow and cheap. Bonhoeffer also warned against a specious, unhealthful solitude that shuns involvement with others in the church: "Whoever cannot stand being in community should beware of being alone." Alienated solitude spirals down into self-preoccupation. When we are called to Christ, it is within the fellowship of the church. Even when physically alone, we remain members of his body. Solitude brings us back to the community refreshed and restored. According to Bonhoeffer, the health of a community depends upon a daily practice of solitary prayer among its members.

Solitude brings us starkly before God, and many of us want to escape that possibility, often without admitting it. For despite our progressive image of a deity positively oozing with "unconditional acceptance," deep down we may dread God, too. Who wants to spend time alone with a God who, knowing us all too well, just might find us wanting? What then?

If we are haunted by the specter of a wrathful, condemning God, who is ever scrutinizing our least mistakes, the only way to banish such an idol from our psyches is through repeated contact with the true and living God. "Whoever has seen me has seen the Father," says Jesus (John 14:9). What we can know of God is most fully disclosed in Christ: "No one has ever seen God. It is God the only Son, who is close to the Father's heart, who has made him known" (John 1:18). And what do we see—what is revealed—in the words and actions of Jesus? From the very start of his public ministry, inaugurated with his baptism by John, Jesus chooses to stand with sinners. He ends up crucified between two notorious bandits, dying as a criminal condemned under the law. Throughout his entire ministry, Jesus scandalized the devout by his familiarity with public sinners, insisting that "the Son of Man came to seek out and to save the lost" (Luke 19:10). Indeed from one standpoint, as Paul would write, Jesus's entire mission could be summed up as the ultimate work of reconciliation: "in Christ

God was reconciling the world to himself, not counting their trespasses against them" (2 Cor. 5:19).

To be sure, warnings about an impending divine judgment resound throughout both testaments, and many of Jesus's teachings and parables speak of such a reckoning. How, we may wonder, do we know whether on the last day we will not find ourselves among the goats rather than the sheep, or cast into "the outer darkness, where there will be weeping and gnashing of teeth" (Matt. 25:30)? These sayings of Jesus must be taken seriously: Moral indifference or a fixed hostility to God has dire consequences. It amounts to an imprisonment in sin, to the darkness of unexamined self-centeredness, to a living hell. But Jesus's teachings on this subject are less a forecast of our eternal destiny than a bracing wake-up call. Jesus told parables for his listeners to hear and take to heart: "Let anyone with ears to hear, listen!" (Mark 4:9). They constitute a summons to conversion, to a radical change in our way of thinking and in our behavior. Hyperbole captures our attention. Defending her habit of populating her stories with grotesque characters and shocking twists of plot, the Roman Catholic fiction writer Flannery O'Conner explained that "To the hard of hearing you shout, and for the almost-blind you draw large and startling figures." The parables and sayings of Jesus have a similar strategy behind them. They are part and parcel of his consistent mission "to seek out and save the lost."

The judgment of Christ, then, is not something to be dodged, but welcomed. Jesus likened himself to a physician of souls: "Those who are well have no need of a physician, but those who are sick. Go learn what this means, 'I desire mercy, not sacrifice.' For I have come to call not the righteous but sinners" (Matt. 9:12–13). We will not be healed if we avoid this physician. As with our physical ailments, we need to say where it hurts, exposing some potentially embarrassing parts. The truth of divine judgment provides an accurate diagnosis, only in this case judgment in itself can liberate and heal, if we allow it to do its work. Sometimes mere encounter with Jesus is sufficient. In the story of Zacchaeus, for instance, Jesus utters not one word of reproach to a man who, in his position as chief tax collector in Jericho, had doubtless practiced extortion upon his neighbors. The experience of being sought out and accepted by Jesus is enough to elicit Zacchaeus's implicit confession in his promise of restitution for ill-gotten gain (Luke 19:1–10).

Yet we do not seek time apart only for those personal matters that may weigh upon us nor solely for the praise and adoration of the God whom we love. As we grow in Christian maturity, we grow in concern for our community, nation, and world. In periods of prayerful reflection, we seek to understand the larger social forces and cultural trends in which we are enmeshed. In solitude, then, we ask for the grace of discernment, the gift of acute insight into what is happening in confusing, obscure, or troubling situations. Only with clarity of vision can we make a graced response to it, personally or communally. The gospels relate a similar dynamic at work in the early public life of Jesus. Immediately after his baptism, he is driven into the desert for a season of fasting, followed by temptation. Fasting is a discipline associated with discernment, and Jesus's temptations all deal in one way or another with his mission and identity as "Son of God," as he has just been named in his baptism. Jesus's parabolic wrestlings with the Evil One are played out against the larger arena of the world: the dizzying heights of the Temple pinnacle or the still more dizzying panorama of "the kingdoms of the world and their splendor" (Matt. 4:1–11). In each case, Jesus responds with a measured word of Scripture.

Christians who have faced political forces of monumental evil, outright persecution, or both, often argue passionately for the necessity of solitude. Alfred Delp, the German Jesuit priest martyred for his role in resistance to the Third Reich, meditated on Christ's retreat in the wilderness as an essential preparation for Jesus's public ministry. From his own solitude in Tegel Prison in Berlin, Delp wrote two days before his trial and less than a month before his execution:

> The fact that our Lord retired into the wilderness shows how genuinely he took to heart the laws and problems of humanity. . . . Great issues affecting humankind always have to be decided in the wilderness, in uninterrupted isolation and unbroken silence. They hold a meaning and a blessing, these

great, silent, empty spaces that bring a person face to face with reality. . . .

Any life that cannot measure up to the wilderness, or seeks to evade it, is not worth much. There must be periods of withdrawal alternating with periods of activity and companionship or the horizons will shrink and life loses its savor. Unless a person consciously retires within himself to that quiet place where he may think out great problems he cannot hope to solve them. . . . (Epiphany 1945)[2]

Like Christ in the wilderness, our initial experience of the interior desert will probably entail struggling with our personal demons: the insidious voices that would undermine our baptismal dignity as sons and daughters of God. Old "tapes" from the past may play themselves out, tempting us to despair or grandiosity, inciting our fears and anxieties, stirring up resentments and disordered passions. We have to face places of guilt and shame within ourselves. Unflinching self-knowledge is hard won. Yet we are not alone in this wilderness. Christ is present in our every experience, and his defeat over the Evil One, both in the desert and finally on the cross, upholds us. It is crucial, then, to refer everything to him in prayer, and not attempt to "sort things out" all on our own. In time, the landscape of our desert solitude shifts to an oasis of consolation. After our Lord's strenuous match with the Tempter, "angels came and ministered to him" (Matt. 4:11). With this turn, far from evading solitude, we begin to welcome it. But whether the inner desert is dry and hard or suddenly blooms in refreshment—and most people swing periodically from one experience to the other—perseverance is crucial.

"Lord, teach us to pray, as John taught his disciples." (Luke 11:1)

One reason we avoid carving out time for prayer is simply that we wonder how to start and what to do. After saying a few familiar

---

2. *Alfred Delp, SJ: Prison Writings* (Maryknoll, NY: Orbis Books, 2004), 82.

prayers or offering up our intercessions, how do we spend the time? This is not a new problem. The disciple who asked Jesus to teach them how to pray had first observed the Lord at prayer and wanted to learn prayer from an obvious master. John the Baptist had evidently instructed his disciples in the art of prayer, and teaching others how to engage God in prayer seems to have been an expected part of the master/disciple relationship. In fact everyone needs to learn how to pray from someone else, whether in person or through books or, ideally, both. Jesus responds to the disciple's request with an example: the Lord's Prayer. The various petitions of this prayer first offer praise to God and then place intercession in its widest context: "Thy kingdom come, thy will be done." These initial petitions also imply a moral commitment to act in accord with them. Everyday concerns ("Give us this day our daily bread") are set beside ongoing spiritual struggle ("Save us from the time of trial"). Jesus names the fundamental disposition of a forgiving heart as the essential preparation for receiving the divine forgiveness we need and seek. It is no wonder, then, that the Lord's Prayer has become the universal Christian prayer. It is recited in every liturgy, and many Christians pray it on their own a few times a day.

In the church, the Lord's Prayer serves as a perfect instance of prayer for personal and communal recitation. It also provides an example for prayer and a standard by which we can assess the character of our own prayers. Clearly, authentic Christian prayer cannot run counter to the petitions and attitudes embodied in it. When Jesus offered this model of prayer, he was himself steeped in the rich traditions of Jewish piety that had shaped his own practice: pilgrimage to the temple for great festivals, synagogue observance, and prayer "in secret." He dies with the words of the psalmist on his lips. Christian prayer over the centuries has also drawn on these deep wellsprings in the course of developing its own traditions of prayer and meditation.

Although some familiarity with various methods of prayer is indispensable, learning to pray involves more than picking up a few techniques. As theologian Hans Urs von Balthasar has noted, "It is not we who force a knowledge of the Absolute by means

of techniques under our control. Of his own accord God freely reveals himself, explains himself in his Son and gives us a Word that satisfies our hungering soul."[3] God takes the initiative in divine self-disclosure. So prayer requires bending our spirits to the movement of the Holy Spirit at work within us. And at least to some degree, we need to understand theologically what is happening when we pray so we can give ourselves wholeheartedly to it.

From the first, we may feel inept about approaching the daunting task of beginning to pray. "For we know not what we should pray for as we ought," Paul candidly admits (Rom 8:26, KJV). To find ourselves at sixes and sevens when we wish to pray has, therefore, a long pedigree! But Paul assures us that God does not abandon us to our own devices. The Spirit supplies what is lacking: "Likewise the Spirit helps us in our weakness." This is the same Spirit of truth Jesus promised his disciples, who would bring to light what is false in the world, elucidate Jesus's teaching, and bring it home to us: "He will glorify me, because he will take what is mine and declare it to you" (John 16:14). Jesus describes the Spirit as our "Advocate," and Paul teaches that this Spirit intercedes for us, creating in us the prayer we ourselves cannot articulate:

> Likewise the Spirit helps us in our weakness; for we do not know what to pray for as we ought, but that very Spirit intercedes for us with sighs too deep for words. And God, who searches the heart, knows what is the mind of the Spirit, because the Spirit intercedes for the saints according to the will of God. (Rom 8:26–27, NRSV alt)

This is an extraordinarily reassuring passage. It teaches that prayer does not start with our fledgling efforts, but with God's Holy Spirit stirring within us. The Spirit prompts that holy restlessness that yearns for contact with God even though we scarcely know how to begin. As the old spiritual puts it, "Every time I feel the Spirit moving in my heart, I will pray." God is no distant deity

3. Hans Urs von Balthasar, *Christian Meditation*, trans. Sister Mary Theresilde Skerry (San Francisco: Ignatius Press, 1989), 11.

who just might listen to us if we could only get our act together or find the right words or formula. God is not a passive-aggressive partner in this affair, eyeing us with detachment as we flail about trying to get his attention. Far from playing hard to get, the Spirit starts the process by wooing us into prayer. The desire that we feel is implanted by the Spirit. We have only to respond.

As Paul portrays the typical experience of Christians at prayer, the spiritual dynamic he describes is thoroughly Trinitarian. Indeed, it is impossible to explain the experience of prayer without reference to the Trinity. The Spirit engenders prayer directed towards God. As we lean into the same filial relation to God that we share with Jesus, the Spirit quickens Christ's life in us. Christ is formed in us as we pray: "When we cry 'Abba! Father!' it is that very Spirit bearing witness with our spirit that we are children of God" (Rom. 8:15–16). Our desire to pray and our first steps towards it confirm the Spirit's prior action.

VOCAL PRAYER

"Prayer is, then, to speak more boldly, a conversation with God." (Clement of Alexandria)

Even if prayer is not a technology of the spirit, we still need something to do. Thomas Keating has likened personal prayer to having a "date with God," and this metaphor highlights its intrinsic freedom and versatility. A "date" is a gift of time spent with someone we love or wish to know better. We do not see it as an obligation, even though we will have to protect this time by adding it to our calendar. Prayer is a gift God wants to give us, not one more duty to add to our "to do" list. Just how we might spend the time with God may be as varied as how we spend time on a date: sometimes conversing, sometimes in an exchange of confidences, sometimes listening attentively, sometimes in silent companionship.[4]

---

4. Frank T. Griswold, *Praying Our Days: A Guide and Companion* (Harrisburg, PA: Morehouse, 2009) offers a beautiful collection of prayers, including some for sacramental and liturgical preparation, along with wise counsel for their use.

Nearest to hand are those prayers that have been prayed by others before us and which are, therefore, steeped in years of grace. There is, as already mentioned, the Lord's Prayer. Slow, thoughtful recitation of each of its petitions, while pondering key words—"our" or "thy will," for instance—can readily inspire meditation on its phrases. Similarly, the psalms offer a treasury of prayer, expressing the full range of human feeling in an attitude of transparency before God. The Book of Common Prayer contains dozens of "Prayers and Thanksgivings" suitable for many occasions and concerns. In addition, the Collects of the prayer book present many beautifully crafted and theologically nuanced prayers, which in one form or another have sustained generations.

Another completely accessible form of vocal prayer is available to us in those prayers in which we address God in our own words. Such words, like the set prayers in the prayer book and psalter, might be spoken aloud or uttered silently in our hearts. Although some people have composed formal prayers, writing them out in polished prose, most people simply speak to God informally and spontaneously. Such conversational prayer, called "colloquy," should have a place in every Christian's prayer life. Jesus calls his disciples "friends," and one characteristic of friendship is the sharing of confidences (John 15:15).

It is reported that St. Francis of Assisi sometimes began his prayer with the query: "Who are you, my dearest God? And what am I?" Conversational prayer is the place to explore both those questions. We expose our thoughts and feelings, troubles and worries, sins and frailties, joys and hopes to the One who already knows the secrets of our hearts better than we do. Unfortunately for some people, awareness of such divine omniscience effectively squashes any impulse towards self-disclosure: Why tell God what God already knows? It seems silly and childish. Yet as we know from every other relationship, self-disclosure does more than impart information. It is how we *give ourselves*. A whole world of feeling is conveyed when we reveal what is significant to us. Releasing our most troubled thoughts or turbulent feelings can be cathartic. We may be surprised when we drill down far enough to discover what is really bothering us, or weighing upon our minds.

Yet colloquy does far more than enhance self-knowledge. Our relationship to God changes when we know that God knows, and we know it *together*. We will not risk such vulnerability without considerable trust that our self-exposure will be honored. Colloquy, then, builds intimacy with God and leads to sanctification. Only when we are willing to lay bare our more tender parts can these dimensions of our psyches be put in order, healed, blessed, expanded, or purified.

"It's me, it's me, O Lord, standing in the need of prayer," sings another inspired spiritual. But who is the "me" coming before God, and what is her need today? Authentic prayer is above all honest prayer. We cannot pretend to be other than we are or to profess aspirations more admirable than those we really harbor. If we come to prayer anxious or bored, perhaps worried that our prayer will be a total flop, it's best to say so. Or maybe we are tired, as many of us often are. As we acknowledge our state before God, what do we want? To rest in God? Or to have the strength and perseverance to accomplish the day's tasks? As in any conversation, after we have sufficiently expressed ourselves, we need to wait in silence for a response. What could we be listening for? Sometimes God does indeed seem to speak to us through words formed in our minds. At other times, we may feel a strong interior nudge, prodding us in some direction. On still other occasions, an apt word or image from Scripture may well up in our imaginations. In response to our fatigue or preoccupation with some problem, Christ may address us: "Come to me, all you that are weary and are carrying heavy burdens, and I will give you rest" (Matt. 11:28). Or perhaps we will recall that Jesus himself found strength for his work simply by aligning himself with his Father's will: "My food is to do the will of him who sent me and to complete his work" (John 4:34). Then again, we may hear a saving word of judgment if we have needlessly piled chores upon ourselves: "You are worried and distracted by many things; there is need of only one thing."

Often we come to prayer concerned about someone, perhaps even ourselves: a state of health, making ends meet, a troubled relationship, employment difficulties. In colloquy we release these worries to our Lord—those we know to be well grounded as well as those we know to be a bit neurotic, so long as they are really ours. In friendship, we feel better just to get these matters off our chests. But when we seek a wise friend's counsel, we do more: We are admitting our state of confusion and our hope for a clarity we cannot furnish for ourselves. We could then search for further light in prayer. We can ask God, "What do you think about all this? What do you desire for me (or us) in this situation? Would you let me share something of your perspective here?" Rather than stew about our anxieties all on our own, going round and round in a fruitless circle of dread, we can face them with God: "Lord, what if ____? What then?" We may need to ask outright: "Will you take care of ____?" Eventually, we may have to make an act of surrender: "I entrust ____ to your merciful hands."

Colloquy may be brief: an "arrow" prayer that shoots straight from the heart. "Short prayer pierces the heavens," wrote the fourteenth-century author of *The Cloud of Unknowing*. Or our colloquy may be lengthy, if we need to get to the bottom of some concern with God. Colloquy might take the form of a lament or an extended petition, as in the case of Hannah, the future mother of the prophet Samuel (1 Sam. 1:9–18). Since transparency is paramount in prayer, we must approach it without a hidden agenda. We are not playing games with God, and God is not teasing us, even when no response seems readily apparent: "Be still, then, and know that I am God" (Ps. 46:11). Yet we never leave prayer unchanged; our inner furniture moves around. No wonder poet George Herbert ended up calling prayer "something understood."

INTERCESSION AND PETITION

"In everything by prayer and supplication with thanksgiving let your requests be made known to God." (Philippians 4:6)

As we more frequently explore conversation with God, colloquy will naturally flower in the principal kinds of prayer: adoration, praise, thanksgiving, penitence, oblation, intercession, and petition (BCP, 856). Of these, the first three—adoration, praise, and thanksgiving—carry us beyond ourselves to a place of wonder and delight in God. Penitence, in which we seek restoration out of love for God, is implied in our baptismal commitment to ongoing conversion and death to sin. Our dignity as a priestly people makes possible oblation, by which we offer every aspect of ourselves in union with Christ. Sometimes oblation is quite specific: when we offer up something definite to God, such as an illness, task, or disappointment. But the final two kinds of prayer, intercession and petition, may pose a quandary for us. At first, seeking some blessing, gift, or favor from God might strike us as the most instinctive form of prayer. But once we give intercession further thought, our efforts may become half-hearted. The fact of divine omniscience and divine goodness may cause us to wonder why we should ever ask God for anything. If God already knows "our necessities before we ask and our ignorance in asking" (Collect for Proper 11; BCP, 231), would it not be better just to trust that God will always provide what is best for us? Making requests of the Almighty seems like a rather primitive form of religion. Are we actually trying to change God's mind when we engage in intercession or petition?

These considerations point to the need to approach prayer with theological integrity. The way we pray has to make sense to us. Our theology of prayer must be congruent with whatever larger theological outlook we embrace. One way of addressing the question of whether we are attempting to "change God's mind" in intercession is to note that it is *we* who are changed by prayer, not God. Jesus enjoins us to "ask, seek, and knock" because perseverance in prayer brings home our dependence upon God and summons us to trust in God's goodness towards us. It is also certainly the case that over time our petitions and intercessions can mature in unpredictable ways. We may begin praying for one outcome—a recovery of health, for example—only to find that with continuing prayer other, more basic desires come to the fore. Our vision may be clarified or widened; our hearts may be expanded in the course of prayer. Our values get sorted out and shaken down. In the long run physical health may seem less crucial than reconciliation or spiritual healing. Or our prayer may shift to pleading for a holy death. Sometimes, too, when confronted with bewildering or unclear situations, we scarcely know what to ask, but are moved to pray for an as yet unknown grace. Then intercession takes the form of silent, contemplative pleading before God on behalf of others.

Jesus further insists that we pray for our enemies. He does not ask us to approve of them or to like them, and prayer for enemies should never be construed as exonerating them for whatever harm they may have done to us or others. Jesus simply says, "Love your enemies and pray for those who persecute you" (Matt. 5:44). Loving in this case begins by wishing them no ill. We pray that God's grace might visit them. We do not need to figure out in advance what form that grace might take. It is better to pray briefly, not rehearsing our grievances over and over. For if we focus more on our enemies than on God, we may end up refueling our rage against them and thus be drawn away from prayer altogether. But if we can simply entrust it all to God's hands, we may find that as we pray for enemies—or even people we find burdensome and irritating—our feelings undergo a change. We discover that it is impossible to pray for someone and still hate or despise that person. When we stand before God, we stand together as sinners, and only God knows the heart.

As we press heaven with our requests, we may find the Spirit pressing us as well. When we pray for peace, God may bring to mind the myriad ways we undermine peace by our impatience, insistence on our way, consumerism, or by holding a grudge. Are we making an effort to serve as peacemakers in our families or as agents of justice in our communities? Since prayer brings us into contact with the Spirit of truth, that Spirit may have some searching questions for us.

How, we may wonder, do we even know whether we are even praying for the right thing, for what is truly God's will? We do not always. Of course, true prayer never asks for something that is against God's revealed will—wishing another harm, for example, or praying for something that panders to our vanity or greed. But even apart from such cases, our prayers are often formed in the dark. We cannot be certain that our requests accord with Christ's prayer, but we offer them anyhow, trusting that the Spirit will lead us to a better prayer, if needed. So we find that intercession—praying for something *beyond* ourselves—begins a process of transformation *within* ourselves. Our prayers of intercession often undergo change across time if we press on faithfully. The crucial thing is continued transparency, for such vulnerability before God exposes us to the action of grace. If we entrust our true desires to God, we give God access to parts of ourselves that may need conversion. Reworking a phrase he found in the *Revelations* of Julian of Norwich, T.S. Eliot once wrote of "the purification of our motive in the ground of our beseeching." In the course of our "beseeching," our motives are sifted and cleansed. Intercessory prayer changes us.

But, we may wonder, does intercession change anything "out there"? After all, that is what intercession attempts to accomplish when we place our needs or those of others before God, asking that the best be done. It would be hard to find the motivation for supplication if we thought it affected only the one who was praying. Doing so might even seem to be something of a mind-game: "I seem to be praying for you, but I'm the only one who will be changed by this prayer." If intercession merely alters our own intra-psychic life, its exercise requires adopting an artificial pose. We would have to offer prayers on behalf of others knowing all the while that our prayers are ultimately ineffective *for them.* We are simply praying for ourselves—perhaps in relation to those others—but for ourselves nonetheless. Yet prayer can and does change things.

The efficacy of intercession only comes to light when we view ourselves not as separate atoms in the universe but as vibrant members of one another in the body of Christ. What one member does, or fails to do, affects every other member. Our lives and destinies are bound up together in Christ. The communion of saints creates a powerful force field. It establishes a network of relationships charged with energy, bursting with potential. It transcends time and death. Hence, our Spirit-inspired prayer for one another releases possibilities into the world that would otherwise not be there. It alters the spiritual environment we inhabit with untold reverberations. God does work though us. If we are scandalized that divine grace could be so dependent on human volition, so vulnerable to human frailty, we have not taken to heart the mystery of the Incarnation, beginning with Mary's "yes." God seeks our cooperation in the work of redemption. Just as our actions make a difference in people's lives, so do our prayers.

Prayer does not begin with us, but with God. In intercession we are not endeavoring to change God's mind or to remind God of some need in the world. It is the other way around. In intercession, the Spirit invites us to participate in the prayer Christ is already offering on our behalf. The Epistle to the Hebrews develops this theme in its portrayal of the ascended and glorified Christ. As our eternal high priest, Jesus is continually engaged in intercession: "He holds his priesthood permanently, because he continues forever. Consequently he is able for all time to save those who approach God through him, since he always lives to make intercession for them" (Heb. 7:24–25). Through intercession we are drawn into Christ's saving love for the world. The Spirit moves us to intercession, however, through very ordinary means. Our entirely natural love for those close to us is an obvious place to begin. Our concern for ourselves and our awareness of our need for grace leads inevitably to petition. In all these cases, we let intercession or petition unfold under the Spirit's gentle pressure, allowing ourselves to be molded by grace over time. If we repeatedly lay before God our heartfelt requests, whatever is unworthy in them will come under divine judgment, be purified, and finally transformed. Whatever is inspired by the Holy Spirit will come to fruition, in this life or the age to come.

If we allow the Spirit's way with us, sharing in the priestly intercession of Christ will finally bring us to the cross. As our love expands, so does our compassion and our pain. Intercession amounts to our taking the suffering, doubt, and anguish of our neighbors into our souls. Over and beyond the situations with which we are personally acquainted, just watching the evening news or reading the newspaper can provide plenty of raw material for prayer. Teresa of Avila spoke of the contemplative vocation as a ministry for a "world in flames." Our own world, sadly, is no less convulsed by violence and grief. In her short story "Greenleaf,"

Flannery O'Connor portrays a habit of intercession that takes the sorrows of the world to heart. It is performed by a most unlikely character, the slovenly yet passionate Mrs. Greenleaf:

> Every day she cut all the morbid stories out of the newspaper—the accounts of women who had been raped and criminals who had escaped and children who had been burned and of train wrecks and plane crashes and the divorces of movie stars. She took these to the woods and dug a hole and buried them and then she fell on the ground over them and mumbled and groaned for an hour or so moving her huge arms back and forth under her and out again and finally just lying down flat. . . .
>
> Mrs. Greenleaf raised her head. Her face was a patchwork of dirt and tears and her small eyes, the color of two field peas, were red-rimmed and swollen, but her expression was as composed as a bull dog's. She swayed back and forth on her knees and groaned, "Jesus, Jesus." . . .
>
> "Oh Jesus, stab me in the heart!" Mrs. Greenleaf shrieked. "Jesus stab me in the heart!" and she fell back flat in the dirt, a huge human mound, her legs and arms spread out as if she were trying to wrap them around the earth.[5]

By some uncanny instinct, Mrs. Greenleaf enacts a ritualized form of intercession by which she participates in the sufferings of others. She does not view the "morbid stories" she cuts out of the newspaper with cool indifference or any sense of moral superiority. She is not relieved to have been spared these tragedies herself. These accounts elicit her tears and groans. Intercession is not for disinterested bystanders to the miseries of creation. When we touch the wounds of the world, they become ours. "Oh Jesus, stab me in the heart!" she cries. Through what she calls her "healing," Mrs. Greenleaf is at one with Christ crucified, whose own side was pierced in death—"stabbed to the heart"—the most powerful intercession ever transacted. Prayer does not deliver us from pain but often intensifies it.

---

5. Flannery O'Connor, "Greenleaf," in *The Complete Stories* (New York: Farrar, Straus and Giroux, 1971), 315–317.

DISTRACTION DURING PRAYER

"It is of great importance, when we begin to practice prayer, not to let ourselves be frightened by our own thoughts." (Teresa of Avila)

Everyone who prays is familiar with the humbling experience of finding one's thoughts straying in countless directions. Sometimes the mind seems to take off on its own. When we finally become aware of a train of thought, we wonder how it ever got started. The experience of such distractions during prayer, especially since they occur over and over, can be so frustrating that we might question the value of even trying to pray. We might conclude that we are simply not the "type" cut out for prayer. But if the presence of distracting thoughts disqualified us for sustained prayer, no one would be eligible: "We know not what we should pray for as we ought." It seems that God is satisfied with the mere intention to pray, but we enact that intention by hanging in. Then the Spirit who searches our hearts expresses prayer for us, often with "sighs too deep for words." We may be disgusted that our prayer seems to lack depth and focus, but we are not the best judges of its worth. When prayer does not please us, it may very well please God. Then we pray purely for love rather than for any spiritual pleasure we derive from it. The impulse to give up is a temptation. Moving away from God can never be God's will for us. So while a host of unwelcome distractions is inevitable, we can learn from them. Our prayer can even mature by confronting them.

The human mind is marvelously complex. We can recite entire prayers while thinking of something else altogether. So when our thoughts wander during the liturgy, as they always do from time to time, it makes sense simply to refocus on where we are along with the rest of the praying community. If we come to the end of the Creed and realize that we have not concentrated on a single phrase, there's no point in trying to catch up by reciting it silently to ourselves. The train has already left the station and we must hop on board. Otherwise we will miss the next prayer. Corporate prayer chugs along. Since we are not in control of the pace, we bend ourselves to the community's movement. It is, moreover, self-defeating to be angry with ourselves for our mental meanderings. Irritation only creates another distraction, and a rather prideful one at that. Who are we to be exempt from the human condition?

The distractions that surface during our periods of personal prayer may need a different sort of handling. A good many of these can be quickly deleted and relegated to the trash file: "Did we remember to lock the door?" "Better put that item on the grocery list." "Can we fit that appointment in before we leave town?" In other words, the flotsam and jetsam of everyday affairs. Most of the time these thoughts have to be endured. When we catch ourselves going off on some tangent, we patiently and without fuss return to the matter of our prayer, perhaps smiling with God at our frailty and susceptibility to distraction. Attention demands effort, and we try once again.

But if we find that time after time we cannot quiet down to pray, our restlessness may signal chronic mental overcrowding. As Kenneth Leech reminds us, "The environment matters, in prayer as in the rest of life."[6] A serious commitment to prayer requires us to consider the context in which we pray. If our lifestyle is frantic and noisy, at the time of prayer we cannot pull some invisible plug, expecting our inner agitation to cease. It is not humanly possible to still our thoughts during prayer if they are racing the rest of the day: the motor keeps running. Physical exercise, a good habit in itself, may help release the tension that inevitably builds up in our bodies. We must maintain vigilance in our use of electronic devices, allowing them to serve us rather than the reverse. Fostering a peaceful atmosphere at home, work, or in the car can help. We could develop a taste for silence. And we can strive to prune our schedules to alleviate needless stress. It is impossible to "practice the presence of God" while engaged in the activity at hand if we are already worried about the next obligation. As we try to cultivate an environment that is conducive to prayer, we discover that a fruitful life of prayer—that is, a rich relationship to God—is not an addendum to life. It calls for deliberation and discipline in the art of living.

---

6. Kenneth Leech, *True Prayer: An Invitation to Christian Spirituality* (San Francisco: Harper and Row, 1980), 52.

There are, however, some distractions worth noticing. In many cases, as soon as we become quiet, our preoccupations and all-too-familiar thoughts rise to the surface of consciousness. Just as our dreams often tell us about matters we have kept at a safe distance from ordinary consciousness, so our waking mind, once we allow it some repose, can bring to the fore material we would rather forget. Old and new resentments, worries, and insecurities start to intrude, as we first suppose, on our prayer time. We wish these thoughts would give us a break and go away. We are tired of them. We see them as "distractions" and push them, once again, to the periphery. But they keep coming back like guests who have overstayed their welcome.

We may be unsuccessful in banishing these intruders because the Holy Spirit is working through them, trying to alert us to their importance. They may not be intruders at all but parts of ourselves we don't especially like. All this old baggage has to be confronted. We cannot know beforehand just what God might wish to do with our inner agitation, but we will not find out until we relax enough to explore this territory under the Spirit's guidance. So rather than ousting these recurrent thoughts and feelings, we could befriend them. These long-neglected, despised, or obsessive aspects of ourselves stand in need of grace. As Martin Smith observes:

> Maybe what we call our "distractions" are the main event. Often God prefers to stay quietly in the background at first when we pray because the real business at hand is setting us free, and only truth sets us free.
>
> Most of us are really bad at telling the truth, and we will never get better at it until we meet our preoccupations and obsessions, the stuff we are always telling ourselves deep down—only we don't realize it until we stop our activity. When we stop to pray, then these preoccupations swim to the surface and start splashing and jostling us. . . .
>
> Instead of pushing them back down, arguing with them, cursing them, or trying to turn your back on them, why don't you try looking them in the face and treating them as parts of yourself clamoring for attention? The feelings they are revealing

could be God's real agenda of prayer. The desires, resentments, memories, and messages that keep on insinuating themselves into your prayer might be the real signposts telling you what to pray about.[7]

The "distractions," then, might signal an invitation to more probing colloquy. The very matters we assumed were taking us away from prayer might be leading us to a more honest engagement with it. Especially when the same conundrums come up over and over, chances are the Spirit is pressing us to face these issues candidly with our Lord.

MEDITATION: THE EXAMEN PRAYER

"Lord, you have searched me out and known me; . . . you discern my thoughts from afar." (Psalm 139:1)

One way of exploring the question, "Who are you, my dearest God? And what am I?" is through the examen prayer devised by Ignatius Loyola, the sixteenth-century founder of the Society of Jesus. In his *Spiritual Exercises* he describes a way of discerning movements within ourselves that lead us either towards God or away from God. Although the examen prayer has five steps, it is basically a flexible method for seeing how God has been at work in our lives over the course of the day.[8] By noticing how our feelings, moods, thoughts, and interior impulses affect our relation to God, we are in a better position to *respond* faithfully to these urgings whatever they may be. Since the Holy Spirit dwells in our hearts (Rom. 5:5), that Spirit is ever seeking to enlarge our identity in Christ. Conversely, Ignatius recognizes other, deleterious influences pressing upon us that may spring from our particular circumstances, from within ourselves, or from the one he calls "the enemy of our human nature." These troublesome impulses or moods he terms "desolations," while the salutary prompting of

---

7. Martin Smith, *Compass and Stars* (New York: Seabury Press, 2007), 81–82.

8. For a full and helpful discussion, see Timothy M. Gallagher. O.M.V., *The Examen Prayer* (New York: Crossroad, 2006).   •

the Holy Spirit are "consolations." It is crucial to note that consolations and desolations are not simply comforting or painful feelings, respectively. Some consolations may hurt at first—such as compunction of heart. Some desolations, such as feelings of apathy or indifference, may masquerade as comfortable indolence. The critical difference between the two is whether the thought, feeling, mood, or impulse tends towards God or away from God.

In the examen prayer, after praying for the enlightenment and guidance of the Holy Spirit, we review our day. We go over ordinary events and our corresponding feelings. Did we get caught in traffic on the way to work? Hear unexpectedly from an old friend? Sense friction with a family member? Feel disheartened listening to the news? Consider taking up a fresh project? After calling these occasions to mind, we reflect on our feelings at the time. What inspired gratitude, joy, courage, or a more lively faith? What had the opposite effect? Here we discover the pressure of the Holy Spirit or the Evil One upon us. Cultivating "the examined life" is not our aim here, even though regular practice of the examen will surely boost self-knowledge. Instead, we are asking God to show us where the Spirit was encouraging or the Enemy discouraging us in everyday life—which is, after all, where growth in Christ takes place. Only after discerning our actual situation can we forge a faithful response: whether we are being called to cooperate with a grace or to resist a temptation. Discernment, then, enhances freedom.

In all likelihood, reviewing the day will elicit our thanksgiving for many special blessings that would otherwise go unnoticed. It might also lead to penitence for ways we have fallen short. Above all, the examen is another version of prayer—that is, a time of deliberate engagement with God—and its integrity requires maintaining this prayerful quality throughout the exercise:

> The examen is a form of prayer. The dangers of an empty self-reflection or an unhealthy self-centered introspection are very real. On the other hand, a lack of effort at examen and the approach of living according to what comes naturally keeps

us quite superficial and insensitive to the subtle and profound ways of the Lord deep in our hearts. The prayerful quality and effectiveness of the examen itself depends upon its relationship to the continuing contemplative prayer of the person. Without this relationship examen slips to the level of self-reflection for self-perfection, if it perdures at all.[9]

The purpose of looking back at the day's blessings and challenges is to equip us to look ahead. We face the future feeling less buffeted by events and more aware of the hidden graces and subtle infidelities lurking beneath the surface. Ignatian spirituality seeks "to find God in all things." By helping us discern the movements of God lodged in our affective consciousness, the examen prayer develops our capacity to notice what is going on at the level of the spirit. By seeing grace at work, retrospectively, in quite ordinary happenings, we are better equipped to perceive God in whatever circumstances lie at hand. We will meet the Lord not just in designated times of prayer but throughout the day, becoming "contemplatives in action" just as Ignatius and his company aspired to become.

To be sure, many before and after the time of Ignatius, without benefit of this particular method, have enjoyed a similar graced discernment. Still, this systematic approach to discerning prayer has proved helpful to many. Ignatius recommended its practice every day for a quarter of an hour. (Members of his community were to practice it twice daily.) Obviously, the examen prayer might well be extended, but not usually shortened to less than ten minutes. Because it aims to survey no more than a twenty-four hour period, most people who practice the examen try to find a regular space for it, ideally towards the evening or nightfall. But opportunities and schedules differ, so a workable time will always be the best practice.

9. George A. Aschenbrenner, S.J., "Consciousness Examen," *Review for Religious* 31 (1972:1), 15.

MEDITATION: DEVOTIONAL APPROACHES

"Jesus is honey in the mouth, music in the ear, and a shout of joy in the heart." (Bernard of Clairvaux)

Repetitive prayers from the liturgy, such as the *Kyrie, Trisagion*, or *Agnus Dei*, lend themselves to rhythmic recitation as we go about our everyday activities or when fashioning a more formal meditation. Inwardly repeating a word or short phrase to still the thoughts and thus enter into meditation has been practiced for centuries across many religious traditions. Because of its demonstrated effectiveness in calming the mind, slowing the heart rate, and other physiological benefits, this method of meditation has been secularized in the West in recent decades. Transcendental Meditation and biofeedback, among other forms of secular meditation, are now practiced by adherents of a variety of religions or none at all.

What turns any form of meditation into prayer, however, is the activity of the Holy Spirit coupled with the intention of the practitioner. For Christians, prayer is "through Christ, with Christ, and in Christ." It is always directed towards God. "Prayer oneth the soul to God," declared Julian of Norwich. In prayer, we discover anew our identity in Christ, the gift of our baptismal union with his death and resurrection. The use of a repeated sacred word can distill and deepen this grace for us. It is an ancient, simplified form of *lectio divina*, in which one simply repeats a short phrase or a single word, often replete with meaning, for the entirety of the meditation.

One of the oldest forms of this practice is the widely used "Jesus Prayer" of Eastern Orthodoxy. Its traditional words combine a double movement of loving aspiration towards God followed by penitential awareness of self: "Lord Jesus Christ, Son of God, have mercy on me, a sinner." The essence of the prayer is the invocation of the holy Name of Jesus, since to do anything "in the name of" evokes that presence and power. The prayer can be lengthened somewhat or shortened, even to the point of the single word "Jesus."

In order to include our bodies in the Jesus Prayer and to slow down the recitation of the words, some people breathe in during the first half of the prayer, then breathe out for the second half. Since the Spirit is also "breath" and "wind," unhurried, gentle breathing can consciously invoke the Spirit's breath of life—inspiration—for our prayer. Traditionally, the Jesus Prayer is recited one hundred times, aided by the woolen strands of a prayer rope of varying lengths—some of one hundred, but possibly fewer, knots. As with a Western rosary, using a prayer rope gives the hands something to do: the body merges integrally with the prayer. Indeed, the unification of the praying self under grace is considered one of prayer's notable benefits. According to the saintly Orthodox bishop Theophan the Recluse (1815–94), in prayer "the principal thing is to stand before God with the mind in the heart." The Jesus Prayer begins with the lips as vocal prayer, engages the mind as one ponders its words, and finally descends into the heart. "Heart" is here understood biblically—not merely as the seat of emotions, desires, and passions, but as the center of the whole person. The "heart," then, includes understanding and intellect, and serves as the basis of the will. Prayer thus unifies the self while uniting the self to Christ:

> The aim of the Jesus Prayer, as of all Christian prayer, is that our praying should become increasingly identified with the prayer offered by Jesus the High Priest within us, that our life should become one with his life, our breathing with the Divine Breath that sustains the universe. The final objective may aptly be described by the Patristic term *theosis*, "deification" or "divinization."[10]

During the Middle Ages, the Marian rosary developed in the Western church. It consists of three sets of five "mysteries," or meditations on the life of Mary and Jesus, based for the most part on biblical events. To "say the rosary" means to pray five decades of prayers associated with the beads—the Lord's Prayer, ten Hail Marys, and a Gloria Patri—while meditating on the joyful, sorrowful, or glorious mysteries. These fifteen mysteries are outlined

---

10. Kallistos Ware, *The Power of the Name: The Jesus Prayer in Orthodox Spirituality*, rev. ed. (Oxford: SLG Press, 1977), 23.

Courtesy of photographer Br. Curtis Almquist, SSJE.

in many places, including *St. Augustine's Prayer Book*, a classic of Anglo-Catholic devotion. In recent years, the rosary has been expanded and updated by various hands, and a distinctly Anglican rosary has come into use as well. Like the Jesus Prayer, the widespread use of the rosary over centuries, with practitioners ranging from peasants to intellectuals, indicates the accessibility of this form of meditation. The repetition of well-known prayers forms a verbal backdrop to the mind's engagement with the mysteries. The hum of the prayers siphons off our usual distracting mental buzz, allowing meditation to pass from one thematically connected mystery to the next. Many people of little education or none, including young children, have thus been introduced to meditative prayer, and some have entered deeply into it.

The Stations of the Cross offer a similarly accessible approach to meditation. The custom of venerating places associated with diverse episodes in the Passion of Christ began in the fourth century with pilgrims in Jerusalem. In time, the number of these places or "stations" became fixed at fourteen, and any place could become the site of the devotion. *The Book of Occasional Services* contains a "Way of the Cross" that honors these stations with versicles, short readings, and prayers that can be used communally or individually. When offered as a permanent foci of devotion, the various stations are usually marked by a cross and sometimes, helpfully, with an artistic rendering of the event. Stations are often set up inside a church or outside of it. Those engaged in praying the stations on their own can therefore linger in meditation at any given station before moving on to the next one. The literal movement from one part of the church to another reproduces in miniature the original movement of the Holy Land pilgrims. Although especially suitable for Lent, the Way of the Cross offers a venue for meditating on the sufferings and death of Jesus suitable for any season. It helps engender heartfelt love for Christ by pondering the cost of his love for us.

PREPARING TO MEDITATE

"Remove the sandals from your feet, for the place on which you are standing is holy ground." (Exodus 3:5)

The Jesus Prayer, the rosary, the Way of the Cross, and the examen prayer all combine vocal, articulated prayer with meditation. Devotional exercises ready us for other forms of Christian meditation. In the examen prayer, the "text" for meditation is our day, its currents and crosscurrents. The examen builds upon and leads back to the meditative practices of *lectio divina*, contemplative gazing, and apophatic prayer without thoughts and words.

Any form of quiet prayer requires thoughtful preparation. Since "the environment matters, in prayer as in the rest of life," just what might help us settle down and settle in? Without shackling ourselves to an ironclad rigidity, most of us need a fairly reliable place and time for prayer. If we leave these practical considerations up to chance, chances are something else will crowd out our best intentions. Even if our schedule changes from day to day, we still need to map out—perhaps a week in advance—where and when we expect to pray. Every Christian needs some time each day to lift the heart to God, however briefly. But if we wish to delve deeper into communion with God through meditation, we must secure a more extensive period of time, perhaps twenty minutes at first, at least a few times a week. This may not be easy, and we may need to rearrange some priorities to make the practice viable. In any case, brutal honesty about our schedule is the only way forward. So is utter realism about our biorhythms. Most people pray best in the morning before the day's concerns overwhelm them. Jesus, apparently, got up before dark to secure the necessary privacy and quiet for prayer. Some of us, however, pray less distractedly in the evening. Such people can more easily "let go" when the day's work is done, yet before the body's need for sleep becomes overpowering. Still others will find their lunch hour or the children's nap time offering the only open space in the day.

Our bodies will help us to pray if we let them. Some physical gestures might move us, literally, into prayer. The profound bows, usually made with the sign of the cross, typical of Eastern Orthodox piety, could express our adoration or intention to pray without using words at all. Or we could adopt the ancient "orans" position by standing straight with both hands uplifted at shoulder height. But if we are to engage in meditation, we will finally be seated, at least most of the time. Standing or kneeling for any length will prove to be uncomfortable and thus distracting. Practitioners of meditation, both East and West, have long known the importance of suitable posture. The ideal posture keeps us alert and receptive without undue strain: spine erect but not rigid, hands relaxed in the lap or on the knees unless we are holding a Bible or other book for a spell. Some may wish to sit cross-legged on a meditation cushion or upon a *seiza* bench—a gently sloping prayer stool that allows the legs to tuck underneath it comfortably. If we sit in a chair, we want one that offers support without our sinking in. It usually takes some time to release the tension in our shoulders, neck, and back. Both feet should be on the floor.

Many of us are drawn into prayer by other visible aids. A prayer rug can define the space for our dedicated time with God. Lighting a candle can signal the beginning of prayer; blowing it out marks its conclusion. A cross, crucifix, icon, or religious picture gives our eyes a point of reference and might serve in itself as the focus of "gazing" meditation. If we pray in a church where the

Sacrament is reserved, the presence of Christ in the aumbry or tabernacle may focus our attention and devotion. Even silent meditation might well begin with a briefly spoken prayer. A short invocation in our own words such as "Come Holy Spirit" or a prayer we know by heart could express our desire to meet God in prayer and our dependence upon grace to pray at all. If we have a particular hope for this time of prayer, we should say what it is. Or we could ask the Lord to help us receive whatever word God may wish to give us. Another way to begin is simply to engage in colloquy until we have said all there is to say and then move on to meditation.

LECTIO DIVINA: PRAYING WITH SCRIPTURE

"Oh, how I love your law! All the day long it is in my mind." (Psalm 119:97)

Meditating upon the Scriptural word is the most ancient form of Christian mediation, with roots in Judaism's devotion to God's revealed word. Psalm 1 declares those blessed whose "delight is in the law of the Lord, and they meditate on his law day and night" (v. 2). Regular exposure to Scripture in the Eucharist and daily offices prepares our minds and hearts for *lectio divina* or "sacred reading." Indeed, the liturgy might well whet our appetite for it. For unlike the reading of lengthy, multiple lessons in the liturgy, *lectio divina* allows us to absorb a single short passage or verse of the Bible. Ancient Christian writers compared the practice to cows chewing their cud over and over, and what this meditation entails is precisely a "rumination" on a sacred text so that we may "inwardly digest" it. The practice first flourished in monastic communities. Because their days were saturated with Scripture through praying the psalms and listening to the lessons of the Office, monks came to know many biblical texts by heart. These formed the basis of continued reflection throughout the day, and especially in the hours given to quiet prayer. *Lectio divina* is not an esoteric exercise. It is accessible to a broad range of people in every walk of life, including youth.

The slow, attentive reading of Scripture, often issuing in prayer, has been a devotional exercise practiced for centuries in many Protestant communities.

Early in St. Luke's Gospel the evangelist presents the meditating figure of Mary who, after the visit of the shepherds, "treasured all these words and pondered them in her heart" (Luke 2:19). He uses much the same expression a bit later when describing her reaction to finding the twelve-year-old Jesus in the temple (2:51). It is as if the gospel writer wishes to coach us right from the start on how to engage his text. Like us, Mary needs time—and a certain interior disposition—to take in the events narrated in the gospel. She is awed and sometimes baffled by the happenings surrounding her son and occasionally by Jesus himself. Sound familiar? But here the evangelist shows us, through the example of Mary, how to relate to Jesus as we read the gospel. As strange as Jesus may be on occasion, Mary does not view him abstractly, as a problem to be figured out. He is decidedly "other," but not distant. She loves him, we may presume, with the full force of maternal affection. Yet like any other parent, she has to learn how to love rightly, with reverence and respect, without attempting to possess him. After the Ascension, we see Mary in the company of disciples at Pentecost (Acts 1:14). What has brought her to this ripeness of faith? All the while she has been "pondering in her heart" the things concerning Jesus. She is now a mature believer.

Some people suspect that meditation on Scripture requires us to jettison whatever we have studied about the Bible or learned from higher criticism. While biblical meditation is not the same thing as biblical study, dividing our mind into two watertight compartments will scarcely lead to a healthy integration. Only a desiccated form of biblical (or literary) criticism treats the text like a cadaver, a dead relic of the dead past, suitable only for dissection and the cold eye of examination. Exposure to such narrow approaches, often reductive or dismissive in their conclusions, can generate reluctance to study the Bible at all: just too hot to handle! As it turns out, neither timidity nor condescension towards the Bible is warranted because the Bible, like all great literature, operates on multiple levels at once. Good biblical criticism, like good literary criticism, has a valuable and vital role to play. It can clear away misunderstandings in our reading of the text and significantly enrich our appreciation of its artistry and message. So we do not have to choose between investigating the Scriptures academically or meditating on them devotionally. Each works constructively, though by diverse methods and at different times, to foster Christian maturity.

We bring our whole self, including our informed study of Scripture, to the task of meditation. Although "meditation" in some contexts simply refers to sustained, reflective thinking, in *lectio divina* reflection takes place in the context of prayer. That is, the entire interior exercise is oriented towards God. It seeks exposure to the Risen Christ, who continues to engage us through the surplus of meanings found in the scriptural word. By frequent encounter with the living Christ, especially engendered by meditation on the gospels, we come to know Jesus not as a revered but remote figure from the past, but as an abiding presence. Because the Holy Spirit animates our meditative prayer—the same Spirit who enlivens the proclamation of Scripture in the Holy Eucharist and Daily Office—the biblical story spills into our lives. Anamnesis takes place here, too, as we participate in the matters about which we are reading while "pondering them in our hearts."

In scriptural meditation we begin by reading a short passage of Scripture slowly. It might be as long as a story or as short as a single verse. If we are new to *lectio divina*, we might well start with a story, especially a familiar episode from the gospels. From our early childhood, stories intrigue us. People have been telling stories and listening to stories from time immemorial. Today we are pulled into stories through novels, film, drama, and television. Why this fascination? Our lives themselves form an unfinished story, still in the process of creation. As we move through our personal, improvisational drama, we are always trying to get a handle on it. All those other stories help us to interpret our own. We are on the lookout for a plot that might make sense. Moreover, we can identify with all sorts of characters: the heroic figures (at least as an ideal), the unsavory ones (if we are honest), and all those in-between. Because our personalities are multi-faceted, we find ourselves empathizing with one, and now another, character, all of whom are us. Art addresses this complexity of ours. By luring us into stories by a combination of curiosity and sympathy, it has power to get behind our defenses. No one leaves a great dramatic performance unchanged.

When we are engaged in scriptural meditation, the Holy Spirit acts as the behind-the-scenes director. Our memories, imaginations, feelings, and thoughts are the raw materials for enacting this play. We give ourselves over to the story we are reading. What do we notice? With whom do we identify on this reading? What associations are stirred in us? The story may set off a memory from the distant past, something laden with emotion. Or we might find ourselves connected to a recent issue—a desire, hope, frustration, or dilemma. As we pass from reading to reflection, from *lectio* to *meditatio*, we allow the Spirit to unearth buried thoughts and feelings. We should avoid preaching to ourselves or cudgeling our brains to come up with some insight. Instead, we allow ourselves to be led. The Spirit might help us make connections or see things in a new light. The meditation could bring healing and blessing. This period of reflection—the "meditation" proper—cannot be rushed. We allow ourselves to feel all these things and to engage them in relation to whatever is going on in the text. Above all, we try to detect how God may be speaking to us through the scriptural text as it addresses the text of our lives.

If we are looking for a plot to our lives, one way or another the gospels press us to situate ourselves in that story. Christian life is life in Christ. We took on another identity in baptism. Or rather, as Paul would put it, "Christ Jesus has made me his own" (Phil. 3:12). So his story must become our story; in fact, it already is, but we may not have noticed exactly how. Meditation helps us to notice—and plunge in. The gospels were written from the perspective of Jesus's death and resurrection. All the parables and teachings and episodes are pulling us into the vortex of that stunning conclusion. We keep getting summoned to wade deeper in.

As Martin Smith writes in his illuminating and thorough introduction to scriptural prayer:

> The overarching story of the cross and resurrection, within which Jesus' stories and the stories about Jesus come together, in turn gathers in the stories of the Hebrew Scriptures so that they become newly laden with transforming potential. . . .
>
> In Christian faith the Story and the stories within it are not illustrations of truths which could be conveyed in another way. There are no philosophical principles which can be distilled from them and the stories then discarded as empty husks. The stories themselves are indispensable sacramental means of encounter with the Word which became flesh.[11]

Lectio divina aims at precisely this encounter with the Word made flesh, the One to whom the words of Scripture bear witness. It is about coming to know Jesus and coming to know ourselves in him. Observing him and drawing near to him we see things afresh. Looking at him, we might sense his invitation to become like him—even more, *to become what he is* through his abiding presence in us.

Out of the mix of thought and feeling, memory and imagination, comes prayer (*oratio*) or direct address to God. We may be moved to vigorous colloquy, as we pose our questions or present our problems. We could engage in intercession, thanksgiving, praise, or penitence for our shortcomings. We might seek guidance or strength to respond unreservedly to the grace we have received. What we have to say might be very brief but heartfelt. Or it could entail a real pouring out of pent-up emotions as the floodgates become undammed.

The medieval monks who habitually engaged in *lectio divina* eventually identified four stages in its practice: reading (*lectio*), reflection (*meditatio*), prayer (*oratio*), and gazing (*contemplatio*). These steps are not hard and fast. Reflection and prayer, especially, are often intertwined, with prayer arising spontaneously

---

11. Martin L. Smith, *The Word is Very Near You: A Guide to Praying with Scripture* (Cambridge, MA: Cowley, 1989), 95.

from our mediation. After speaking directly to God, we may then be drawn back into mediation. Or we might begin the process over again, resuming our slow reading, reflecting on what we have read, allowing feelings and associations to well up, and then finally speaking to God from the depths of the heart.

Often this is how meditation ends, and we could round it off with a brief prayer of thanksgiving, praise, or self-dedication. But sometimes we seem encouraged to take another step—to rest in God or quietly take in an insight or fresh truth. An image from the text—and the Bible is chock full of images—may compel our contemplation: a silent, simple gazing with the eye of the heart. This is the fourth step—*contemplatio*—of classical *lectio divina*.

The grace of this final step, contemplation, is not always available to us. Sometimes our prayer ends inconclusively, with a question still hanging in the air. Often, we need to return to the subject of our meditation: we sense "unfinished business" with the Lord. On other occasions, though, our meditation ends peacefully or with a powerful sense of grace. Then we are called to absorb that grace or contemplate what we have glimpsed of God.

For some people, resting in a word or brief phrase from Scripture, or gazing upon a verbal image, may become habitual. This is not how their meditation ends; it defines the whole process. Many arresting verses lend themselves to this simplified form of meditation: "Your life is hid with Christ in God," "Fear not, it is I," or "I am the living bread," for example. The method of meditation now consists in repeating the words from time to time, letting them sink in. We immerse ourselves in the truth, beauty, comfort, or challenge of the words without extensive analysis. The rhythm of repetition is not mechanical but organic, an aspiration interspersed with silence. This is "rumination": a slow, steady chewing on the word. As we repeat the phrase, it may take on new resonances for us. Although we have not been analyzing the words (what they mean is usually clear enough), fresh associations may surface. If we begin to meditate on "Fear not, it is I" conscious of a particular anxiety gripping us, in time we may find our Lord addressing other fears, submerged beneath our immediate awareness. Or our whole attention could shift to the second half of the phrase as we become more alert to the presence of Christ: "It is I." The Spirit blows where she wills. In prayer we allow the Spirit to move and direct us. In the course of meditation or near the end, we make some response in prayer. *Oratio* may punctuate our meditation or conclude it.

Obviously, much material in the Bible is not narrative: the Sermon on the Mount, the long discourses in John, the epistles, the psalms, and the rest of the wisdom literature, among other books. As in meditation on the Bible's stories, we begin with *lectio* or slow reading, continuing until a word or phrase echoes within us. We don't have to understand why something resonates with us. It is enough that we pay attention and stop. We may not get far in our reading, but here we are seeking depth rather than breadth. Once something stands out, we then go back and re-read the passage, phrase, or word. If we have been meditating on the Beatitudes, we might have paused at the very first word: "blessed." How long has it been since we felt blessed by God? Since we allowed ourselves to take in God's blessing? Or we might have halted at "poor" with all its myriad associations, repeating the phrase "Blessed are the poor" until the Spirit sheds light on its significance for us. We should refrain from trying to force meanings or messages, however edifying they may be. For a while we may be in the dark. After a time, the Spirit will act upon our intuition, and we will be ready to respond in prayer.

How do we decide on a text for our meditation? There are many options. Sometimes a spiritual director or retreat leader counsels meditation on a specific passage. When on our own, we could select a reading from the Sunday eucharistic lectionary. After looking over the lessons from the previous or forthcoming week, we choose one—not all three! Meditating on these lessons, which are often geared to the liturgical year, enhances our sense of the church season and certainly enriches our participation in the Liturgy of the Word. Another fruitful approach involves gradually working through an entire book of the Bible. Regularly encountering Jesus through the course of a gospel, with all its varied episodes and events, develops our relationship to him as nothing else can. If we happen to be blessed with a lively imagination, using it in meditation can bring us right into the scene. Some people can see, hear, and even smell what is going on. But whether or not that approach appeals to us, the crucial matter is engaging the living Christ mediated by the living words of Scripture.

Sometimes we choose an image or text based on our current situation. A woman who has lost her child could seek companionship with the bereft mothers of Bethlehem (Matt. 2:18; Jer. 31:15) or Mary at the foot of the cross. Those sensing vocational upheaval in middle or late life might spend some time with the call of Abram and Sarai (Gen. 12). When faced with an excruciating test of fidelity, we might find ourselves with Christ in Gethsemane (Mark 14:32–42). But we do not go to the Scriptures merely to secure confirmation of our position and outlook. By and large, when we meditate on parallel instances in Jesus's life and ministry, we cannot identify with him in every respect. Our thoughts and feelings will not always be validated. Jesus may comfort, but he also may confront. Either way, the engagement is transformative. When we view our situation vis-à-vis Christ, the context is enlarged and our perspective inevitably shifts.

Certain handbooks propose suggestions for Bible reading based on felt spiritual need. *The Word is Very Near You* offers an extensive range of passages profitable for meditation organized around thematic clusters. Over time, and with continued exposure to the variety within Scripture itself, we may find ourselves returning to certain stories, passages, phrases, or images that we have come to treasure. It should not surprise us that God continues to speak to us through parts of Scripture that have become laden with meaning for us. We should not hesitate to let ourselves be refreshed by them again and again. Finally, the practice of *lectio divina* can be used fruitfully with some non-biblical texts, such as the writings of the saints or contemporary authors, which feed our meditation and prompt our prayer.

GAZING: PRAYING WITH ICONS

"And all of us, with unveiled faces, seeing the glory
of the Lord as though reflected in a mirror, are being
transformed into the same image from one degree
of glory to another." (2 Corinthians 3:18)

In recent years the devotional use of icons, a tradition embedded
in Eastern Orthodoxy, has increasingly attracted Western Christians. Why now? Perhaps the discovery of icons in the West reflects
our decidedly visual culture. Since the invention of television in
the mid-twentieth century, most of us spend many hours each day
looking at a screen of some sort. But what images are feeding our
imaginations? Advertisers bombard us with pictures that alterna-
tively play upon our insecurities, vanity, or greed. We get a regular diet of violence and vulgarity mixed in with some magnificent
scenes. Henri Nouwen addressed this challenge decades ago in the
Introduction to his tender meditations on four Russian icons:

> We are forever seeing. When we dream, we see. When we
> stare in front of us, we see. When we close our eyes to rest, we
> see. . . . But what do we really choose to see? . . . Just as we
> are responsible for what we eat, so are we responsible for what
> we see. It is easy to become a victim of the vast array of visual
> stimuli surrounding us. The "powers and principalities" control
> many of our daily images. Posters, billboards, television, video-
> cassettes, movies and store windows continuously assault our
> eyes and inscribe their images upon our memories.
>
> Still we do not have to be passive victims of a world that
> wants to entertain and distract us. A spiritual life in the midst
> of our energy-draining society requires us to make conscious
> steps to safeguard that inner space where we can keep our eyes
> fixed on the beauty of the Lord.[12]

The popularity of sacred icons nowadays may manifest a salutary instinct on our part since they enable us to "keep our eyes

---

12. Henri J. M. Nouwen, *Behold the Beauty of the Lord: Praying with Icons* (Notre Dame,
IN: Ave Maria Press, 1987), 12.

fixed on the beauty of the Lord." When many images around us cheapen and degrade, icons open another world. Gazing upon them with prayerful receptivity, we step into that realm: the kingdom of God. For icons are not decorative art; they exist to be contemplated. Often described as "windows" into eternity, icons are to be *looked through* rather than *looked at*. Contemplating an icon of our savior, we are not simply viewing a picture of Jesus. The prayerfulness of the icon writer combines with the prayerfulness of the icon gazer. The Holy Spirit, active across time, brings us into the presence of Christ through the icon. Speaking of his experience of life in Christ, St. Paul declares: "And all of us, with unveiled faces, seeing the glory of the Lord as though reflected in a mirror, are being transformed into the same image from one degree of glory to another" (2 Cor. 3:18). It is precisely this transformative vision that icons seek to impart.

In Eastern Orthodox spirituality, icons are reverenced with bows and kisses, and they are incensed during worship as holy objects. Such veneration is entirely appropriate, for within the context of prayer, icons mediate the mysteries they represent. Some Protestant churches, however, regard representational religious art as a form of idolatry, a violation of the First Commandment. While evidence indicates that Christians have been employing such art forms from very early times, it was the "iconoclastic controversy" of the seventh and eighth centuries that inspired the most probing theological deliberation on the issue. For theologians such as John of Damascus (675–749), everything turns on the Incarnation of the divine Son. By becoming visible in the Incarnate Word, God rendered obsolete the ancient prohibition against image-making. The New Testament declares that Christ "is the image (*eikon*) of the invisible God" (Col. 1:15) and "is the reflection of God's glory and the exact imprint of God's very being" (Heb. 1:3). Jesus himself asserts that "Whoever has seen me has seen the Father" (John 14:9). Because God became flesh in the human Jesus, such a human being can be depicted and worshipped. The Second Council of Nicea (787) argued that because Jesus's divine and human natures cannot be separated, an icon represents his whole, enfleshed person: "In depicting the

Saviour, we do not depict either His Divine or His human nature, but his Person in which both these natures are incomprehensibly combined."¹³ This is the one human being whose entire self is saturated with God. By various artistic techniques, icons seek to convey this divine reality embodied in Jesus.

Icons extend the incarnational principle to paintings of biblical scenes, saints, angels, and especially Mary, named as "God-bearer" (*Theotokos*) by the Third Ecumenical Council of Ephesus (431). In none of these cases does the iconographer intend a photographic or historical likeness. Biblical events are not passing episodes on the timeline of history but mysteries of unfathomable significance. Jesus, Mary, and the saints gaze at us from the other side of the eschaton. While each figure is fully recognizable, the icon stretches our imaginations to portray a humanity transfigured. Through a combination of spiritual practices and artistic techniques refined over centuries, iconographers seek to transmit this vision. Before ever applying a stroke of the brush, they have fasted and prayed for weeks, meditating upon the subject of the icon. Icons emerge out of prayer in order to elicit prayer.

To convey a sense of transformative grace, icon painters offer a deliberately stylized rendition of their subjects. Strict artistic conventions govern their creation: a typical frontal look and wide-open eyes portrays an abiding illumination. The small mouths of saints suggests their ongoing inner work of contemplation. The poise of the subject and beauty of composition generate a feeling of unearthly harmony. The technique of reverse perspective creates a double movement: It draws the viewer into the icon while allowing eternity to spill into the present. We are not disinterested spectators, but participants in the scene. If the icon radiates the transformation of resurrection life, gazing upon it can transform us, too. Speaking of the aim behind the various distortions of perspective and impossible architecture found in icons, John Baggley observes:

13. Leonid Ouspensky, "The Meaning and Language of Icons," in Leonid Ouspensky and Vladimir Lossky, *The Meaning of Icons*, rev. ed., translated by G.E. H. Palmer and E. Kadloubovsky (Crestwood, NY: St. Vladimir's Press, 1982), 32.

This can lead to the recognition that our normal everyday world is also the scene where events of an inner or higher spiritual world are taking place, a world where our normal values and assumptions are turned upside down. To enter this world our minds must be converted, we must pass through the narrow gate that leads to eternal life (Matthew 7:13–14). . . .

The "unrealistic" buildings are part of the visual language of the icon painters; they can represent the setting of the event portrayed, but by being non-naturalistic these buildings help show that the event and its significance are not confined to a precise historical moment of time and space; they belong to the world of the spirit. . . . The wider significance of the events portrayed has to be worked out in the soul of those who behold the icon.[14]

In his brilliant meditation on the icon of the Transfiguration, Rowan Williams considers the trans-historical implications of the gospel rendered through the vision of the icon. In the case of the Transfiguration of our Lord, the bending of time is evident in both the original story in the synoptic gospels and its interpretation in the icon. In both story and icon we see Moses and Elijah, who lived centuries before Jesus, conversing with him as contemporaries. And what about us, who live centuries after the events described? We are there, too:

In Jesus, the world of ordinary prosaic time is not destroyed, but it is broken up and reconnected, it works no longer in just straight lines but in layers and spirals of meaning. We begin to understand how our lives, like those of Moses and Elijah, may have meanings we can't know of in this present moment: the real depth and significance of what we say or do now won't appear until more of the light of Christ has been seen. . . . Christ's light alone will make the final pattern coherent, for each one of us as for all human history. And that light shines on the far side of the world's limits, the dawn of the eighth day.[15]

14. John Baggley, *Doors of Perception: Icons and their Spiritual Significance* (Crestwood, NY: St. Vladimir's Press, 1988), 81–82.

15. Rowan Williams, *The Dwelling of the Light: Praying with Icons of Christ* (Grand Rapids, MI: William B. Eerdmans, 2004), 8–9.

Icons, like all true manifestations of prayer and especially the sacraments, bring us to the frontier, the threshold of the eschaton. So we begin to pray before icons as we begin every kind of prayer: anticipating deeper conversion. "Looking at Jesus seriously changes things," writes Williams. "If we do not want to be changed, it is better not to look too hard or too long."[16]

The approach to this form of contemplation would be similar to our way of entering into other methods of personal prayer: We find a time and place, perhaps light a candle, settle ourselves physically. Praying with an icon lends itself to various forms of engagement with God. We can just gaze upon the icon in contemplation, letting ourselves be drawn in. We can intersperse our looking with occasional colloquy or *lectio divina*. We can perform the examen prayer. Or we can lovingly direct our attention towards God in silent communion for short or extended periods of time. This "prayer of loving regard," as it is sometimes called, may be performed with or without a sacred image before us. The Curé of Ars, a sainted, early nineteenth-century French priest, once asked an old peasant in his parish what he did, sitting for hours in church. The man replied: "I look at him, and he looks at me, and we are happy together."

APOPHATIC PRAYER AND THE NEGATIVE WAY: UNION WITHOUT THOUGHTS OR IMAGES

"By love He may be gotten and holden; but by thought, never." (*The Cloud of Unknowing*)

It sometimes happens that we wish to pray, but words fail us. Perhaps we have no more words left, having said everything to God that there is to be said, at least for now. Sometimes we are plunged into a season of grief, confusion, or darkness that no words can express. Or we may be struck by the utter inadequacy of our words to address the awesome mystery of God. Moreover, it often happens that meditation on Scripture, after long practice,

---

16. *The Dwelling of the Light*, 13.

eventually becomes impossible. *Lectio divina* feels forced and artificial. Thought and language seem to have run their course. Yet we still want to be with God in prayer. We are attracted to the silence of prayer but are at a loss for what to do.

It may be a relief to learn that in these circumstances we are occupying well-traversed spiritual terrain. There comes a time in which words must give way to sheer silence: "For God alone my soul in silence waits," prays the psalmist (Ps. 62:1). There is a way of praying without words, thoughts, or images, and such prayer has a solid theological basis. For God exceeds all our imaginings. God is the ever-greater, outstripping our most superlative ideas of the Divine.

Most of Christian theology and spirituality builds upon God's revelation to us through creation, Scripture, Jesus, and the church. Creaturely things can become vehicles of grace for us because the incarnation of the Word has sanctified creation and Christ's resurrection has transfigured it. In Christian theology there is at base a decided affirmation of the material world and human culture. In its most developed form, this *via affirmativa* yields a sacramental view of the universe: a vision of the world as a communicating symbol of the divine. The suppositions of affirmative theology support liturgy, religious art, theological discourse, and all forms of prayer that make use of words, images, or concepts. In practice, then, the Christian faith is largely a religion of the affirmative or *kataphatic* (Greek: affirming) way.

Yet some of our earliest roots suggest certain dangers inherent in this path to God. The ancient prohibition against graven images—a prominent issue in the iconoclastic controversy—underscores the perennial human tendency towards idolatry. And the more ethereal the image, the more it is apt to be mistaken for the Real. The *via negativa* insists that God cannot be reduced to any of our notions, words, or images of the Divine. Negative or *apophatic* (Greek: denying) theology emerged from the perception that God is always beyond—beyond our words, our ideas, or even our experience of God. All human notions of God are inadequate to the Divine Reality. While appreciation for liturgy, icons, sacred music, or theology usually supports our devotion to God, these things can also become a snare—an idol—if we become too attached to them. "Seek God," one of the desert ascetics said, "not the place where God lives."

The affirmative and negative ways are not opposites nor even alternate routes to God. Instead, they represent complementary theological truths. Both are necessary for an adequate and comprehensive Christian theology. On the one hand, the apophatic insight that God is always greater than anything we can say or think of him is a crucial component of Christian theology as a whole. It fosters humility and reserve in theological work and serves as a counterweight to naïve or falsely literalistic readings of scriptural metaphor. It reminds us that all theological and liturgical language proceed by analogy. On the other hand, the richness of the affirmative way rests upon nothing less than God's gracious self-communication. Hence, we can never bypass or discard divine revelation, even though it is inevitably tailored to our human limitations of language, thought, and culture. How else could God communicate with us?

The complementarity of the affirmative and negative ways is found, at least in germinal form, in Scripture itself. The Hebrew tradition affirms that God is self-communicating; hence the stupendous gift of revelation. Creation first manifests something of God: "The heavens declare the glory of God, and the firmament shows his handiwork" (Ps. 19:1). Then the Scriptures as a whole bear witness to God's words and saving acts. At the same time, the Bible recognizes that we can never know God fully: God always remains "Other" and beyond our comprehension. A long tradition asserts that no one can "see" God—that is, enjoy a direct, unmediated vision of God—and live. The Divine Name revealed to Moses in the great theophany of the burning bush bespeaks an elusive identity (Exod. 3:14). When Jacob wrestles with the angel (or river demon), this emissary of the Most High refuses to reveal his name (Gen. 32:29). Behind these and many other stories lies the reverent recognition that humans cannot control or "possess" God. The Deuterocanonical Book of Sirach presents an affirmative path of praising God's greatness yet with an apophatic twist. As the author recounts the wonders of creation, in the end he knows he cannot find words adequate to extol their Creator:

> We could say more, but we could never say enough;
> let the final word be: "He is the all." . . .
> Glorify the Lord and exalt him as much as you can,
> for he surpasses even that. (Sir. 43:27, 30)

The Prologue to St. John's Gospel sums up both sides of this insight succinctly: "No one has ever seen God. It is God the only Son, who is close to the Father's heart, who has made him known" (John 1:18). Jesus is the consummate revelation of God. Yet we never finish exploring the mystery of Christ.

Early in the life of the church the insights of apophatic theology issued in apophatic approaches to spirituality. The *via negativa* can be traced at least as far back as St. Gregory of Nyssa (330–395). Its classic expression, however, is embodied in the works of an unknown sixth-century Syrian monk, who called himself "Dionysius"—St. Paul's Athenian convert mentioned briefly at the conclusion of Paul's speech at the Areopagus (Acts 17:34). His successful use of his pseudonym—one closely associated with an apostle—afforded the writings of "Dionysius the Areopagite" an almost biblical sanction for the Middle Ages and beyond. Commenting on one of Dionysius's works, St. Thomas Aquinas noted that "the highest knowledge we can have of God in this life is that God transcends anything we can think about him."[17] This from the pen of the most renowned theologian of affirmative theology!

In his short work entitled *The Mystical Theology*, Dionysius outlined a method of meditation based on apophatic theology. It consisted of systematically negating every quality that could be posited of God. He begins by eliminating patently mundane characteristics such as corporeality, and he ends up denying even the properties traditionally associated with God—goodness, for instance, or being. We can deny these attributes, too, according to

---

17. *De Divinis Nominibus*, I, lect. 3 (Parma ed., XV, 271).

Dionysius, because our human conception of them inevitably falls short of the supreme reality they are attempting to convey. All our notions of God's attributes—wisdom, beauty, and so on—are based solely on our limited human experience of them—not on the absolute reality itself. When at last we find ourselves bereft of all mental concepts of God, we enter a "darkness of unknowing." At this point theological method is transformed into prayer, because in this intellectual darkness we can be mystically united to the unknowable God and possess a "knowledge that exceeds understanding."

The influence of Dionysius on the subsequent tradition of apophatic spirituality can scarcely be overestimated. The fourteenth-century English author of *The Cloud of Unknowing*, also anonymous, conveyed the substance of the Dionysian teaching but offered more explicit direction about how to engage the "darkness of unknowing." In company with earlier medieval commentators, he places the accent on love: "By love He may be gotten and holden; but by thought, never." Energetic, passionate desire for God is the driving force of this prayer. When all particular thoughts—whether about created things or about God—are temporarily set aside, cast under a "cloud of forgetting," there exists yet another barrier between the practitioner and God: a "cloud of unknowing." Since all our thoughts about God are inevitably contaminated by our imperfect conceptualizations, we can never fully penetrate the divine mystery. Thus suspended between deliberate forgetting and reverent unknowing, the practitioner still has something to do. He must beat incessantly upon the cloud of unknowing "with a sharp dart of longing love." The loving will repeatedly orients itself towards God. In this exercise prayer is reduced to its most basic terms: a "naked intent unto God." Like St. Paul's "sighs too deep for words," prayer in *The Cloud* has become utterly simplified.

Apophatic mysticism runs like a thread through the history of Christian spirituality. St. John of the Cross extolled the "luminous darkness" of the *via negativa*. As a spiritual guide, he noted that the onset of an inability to engage in "discursive meditation"—that is, meditation using ordinary thought processes—indicated a probable call to this more austere prayer of pure faith. He does, however, presuppose ample experience with forms of meditation that do employ such thinking and prayerful reflection. Hence St. John, along with the preponderance of tradition, urges continued meditation on Scripture and other spiritual topics until such meditation becomes impossible. He refers to this incapacity as a "ligature"—literally, a "binding" of the mind. Of course, the liturgy—the Eucharist, office, and a full sacramental life—continues to ground life in Christ. Apophatic prayer, like all personal prayer, it is situated within the communal forms of prayer incumbent upon all Christians.

In the twentieth century, T.S. Eliot captured the way of unknowing he learned from John of the Cross in a section of his monumental poem, *Four Quartets*. Through the language of contemporary poetry, Eliot illuminates both the appeal and the demands of the negative way:

> I said to my soul, be still, and wait without hope
> For hope would be hope for the wrong thing; wait without love
> For love would be love of the wrong thing; yet there is faith
> But the faith and the love and the hope are all in the waiting.
> Wait without thought, for you are not ready for thought;
> So the darkness shall be the light, and the stillness the
>   dancing. . . .
>
> To arrive where you are, to get from where you are not,
> You must go by a way wherein there is no ecstasy.
> In order to arrive at what you do not know
> You must go by a way which is the way of ignorance.
> In order to possess what you do not possess
> You must go by the way of dispossession.
> In order to arrive at what you are not
> You must go through the way in which you are not.
> And what you do not know is the only thing you know
> And what you own is what you do not own
> And where you are is where you are not.

("East Coker," III)

Since the early 1980s the Centering Prayer movement has taught a version of apophatic prayer to countless numbers of people seeking greater depth in their relation to God. Weaving together strands from this tradition, including a gently repeated "sacred word," Centering Prayer offers a way into silent communion with God. In this practice as in other forms of apophatic prayer, one sets aside all thoughts of God, self, and creatures during the time of meditation. When thoughts occur, as they inevitably do, one notices them and then releases them without fuss. M. Basil Pennington, one of the earliest exponents of Centering Prayer, sums up its method:

> *Rule One*: At the beginning of the Prayer we take a minute or two to quiet down and then move in faith to God dwelling in our depths; and at the end of the Prayer we take several minutes to come out, mentally praying the "Our Father" or some other prayer.
>
> *Rule Two*: After resting for a bit in the center in faith-full love, we take up a single, simple word that expresses this response and begin to let it repeat itself within.
>
> *Rule Three*: Whenever in the course of the Prayer we become *aware* of anything else, we simply and gently return to the Presence by the use of the prayer word.[18]

The simplicity of Centering Prayer has made silent, contemplative prayer accessible to many who otherwise would never have known of it. Many Western Christians have had little if any exposure to the meditative traditions that are their heritage. Because of the commitment of the Contemplative Outreach movement, it has reached a broad spectrum of people in all stations of life. Contemplative depth is not reserved to some spiritual elite, but is the calling of all Christians.

There is pastoral wisdom, however, in the long tradition that warns against embarking upon the negative way without

---

18. M. Basil Pennington, O.C.S.O., *Centering Prayer: Renewing an Ancient Christian Prayer Form* (Garden City, NY: Image Books, 1982), 65. See also *Thomas Keating, Open Mind, Open Heart: The Contemplative Dimension of the Gospel* (Amity, NY: Amity House, 1986) for clarification of the Centering Prayer method and typical difficulties.

considerable exposure to the more ordinary modes of meditation found in the *via affirmativa*. The mind usually needs something to do in prayer, and *lectio divina* and other forms of affirmative meditation fill that gap. It moves us to conversion of mind and the affections. Meditation on Scripture, moreover, offers the opportunity of coming to know and love Jesus as he is mediated through the gospels. For Christians, this is no small matter.

Yet when people are powerfully drawn to silent communion with God, it suggests that the Spirit is leading them to some version of the *via negativa*, perhaps to Centering Prayer. Sometimes, for a variety of reasons, we cannot pray or meditate with words, thoughts, or images. Sometimes we feel saturated with words because of our work or environment. Our words then need the cleansing tonic of silence, and we yearn for contact with God beyond our conceptions of him.

There is one bias in the apophatic tradition about which we might exercise caution. Much of the literature of Christian mysticism assumes that entrance into apophatic prayer signals a kind of graduation from kataphatic meditation. This would seem to discount kataphatic mystics such as Bernard of Clairvaux, Julian of Norwich, and Teresa of Avila, to name but a few. Moreover, experience indicates that the ligature is not always permanent. People are drawn to pray with words, thoughts, and images during some seasons of their lives, then engage in silent prayer for a spell, and then move back into *lectio divina*. Although most people settle into something of a default position, relying on a particular method for months if not years, there is more fluidity in the spiritual life than some of the older treatises might lead us to believe. The crucial thing, the wise Benedictine John Chapman (d. 1933) counseled in one of his letters of spiritual direction, is this: "Pray as you can; and do not try to pray as you can't. Take yourself as you find yourself, and start from that."[19]

---

19. John Chapman, *Spiritual Letters* (London: Sheed and Ward, 1976), 109. Letter dated September 4, 1932.

CHAPTER FIVE

Practices for the Journey

"Do not be daunted immediately by fear and run away from the road that leads to salvation. It is bound to be narrow at the outset. But as we progress in this way of life and in faith, we shall run on the path of God's commandments, our hearts overflowing with the inexpressible delight of love."

—"Prologue," Rule of St. Benedict

RULE OF LIFE

We may not be inclined at first to imagine that principles formulated centuries ago for celibate monks can enlighten our own way of life and faith today. Yet because many people who are not monastics confirm that the Rule of St. Benedict offers an invaluable pattern of practice for themselves, it is worth considering just how and why this is so. When in the sixth century St. Benedict committed his Rule to writing, he was drawing on earlier monastic precedents as well as his considerable personal experience in guiding the monasteries that took shape under his leadership. Contemporary readers of his Rule are often surprised to find in it scant spiritual teaching, although sprinkled here and there are such memorable instructions as "All guests who present themselves are to be welcomed as Christ."[1] For the most part, however, the Rule concerns itself with the practical details of organizing prayer, work, and the common life: how the psalms should be arranged for recitation, the rotation of kitchen servers, the duties of the abbot, and the distribution of clothing, for example. Only when taken as a whole does the order and balance of the Rule,

---

1. All citations are from *The Rule of St. Benedict in English*, ed. Timothy Fry, O.S.B., (Collegeville, MN: The Liturgical Press, 1981).

for which it is justly famous, shine through. Rather than create a monastery functioning like a well-oiled machine, Benedict aims for the organic harmony of a disciplined yet adaptable community. Practices support this life and direct it to its final purpose: "let us set out on this way, with the Gospel for our guide, that we may deserve to see him who has called us to his kingdom" (Prologue: 21).

Practices matter. They slowly shape our character and relationships, including our relation to God. If we fail to give thought to them, we will often find ourselves frustrated, dancing to other people's tunes or simply reacting to each day's pressures. Our own aspirations and values will get sidelined. To help protect what is essential but often fragile, the ascetical tradition recommends devising a "Rule of Life." Such a Rule is primarily concerned with a "Rule of Prayer," but often contains other practices that uphold our spiritual, emotional, and physical wellbeing.

The very word "rule" can conjure up images of a spiritual straitjacket, and we may well feel that we already have plenty of obligations without adding to them. But the purpose of Benedict's Rule is to foster regularity, not bind us to ironclad laws. It seeks to develop the balance and harmony often lacking in contemporary culture. It creates space to safeguard practices in tune with our deepest desires—goals usually at odds with our driven, consumerist culture. It helps us put ends and means together: What kind of person do we want to become and how will we get there? What is most important—the "one thing needful"? What might God desire for us? These are questions to explore with God in prayer, for framing a Rule of Life is no exercise in spiritual self-perfection, a Christian version of the quest for personal culture. It instead attempts to orchestrate a faithful response to our Christian vocation.

That calling already commits us to basic practices that are part of our common life in the community of faith. The Baptismal Covenant, as we have seen, aligns us with the corporate Rule of Life first attested in Acts 2:42: "They devoted themselves to the apostles' teaching and fellowship, to the breaking of bread and the prayers" (cf. BCP, 304). Our Rule of Life, then, does not begin from scratch. It is more a fleshing out of specific practices, in accord with our personal circumstances, within an inherited organizing pattern. And because life in Christ is a life situated within the "fellowship," it is prudent to consult with others, usually our pastor or spiritual director or a wise Christian friend, when pondering the details of our Rule. It is also sensible to begin with a simple, uncomplicated Rule that challenges us without strain. If our Rule of Life represents an impractical ideal, we will quickly give up, as our practices go the way of many New Year's resolutions. It is better to start out with something entirely attainable, and later intensify our practice, if possible. St. Benedict himself recognized the value of moderation in the provisions of his Rule: "In drawing up its regulations, we hope to set down nothing harsh, nothing burdensome" (Prologue: 46). We should experience a Rule of Life as an aspect of the discipline of Christ, whose "yoke is easy" and whose "burden is light" (Matt. 11:30).

It has long been noted that Anglican spirituality is imbued with a strong Benedictine coloring, highlighting balance, harmony, and bending oneself to the demands of common life rather than to feats of individual asceticism. Perhaps this springs, as Esther de Waal and others have speculated, from the daily rhythms of prayer and work in the numerous English cathedrals that for centuries also happened to be abbey churches, at least until the Reformation. Certainly the significance of the Daily Office in successive Books of Common Prayer reflects these Benedictine roots. In a similar vein, mid-twentieth century Anglican pastoral theologian Martin Thornton, in his widely read *Christian Proficiency*, identified a threefold Rule of Prayer consisting of Eucharist, Daily Office, and personal prayer. This straightforward and comprehensive outline for spiritual practice embodies the scriptural model found in Acts.

What practices, then, would we include in our Rule of Prayer? Primacy must be given to the Holy Eucharist, "the principal act of Christian worship on the Lord's Day and other major Feasts" (BCP, 13). From the first, Christians have gathered on Sunday, the Day of Resurrection, for the breaking of bread. Through the Eucharist we also participate in those mysteries of Christ commemorated by the major feasts—the Lord's Nativity, Transfiguration, or Ascension, for example—or renew our communion with the great saints of the church. Participation in the Eucharist "on the Lord's Day and other major Feasts" thus marks Anglican spirituality as a defining though scarcely unique trait. Moreover, the abundant grace of the Eucharist prompts some Christians to attend on still other days, especially if the parish offers regular weekday celebrations. Such people might want to include a daily or weekday Eucharist in their Rule of Prayer.

Unfortunately, since few parishes offer Daily Morning or Evening Prayer, incorporating recitation of the Office into our practice can seem daunting, even esoteric, especially if we have never been exposed to a community that prays the Office each day. Yet the rhythms of the Office, alternating between morning and evening, and connecting us to the round of liturgical seasons, situates us each day in the larger community of the praying church. An ancient practice with roots in Judaism, the Office anchors the soul in the community of faith and can sustain it in times of distress or dryness. Use of the Daily Office is a characteristic feature of Anglican spirituality, which has never regarded its recitation as an exclusively clerical endeavor. If we are unfamiliar with the Office, we can begin to enter its rhythm very modestly, perhaps using one or more of the "Daily Devotions" found in the Book of Common Prayer, saying Compline at the end of the day, or just reciting the Lord's Prayer at key intervals. Once we establish a pattern of praying with the church throughout the day, we can build on it over time.

Daily personal prayer forms the final, crucial piece in the threefold Rule of Prayer. As discussed in the previous chapter, we have many options at hand for engaging in this intimate mode of communion with God. What we do, how much time we allocate to it, and whether we engage in any form of meditative prayer, will require deliberation and the most searching honesty. While a few contemplative souls find their natural home in solitary prayer, most people struggle with it. Avoidance typically takes the form of "not having any time for it." But when all is said and done, the only way to have a life of prayer is to pray. Without a space for personal prayer, sooner or later liturgy becomes wearisome and our ministries, shallow. Hence a realistic commitment to personal prayer as an element of our Rule can support and strengthen our resolve. Eventually we may find, like Benedict's novice, that with practice we "run on the path of God's commandments, our hearts overflowing with the inexpressible delight of love." As a woman new to the life of prayer once said, "When you show up, God shows up. It's amazing!"

Just as we must find equilibrium along the axis of liturgical/ personal prayer, so we require balance among other facets of our humanity in order to live fully and faithfully. Depending on where we sense chronic one-sidedness or distortion, incorporating a few other practices into our Rule could help. For instance, if we are given to persistent overwork or bouts of depression, commitment could take the form of scheduling ways to sustain relationships or engage in forms of recreation that renew our spirits.

Then there is the crucial balance of body and spirit. Our relation to our bodies has been transformed by our union with the resurrected body of Christ. They are "members of Christ" and a "temple of the Holy Spirit." St. Paul further urges us to "glorify God in your body" (1 Cor. 6:14, 19–20). We are to treat that part of creation uniquely entrusted to us with proper honor. So unless our occupation entails physical labor, we will probably need to engage in regular exercise, according to our ability, in order to keep fit. Like finding time for prayer, scheduling exercise demands realism about the flow of our day and level of energy. As in all other aspects of our Rule, it is better to begin on a small scale in order to establish the habit. Our Rule of Life might also set parameters around our use of food and drink. Using these gifts with thankfulness and joy—as well as appropriate self-control—frees us from our cultural obsession with dieting and body image. By contrast, the church has long maintained a satisfying rhythm of feast and fast, with most days characterized by moderate, healthful habits. Recovering the sense of feast days as truly celebratory, and fast days as occasions of real self-denial, can embody this balance for ourselves and our households.

In drawing up a Rule of Life, then, we take into account the practices expected of all the baptized (Acts 2:42) as well as our particular circumstances and propensities. With respect to elective practices, we might recall the advice Teresa of Avila gave to her community of sisters: "Do that which most engenders love in you." If we are consistently failing to observe some aspect of our Rule, or if it no longer seems sufficient, it may require revision, best undertaken in consultation with a spiritual guide. It sometimes happens that because of illness or emergencies, we need to set aside our Rule for a while, later to be resumed. A Rule of Life is embraced not as a set of wooden obligations, but as a flexible instrument. It puts flesh on God's call to fullness of life in Christ.

SPIRITUAL DIRECTION

"Who is wise? Attach yourself to such a one." (Sirach 6:34)

"Teach us to pray." Like the disciple who turned to Jesus, we sometimes need help in navigating our relationship with God. The disciple had observed Jesus at prayer: Here was someone who clearly lived on the closest terms with God and who could, therefore, be trusted. And Jesus was a consummate teacher, a "rabbi" as his disciples spontaneously called him, who taught "with authority." Judaism, especially in the Wisdom books, had stressed the importance of assimilating the ways of God by placing oneself under the tutelage of a wise teacher. As valuable as private study of Torah might be, a community of disciples learning together could offer even more, especially under the supervision of a recognized teacher.

The community of disciples gathered around Jesus continues as the community of the church. Within that body, the Spirit has unleashed a variety of gifts "for the common good" (1 Cor. 12:7). These include the "utterance of wisdom," "the utterance of knowledge," and the "discernment of spirits." We are to "teach and admonish one another in all wisdom" (Col. 3:16). The exercise of these gifts within the contemporary church takes a variety of forms. Many parishes and other Christian communities sponsor prayer and meditation groups. These typically include instruction in the art of prayer. Participants can air their difficulties as well as the breakthroughs that prayer affords, receiving guidance from other members or the leader.

The cultivation of spiritual friendships in the church, whether based in such groups or not, offers another treasured venue for "teaching and admonishing one another in all wisdom." What makes a spiritual friendship different from other friendships, even friendships with other Christians, is its deliberate focus. Spiritual friends come together to speak specifically of their journey in Christ. They discuss where, since their last meeting, they have experienced blessings or setbacks, insight or confusion, and seek each other's counsel. Usually their conversations are framed in silence and prayer, and they generally meet at set intervals. As in all friendships, such relationships are entered freely, with mutual respect as a foundation. Above all, spiritual friends seek God's will together; they want to build each other up in faithfulness to Christ. A spiritual friendship may consist of two or more friends who pray for each other between gatherings. Clearly too large a group might hamper the depth of exchange. And a regular meeting of two friends of the attractive sex—if either one is already committed in marriage or to celibate life—poses obvious dangers.

The ministry of spiritual direction includes many characteristics of spiritual friendship, entailing as it does a special companionship within the company of believers for the sake of enhancing faithful discipleship. But while spiritual direction usually builds upon, or develops into, a warm personal relationship, it is not a mutual ministry. The director is there for the for the sake of the person being directed, not vice-versa, and the director bears primary responsibility for maintaining appropriate boundaries. Although the term "spiritual direction" can, unfortunately, convey excessive control or an aura of authoritarianism, the alternatives of "soul friend" or "spiritual companion" can also give the wrong impression. Spiritual direction is a pastoral ministry in which friendliness rather than friendship sets the tone.

Alan Jones, himself a renowned spiritual director, has described his own first encounter with spiritual direction when he was a young seminarian in England. For him, the role of the praying community, which upheld him at a time when he could not get his own bearings, was crucial. Then the dean of the seminary intervened with a pastoral conversation he never forgot:

> I first came into contact with a spiritual director in my early twenties and my initial experience of spiritual direction was one of rescue. I was a confused and rebellious Christian drawn into the fellowship of the Church in the hope that what was preached might possibly be true. I was then a seminarian at the College of the Resurrection where young men were trained for the priesthood in a monastic context. . . . I thought the extremity of monasticism would help me see not only if Christianity was real, but if I was.
>
> I had never experienced such isolation. . . . My me began to disintegrate, not in the benign disintegration of a person in the act of loving self-surrender. Mine was the kind of dissolution that placed everything on quicksand. I did not so much doubt God as I doubted myself. I even doubted my doubts. . . .
>
> Rescue came in two ways. . . . The first was the sustaining power of a worshipping, compassionate, and believing community. For a while I was carried by the lively tradition of the Church, by the liturgical rhythm of the community, and the compassionate presence of my fellow Christians. For a few weeks, then, I was sustained by the faith and faithfulness of the Christian community at a time when I felt that I had no faith at all or, rather, I felt there was no "I" to have faith. . . .
>
> The second part of the rescue operation was a summons from the dean of the seminary to go for an afternoon walk with him across the moors. I had no choice. . . . At the time I had no real notion of his own hurts. I received nothing but receptivity and love and it was this that influenced me deeply. It was as if he could see into my deepest self. He was able to show me that God loved me all the way through. He was the bearer of the miracle that I mattered. This doctrine that I matter, that people matter, was and is the hardest thing for

me to believe. My struggle with other aspects of Christian belief are insignificant compared with the difficulty I have in accepting that I am loved.[2]

Somehow the seminary's dean could "see into" Jones's "deepest self." This kind of startling insight into another's soul is by no means uncommon in spiritual direction. It is a special but not altogether rare gift. Discerning Jones's inner turmoil and deepest desires, the dean could express and embody the kind of love the young Jones craved but dared not hope for: "the miracle that I mattered." Yet this graced combination of discernment and love might have been just a passing consolation without the sustaining network of the church: the compassionate, praying community that supported both of them.

Thomas Merton once defined spiritual direction as "a continuous process of formation and guidance, in which a Christian is led and encouraged *in his special vocation*, so that by faithful correspondence to the graces of the Holy Spirit he may attain to the particular end of his vocation and to union with God."[3] Spiritual direction deals with the most fundamental, sacred, and intimate relationship we enjoy: our relationship to God. Merton names its ultimate goal as union with God: a union begun at baptism with immersion into the death and resurrection of Christ. It grows as we participate ever more fully in divine love manifested, as Merton shrewdly observes, through fidelity to our particular vocations. Holiness is never abstract. The Spirit sanctifies the flesh of everyday life amid its precise pressure points. In the warp and woof of ordinary vocation—parent, worker, student, citizen, and so on—the fruits of the Holy Spirit are formed in us: "love, joy, peace, patience, kindness, generosity, faithfulness, gentleness, and self-control" (Gal. 5:22–23). There is no better test of the authenticity of our prayer than these objective manifestations of grace—not our feelings nor even our insights.

2. Alan Jones, *Exploring Spiritual Direction: An Essay on Christian Friendship* (New York: Seabury Press, 1982), 5–6.

3. Thomas Merton, *Spiritual Direction and Meditation and What Is Contemplation?* (Wheathampstead, England: Anthony Clarke Books, 1975), 14–15.

Because divine grace flows through the whole of our lives, any aspect of our multiple vocations or relationships might come under discussion in the course of spiritual direction. But while it will always include attention to our experience of God in prayer, spiritual direction deals with more than our devotional practice. We meet God everywhere, though much of the time we just do not notice. Spiritual direction penetrates beneath surface phenomena, picking up on the Spirit's movements in our lives. By a more acute discernment of God's ways with us—or, conversely, by perceiving the subtle, undermining pressure of the Evil One— our true freedom in Christ is enhanced. We can better embrace a grace or resist a temptation when our eyes are open.

The broad scope of concerns that can be brought to spiritual direction might suggest a superficial resemblance to therapeutic counseling. But there are crucial differences. The various forms of therapy work toward the resolution of inner conflict, the psychic healing of individuals or their relationships, or simply problem-solving of a serious order. Christians, like other people, should pursue such means of healing whenever necessary: the restorative touch of Christ comes in many ways. But even though some degree of healing usually follows upon deeper conversion, spiritual direction does not directly aim to achieve it. And while some dilemmas are occasionally untangled through spiritual direction, many of our problems cannot be resolved. They instead require *interpretation* in the light of the gospel so we can bear them with grace. Spiritual direction also differs from therapy in its explicitly religious setting. It takes place within the community of the church and is itself an aspect of our common life: "Bear one another's burdens, and so fulfil the law of Christ" (Gal. 6:2). Its context is thus the vigorous life of faith: the Scriptures, sacraments, worship, and fellowship of the church.

First and foremost, spiritual direction supports our relationship to God through careful discernment. It helps us notice how God is already active in our lives, and it encourages a generous response to grace. What experiences, whether in ordinary events or in interior movements, have shored up our faith and trust in God? What activities, impulses, or settings tend to make us feel discouraged? How have these things affected our behavior? What has prayer been like? In spiritual direction, we are encouraged to grow in the affective discernment characteristic of the Examen Prayer. Here, however, we also benefit from the more detached perspective of another seasoned Christian. In the end, as Merton explains, the goal of this ministry is union with God. Spiritual direction is oriented towards sanctification, our transformation in Christ. Or as the Epistle to the Ephesians puts it, "to unity of the faith and knowledge of the Son of God, to maturity, to the measure of the full stature of Christ" (4:13).

The tradition of spiritual direction in the church began with the desert ascetics of the late third and fourth centuries. When thousands of men and women fled to the remote deserts of Egypt, Palestine, and Syria seeking solitary communion with God, they discovered that they had brought their inner turmoil, conflicts, and temptations with them. Since they wanted to pursue that purity of heart by which alone one "sees God" (Matt. 5:8), they turned, understandably enough, to the most mature among them for guidance. Still other spiritual seekers travelled to the desert briefly, hoping for "a word" of insight from these *abbas* and *ammas* ("fathers" and "mothers"). Fortunately, their disciples committed many of their pithy sayings and pungent stories to writing. It is noteworthy that the vast majority of desert Christians were lay men and women; and even after monastic life became more communally organized, it still retained its largely lay character for several centuries. For this reason the authority of the spiritual director has long been recognized as charismatic—that is, dependent on a particular gift or charism of the Holy Spirit rather than on the grace of ordination. The first *abbas* and *ammas* were consulted because they lived manifestly close to God. Such familiarity with the Lord created a "taste" or innate perception of divine things. They knew from experience what "smacks" of God and what does not. Later scholastic tradition would call this "connatural knowledge": the wisdom and knowledge born of abiding in God.

Today we still turn to those Christians among us whose maturity, steadiness, and peace inspire our confidence. The journey of faith is often obscure, and the life of prayer is neither obvious nor easy. Since we sometimes need coaching in our human relationships, counsel is all the more vital in our relationship to God. We are subject to many influences, both within and without, pressing us to do one thing or another. We may wonder how God is leading us, or how to read our own spiritual state of affairs. We may fear self-deception, and sometimes this fear can become crippling. We may feel blocked in prayer or just treading water. Often a single conversation with a trusted Christian friend or our pastor can clarify our situation and set us on our way, as the case of Alan Jones illustrates. In a few months, we might want to check in again. Such occasional guidance seems to have been the usual practice in the desert tradition.

Some people, however, benefit from more consistent spiritual direction, the "continuous process of formation and guidance" about which Merton wrote. They typically meet with a director once a month for about an hour. Both parties will need to agree upon scheduling and other logistical details. In this collaborative and prayerful partnership, they meet in the Name of Christ, attending to the movements of the Holy Spirit. Often an early session will be spent reviewing or refining the Rule of Life of the person being directed, since the fruitfulness of spiritual direction depends upon an active life of prayer. After that, the one seeking direction usually supplies the material for discussion and discernment: What concerns does he or she bring to today's meeting? Good directors listen much and speak sparingly. They do not endeavor to foster dependence on themselves but rather work to enhance the maturity and inner resources of those under their direction. They remain on the lookout to support God's distinctive ways with each person.

Those being directed must, for their part, cultivate honesty and openness with the director. Important matters cannot be hidden. We have to be as "real" in direction as we possibly can, letting go of any wish to save face or keep up a respectable façade. We have to be frank about our motives and willing to admit to thoughts and feelings that may bring us shame. Some people find it even more embarrassing to speak about their sense of God and their brushes with the divine—the graces that come their way. We have to lay bare the desires of our hearts in transparency and vulnerability.

An atmosphere of freedom surrounds the entire spiritual direction relationship. Both parties enter the relationship freely, and either one can withdraw from it at will. In the first few months particularly, both sides will be testing the relationship to determine whether it seems to be a good fit. In any case, termination should not be abrupt; a final discussion should offer some closure to this intimate spiritual partnership. When during a meeting directors offer an interpretation of the situation, they usually present such a discernment tentatively, since only God fully knows the heart. So while the director might suggest, prompt, or challenge, those under direction must confirm the director's reading of the data. It has to ring true to them. Some matters do not lend themselves to immediate discernment. These must be left open to further prayer and leading by God. In many cases, directors need only endorse the discernment of those they are directing, strengthening and encouraging their graced intuitions. Often directors will suggest a passage of Scripture for future meditation or as a starting point for prayer, either to assist in further discernment or to appropriate a grace that has been freshly recognized.

Spiritual direction offers a warm and often comforting companionship in Christ, but it also demands a serious commitment on both sides, especially to regular and sustained prayer. It can be enormously beneficial for those willing to work at it. Finding a spiritual director is not always easy. As in the desert tradition, certain people in certain locales are simply known as wise and reliable guides in the life of the Spirit. Ideally, we wish to entrust ourselves to someone well acquainted with the temptations and pitfalls of discipleship. Directors should know the spiritual terrain and the landscape of grace. They will have spent considerable time in the interior desert and, though still engaged in their own struggles, have won through to a real measure of peace. As lovers of souls, they are willing to stand with us at the foot of the cross. Above all, directors must be confident in divine mercy and grounded in hope. If you are not yourself familiar with such a guide, someone's personal recommendation is the best way to find one. Your priest, deacon, bishop, or a person you know to be already under direction, might be able to make a suggestion. Monasteries and retreat houses usually have experienced spiritual directors available, if you happen to reside near one.

Nowadays, it is possible to receive training for spiritual direction at some retreat centers and theological schools. While education in the ascetical tradition is extremely valuable for this ministry, in the end it depends, as it always has, on a charism from God, rather than on any certificate or degree. Finally, because spiritual direction is a pastoral ministry and not a service-for-fee, financial compensation falls outside the norm. If, however, the director has limited means or is a member of a religious community, an offering to support this ministry is appropriate.

THE SACRAMENT OF RECONCILIATION

**"Therefore, confess your sins to one another, and pray for one another, so that you may be healed."
(James 5:16)**

In his instructions about beginning contemplative prayer, the author of *The Cloud of Unknowing* insists that none undertake this exercise "before they have cleansed their conscience of all the particular sins that they have committed beforehand according to the ordinary direction of holy Church" (Chapter 28). Such pastoral advice in the fourteenth century would strike us as unexceptional. Indeed, the Fourth Lateran Council of 1215 had made annual confession to a priest during the Easter season mandatory for all Western Christians. But beyond the common, expected practice of sacramental confession, the *Cloud*-author has reasons of his own for recommending it. Apophatic prayer requires exceptional clarity and single-minded attention to God. All other thoughts must be put under a "cloud of forgetting." A troubled conscience could undermine the exercise by creating a constant distraction and downward drag. But simply "forgetting" sin would be tantamount to a psychologically unhealthy and spiritually damaging denial. So he directs his reader to the Sacrament of Penance. By acknowledging sin and receiving absolution, this fledgling contemplative would be prepared for apophatic prayer which, the author maintains, goes on to destroy the "root and ground of sin" that still lingers in us all.

Sin operates in every adult Christian life. In the course of our own baptismal liturgy, the candidate is asked: "Will you persevere in resisting evil, and, whenever you fall into sin, repent and return to the Lord?" (BCP, 304). The unblinking expectation is that we will fall many times and that we will need to repent as often as we do. We fall in all sorts of ways. But how will we repent? People have expressed repentance in various ways over the course of church history. As the Lord's Prayer suggests in its petition, "Forgive us our trespasses," prayer remains the indispensable first step in seeking God's forgiveness. We also have each other in the church for encouragement and mutual prayer. Thus, as the Epistle of James testifies, Christians have from early days confessed their sins "to one another" as a means of spiritual and even physical healing. The first-century document, the *Didache*, recommends the same mutual confession before participating in the Eucharist (*Didache* 14.1).

The desert tradition took this practice a step further, often including a wide-ranging "disclosure of thoughts" by the one seeking guidance from an *abba* or *amma*. What was presented for discernment would be the whole gamut of troublesome thoughts and feelings along with overtly sinful words and actions. Spiritual direction and confession of sin were thus intertwined. The Rule of St. Benedict incorporates this desert discipline when it advises, "As soon as wrongful thoughts come into your heart, dash them against Christ and disclose them to your spiritual father" (4:50). Finally, private confession became the norm through the influence of Celtic Christianity. Because the churches of Britain and Ireland developed with monastic settlements forming the center of Christian life, confession of sins followed the monastic pattern. This practice eventually become so widespread on the European continent that by 1215 the Fourth Lateran Council could codify it as canon law.

At the time of the Reformation private confession came under exacting scrutiny. Reformers argued that since auricular confession had not been instituted by Christ, it could not be considered a sacrament. Nor could its use be compulsory. Many reformers, however, including Luther, continued to recognize its value for relieving individual consciences burdened by sin. The Exhortation in the first Book of Common Prayer (1549) urged "secret confession" to a priest for those whose consciences were troubled. The same prayer book directed that the absolution prescribed for the Visitation of the Sick be used as well for "all private confessions." So while the practice of private confession has waxed and waned in the course of Anglican history, it has never entirely disappeared.

Today we recognize the evolution of sacramental rites in the church over time—a perspective not available in the sixteenth century. Many have found confession to a priest to be a palpable vehicle of divine mercy, mediating sacramental grace. The classic Anglican adage about using this sacrament is pastorally wise and judicious: "All may, none must, some should." With the liturgical renewal of recent decades, it has received a full rite of its own in many prayer books throughout the Anglican Communion, including the 1979 Book of Common Prayer of the Episcopal Church.

But since the Book of Common Prayer also provides for a General Confession and Absolution in the Eucharist and other liturgies, why go through the embarrassment of making a personal confession to a priest? The relationship between these two forms of reconciliation is complementary, and neither should undermine the other. The General Confession serves the pastoral need of Christian people to acknowledge their sinfulness and be absolved. As a corporate act of the praying community, however, it expresses our failings precisely *as a community*. We are a sinful people, entangled in the destructive forces at large in our society, both known and unknown to us. We also stand guilty of personal sin. The General Confession is roomy enough to include these particular sins of ours, which also of course compromise the spiritual health of the community. The reach of absolution in the General Confession, then, extends to both personal and corporate sin. As in every case of penitence, it presupposes a resolve for amendment of life, coupled with a determination to reduce the harm we have caused to whatever extent we can. For many, the corporate confession of sin and words of absolution in the General Confession offer an entirely sufficient means to receive God's forgiveness.

For others, though, the repetition of a generic confession week after week loses its force over time, and people often have no clear notion of what they are actually being absolved of. Attempts in some quarters to remedy this deficiency by devising liturgies that name more specific—usually social—sins has not helped, either, as people find themselves mouthing a confession of sins for which they feel scant personal conviction. Absolution again seems hollow, a mere comforting noise.

Yet reconciliation stands at the heart of the gospel. Jesus, echoing the message of John the Baptist, begins his ministry with the twin summons, "Repent, and believe in the good news" (Mark 1:15). St. Paul describes the *missio Dei* and the ministry of the church in just such terms of reconciliation: "in Christ God was reconciling the world to himself, not counting their trespasses against them, and entrusting the message of reconciliation to us" (2 Cor. 5:19). The ministry of reconciliation extends to the whole of creation and embraces everyone, bringing Christians to the forefront of witness for justice, truth, and peace. Because of our baptism into Christ, we share in his reconciling work. Yet from time to time we also stand in need of reconciliation, "whenever we fall into sin." Conversion of life is a slow, ongoing process.

The Reconciliation of a Penitent offers a compelling vehicle of repentance and forgiveness for those who desire it. It provides a potent way of dramatizing and enacting both penitence and divine mercy. For a good many Christians, forgiveness of sin is something they believe in but do not experience. In their case, forgiveness seems to exist only in the realm of ideas. The powerful dynamic at work in the rite of reconciliation shifts forgiveness from the head to a heartfelt appropriation of contrition and joy. St. Ambrose of Milan once wrote: "You have shown yourself to me face to face, O Christ: I meet you in your sacraments." The experience of Ambrose has been repeated millions of time, as Christian people encounter Christ in the sacraments. In the sacrament of reconciliation, Jesus embraces us as our merciful savior. Contact with him is transformative.

Because sacraments are rooted in the human experience of time, they offer a clear sense of before-and-after. They work as rites of passage. In reconciliation, one's sinful past is annulled and a new stage commences. This holds true even for those who regularly use confession, for whom it might not signal a dramatic turning point. It still offers a fresh start and a vibrant sense of renewal. Confession in the presence of a priest also diminishes our loneliness in sin. We reach out to the community represented by our confessor, aware that both sin and salvation have corporate repercussions. Our sins damage the body of Christ, and salvation occurs within the community of faith. The term "private confession," then, while useful to distinguish it from the General Confession, is somewhat misleading. Although the administration of this sacrament requires the utmost privacy, it remains a liturgy of the church, not a "private" meeting between priest and penitent. In the sacrament of reconciliation, the smallest quorum of the church comes together: "Where two or three are gathered together in my name, there I am in the midst of them."

Confession helps us be specific in our repentance. Although all Christians have a duty of self-examination, it is easy to neglect this practice. Many of us carry around vague feelings of guilt or remorse. We know we are not quite what we ought to be, but our sense of inadequacy remains fuzzy and generalized. The grace of confession begins even as we prepare for it. In honest and thorough self-examination we endeavor to discard obsolete images of ourselves—the false and deficient stories we have been telling ourselves for years. We try to set aside erroneous notions of guilt or blame, assuming genuine responsibility for our omissions and transgressions. Because in confession we need to make ourselves intelligible to another, we must find words to name our particular sins. We commit ourselves to being comprehensive and straightforward. We move past the blur of hazy guilt feelings to sharp and liberating penitence.

If we have never made a confession before, we may feel overwhelmed by the prospect of getting ready for it. Martin L. Smith's

Reconciliation: Preparing for Confession in the Episcopal Church was designed to fill this need, and it remains a valuable tool not only for those making a first confession but also for those who regularly use the rite.[4] In the course of looking back over our life, or the time since our last confession, some sins will stand out. Our consciences, however, need the additional, penetrating light of Scripture: the Ten Commandments (Exod. 20), the Sermon on the Mount (Matt. 5–7), the Fruits of the Spirit (Gal. 5:22–26), and the Way of Love (1 Cor. 13). Preparation, especially for a first confession, should be neither rushed nor overextended. It is a time of introspection, to be sure, but it should never dissolve into a self-absorbed preoccupation with our deficiencies. In self-examination we seek the light of the Holy Spirit to see ourselves as God sees us. Like the sacrament itself, it is first and foremost a prayerful encounter with our merciful savior.

Confession brings damaging secrets into the open so healing can begin. Psychotherapy and twelve-step programs borrowed this wisdom from the church to great advantage. For centuries the church has provided a safe place to tell the truth about our pained and troubled self, bringing the shadowy side into the light. The ancient practice of "disclosure of thoughts" was grounded in the recognition that sin and other destructive forces begin to lose their power over us when finally named. Saying our sins aloud makes them real to us, deepening our penitence. And by handing our sins over to God through confession, we find ourselves unburdened. Moreover, we can rest confident that what we confess will never be disclosed to anyone in any situation whatsoever. The Book of Common Prayer safeguards the ancient discipline regarding the secrecy of a confession as "morally absolute for the confessor, and must under no circumstances be broken" (BCP, 446).[5]

---

4. Martin L. Smith, *Reconciliation: Preparing for Confession in the Episcopal Church* (Cambridge, MA: Cowley, 1985). Both *Praying our Days: A Guide and Companion* and *St. Augustine's Prayer Book* also offer material to prepare for the rite.

5. For a fuller discussion of the pastoral ramifications of this discipline, see Julia Gatta and Martin L. Smith, *Go in Peace: The Art of Hearing Confessions* (Harrisburg, PA: Morehouse, 2012), 53–56.

While confession can be profoundly cathartic, it is not a religious form of therapy. It offers instead a sacramental encounter with Christ through the ministry of the church, whose purpose is forgiveness of sin. By the grace of God, forgiveness is itself healing, and the whole process of contrition, confession, amendment, and absolution is restorative. We take responsibility for our lives and make amends whenever possible and beneficial. If we need to make restitution of property, harmony, or reputation, but are unsure where our obligation lies, our confessor can counsel us how to proceed. After we have finished confessing our sins, we may ask for direction about something that is particularly troubling. In any case, the priest will usually offer brief counsel. Since confession is not the place for probing analysis of our situation, our confessor may suggest discussing some matter with us at greater length in a later session of counseling or spiritual direction. Such proposals are rare, and acceptance of such an offer is entirely up to the penitent. If we follow up on this opportunity, the subsequent conversation continues to be protected by the seal of confession. In most cases, however, our confession is simply surrounded by words of encouragement and grace as the gospel is applied to our specific condition.

The Reconciliation of a Penitent supplies a vigorous renewal of baptismal grace. It liturgically enacts the painful death to sin, after which absolution raises us to joyful new life in Christ. Since baptism entails immersion into the death of Christ, the forgiveness of sin brings a fresh exposure to the cross. The anguish we feel in naming our sins before another withers pride, one of the roots of sin. It goes against our concern with self-image. It means taking off a mask, exposing our fallibility and hurt and capacity to hurt others. The costliness of confession is a participation in the costliness of the cross. Like the resurrection itself, absolution always comes as a surprise. The risen Christ breathes his Spirit of life and peace into our souls.

Some people seek the Reconciliation of a Penitent when weighed down by a particularly heavy remembrance of wrongdoing. They need the church's maximum help to entrust themselves to the Lamb of God who alone takes away the sin of the world. Others use the occasion of a retreat for this sacrament. Since in retreat our relationship to God comes under review, making a confession supports this renewal of our life in Christ. Confession is a particularly appropriate way to prepare for the grace of other sacraments or major life transitions: confirmation, marriage, ordination, taking up a new ministry, after a divorce, or before becoming a parent. Still others avail themselves of the rite at regular intervals, perhaps linking it to the rhythms of the liturgical year. As penitential seasons, Advent and Lent lend themselves to the practice, but we might find other occasions suitable for confession, as well. If, as the desert tradition observes, "We fall down and get up, and fall down and get up" through the whole of life, our need for Christ's forgiveness will always press upon us. In the rite of reconciliation we can experience this grace, upheld and restored to resurrection joy.

To whom should we turn for this most intimate sacrament? If we are under spiritual direction and our director happens to be a priest, combining those two ministries in the same person makes sense in many ways. Since directors are already familiar with our souls, they are well positioned to serve as our confessor. The two ministries, however, should be kept distinct in practice, even if that simply means deliberately setting aside time before or after a session of direction for the liturgy of confession. If material comes up in direction that might need to be repeated more succinctly in confession, it is nonetheless crucial for the seal of confession and the integrity of the rite that the boundary between the two not be blurred. If our director is a deacon or lay person and is willing to hear our confession, the Book of Common Prayer offers a "Declaration of Forgiveness" that can be used in these cases. Normally, though, confessions are heard by bishops and priests since they alone represent the church's authority in granting absolution. In any case, we have complete freedom in selecting our confessor. We may use our spiritual director or not, and some find it better to keep these offices entirely separate.

As in the case of selecting a spiritual director, it is best to follow a trusted personal recommendation when seeking a confessor. It may be that our own parish priest is the right person for us since the sacrament of reconciliation is a decidedly pastoral ministry. However, just as it is necessary for spiritual directors to be themselves under direction, it is essential that those who hear confessions use the rite regularly themselves. What matters here is not whether the priest has heard many confessions but whether the priest makes habitual use of the rite as a penitent. We learn how grace is released in this sacrament by experience; there is no other teacher. Unfortunately, many Episcopal priests have little or no familiarity with the Reconciliation of a Penitent as penitents themselves, and such inexperience effectively disqualifies them from administering this sacrament except in emergencies. Also, for both the ministries of spiritual direction and confession, we must go outside our circle of family, close friends, and those who exercise immediate authority over our work. The abundant grace available to us in direction or confession will be compromised if we are inhibited by relationships that, while enriching in themselves, are already complex. Rather than limit us, these traditional norms enhance our freedom in Christ. Nothing should obstruct our Lord's invitation, "Come to me, all you that are weary and are carrying heavy burdens, and I will give you rest" (Matt. 11:28).

RETREAT

"The apostles gathered around Jesus, and told him all that they had done and taught. He said to them, 'Come away to a deserted place all by yourselves and rest a while.' For many were coming and going, and they had no leisure even to eat. And they went away in the boat to a deserted place by themselves." (Mark 6:30–32)

We have already observed how Jesus moved between periods of intense engagement with people and interludes of solitary communion with the One he called his Father. He also summoned his disciples to times of retreat together, with him. The invitation recorded by St. Mark comes after the first mission of the Twelve. They have returned to Jesus after a stint of preaching and healing, and they are exhausted. The workload has been so demanding that even physical necessities like regular meals have been put on hold. Ours is not the first generation to be totally stressed-out by work! Jesus knows when enough is enough: "Come away to a deserted place all by yourselves and rest awhile."

Jesus calls them out to "a deserted place" (Mark 6:31). The KJV had translated *erēmos topos* literally: "a desert place." In biblical tradition the Greek word *erēmos* speaks of an isolated and barren locale, yet because of its very isolation and barrenness, a site conducive to spiritual growth and renewal. An extended stay in such a place, for the purpose of renewal in Christ, is a retreat. Jesus himself entered such a retreat before beginning his public ministry, when after his baptism the Spirit drove him into the Judean desert for forty days (Mark 1:12–14). Today people often go on retreat when they are at a similar crossroads: when they are discerning their vocation, before taking up a new calling, or before making a critical decision. Others come to retreat in search of healing. They hope to be comforted and restored by Christ after a job loss, a miscarriage, the breakup of a relationship, or a troubling diagnosis, for instance. Because of what transpires during retreat, they leave able to take up their future, whatever it may be, in the strength of the Lord. For some, the crisis may be entirely spiritual. Still others just need to pull back from the hectic pace of life to gain fresh perspective on themselves and their relationship to God—the relationship that undergirds all other relationships and activities.

Jesus invites his disciples to "Come away and rest a while," and almost everyone who goes on retreat needs to do just that: rest. Many of us suffer from chronic fatigue due to lack of sleep or overwork, or both. Retreat often begins with letting our Lord give us the gift of rest: "for he gives to his beloved sleep" (Ps. 127:3). Going to bed early and taking naps is in order. So is more thoughtful care of our bodies. Some people use retreat as an opportunity to engage in fasting, but anyone on retreat should eat moderately and healthfully which, while a beneficial practice in itself, also enhances sleep and prayer. Consideration of our physical self includes such daily exercise as is possible for us. It is not uncommon to take a day or more for "pre-retreat," during which we clear off our desks, catch up on correspondence, get the sleep and exercise we need, and engage in forms of recreation that refresh us. We can then enter the retreat more fully present to its graces and ready for its challenges.

An annual retreat of five to eight days can re-center us in Christ and open possibilities as nothing else can. This is largely a result of the power of silence. Although today various sorts of planning or re-focusing conferences, even among businesses, are styled "retreats," a true retreat is a period of silent, intense engagement with God. We give ourselves over solely to our relationship with God, thereby witnessing to the priority it holds for us. The silence, especially after a few days, enlarges our capacity to listen. In the first few days of retreat we are likely to hear mostly the chatter in our own heads, the concerns and preoccupations we brought into our time away. Sometimes in the silence memories are dislodged which may be significant or a distraction. Discernment is needed to know whether to ignore or pray about this material. In time, as the silence enfolds and penetrates us, we often sense the deeper voice of God and the subtle movements of the Spirit.

Silence is more than a matter of refraining from speech, although it begins there. Most monasteries and retreat houses, the most likely settings for retreat, support silence with meals free of sociable conversation. It is important to find a place of retreat that is, in fact, silent, for once silence is broken, it takes days to recover its benefits. Sometimes parishioners or other groups go on retreat together. Although at first it may feel awkward to hold back from our usual modes of conversation or comments, respecting each other's silence allows for a communion with one another that goes deeper than words. The same holds true if we are with a group of retreatants who are strangers to us. Real silence is rare in our culture; it is a precious and irreplaceable gift we can offer one another.

Silence also means completely disconnecting electronically. If we want to be reached in case of emergency, we can leave the telephone number of the place where we will be staying with a responsible person. Having given notice to family members or colleagues that we are going on retreat and cannot be contacted, we then turn off our cell phone and laptop and leave them at home, or in our suitcase, for the duration of the retreat. This may be the hardest discipline of all because we have become dependent on a continuous flow of communication. But if we are distracted by other people or the news (including reading newspapers) during our retreat, in the profound silence of the retreat these things will lodge in our minds and take up disproportionate space. We will be like the person in the gospel who swept out one demon only to have seven others move in, worse than the first (Matt. 12:43–45).

Obviously, a retreat is no time to catch up on work, letter writing, or even reading. It is devoted solely to prayer and those quiet physical activities that support prayer—long walks, working in the garden, some forms of handwork or art. The usual retreat entails three periods of meditation a day spaced fairly evenly. If we are at or near a monastery or convent, we might well take part in the public liturgies. The rest of the day is spent in "holy vacancy," available to the intuitions that may come to us at any time. It is all right to be bored. Boredom may be an aspect of our desert experience—the barren wilderness—no matter how lush the retreat setting. Filling in the time with reading, unless it serves *lectio divina*, is a way of escaping the silence and hinders our accessibility to God.

People sometimes call a retreat a "vacation with God," but the analogy can give the wrong impression. Retreats, while physically restful, often involve hard interior work. In the desert Jesus engaged in spiritual combat with the Tempter. The character of any retreat, whether it is full of consolation and peace or energetic and arduous—or some mixture of both—is impossible to know ahead of time. It depends, in part, on what we bring into the retreat; but it depends even more on the unpredictable leading of the Spirit.

A retreat of five to eight days is a strenuous undertaking, although the classic Ignatian retreat entails four full weeks. It is best to work up to any period of prolonged silence. Quiet days offer a brief period of retreat. Even if we take a long annual retreat as part of our Rule, periodic Quiet Days let us step back and take stock of our relationship with God at regular intervals. It is a bit like bringing a car in for scheduled maintenance: Nothing seems to be seriously awry, but we don't really know until we check in. When he was archbishop of Cape Town and a busy man indeed, Desmond Tutu set aside one Quiet Day each month for reflection and prayer—and no work. Eventually, we can undertake a weekend retreat. Since some of these juxtapose silence with discussion or other endeavors (journaling, icon painting, yoga, and so on), such retreats help us ease into an enhanced capacity for silence. Talking, however, always involves the ego: We inevitably want to be understood or to get our ideas across. Sooner or later we come to the point where we want to shed our ego-driven selves for a while and simply be with God in silence.

The silence of retreat brings God intensely close. Not every retreat is dramatically life-changing, but some are. God always changes us in prayer; we are never quite the same after retreat as before. We fall more deeply in love with God. Almost as a correlative, charity towards others and even ourselves suddenly springs up, too. Describing the wonder of silence before God, the Rule of the Fellowship of St. John the Evangelist teaches:

> The gift of silence we seek to cherish is chiefly the silence of adoring love for the mystery of God which words cannot express. In silence we pass through the bounds of language to lose ourselves in wonder. In this silence we learn to revere ourselves also; since Christ dwells in us we too are mysteries that cannot be fathomed, before which we must be silent until the day we come to know as we are known. In silence we honor the mystery present in the hearts of our brothers and sisters, strangers and enemies. Only God knows them as they truly are and in silence we learn to let go of the curiosity, presumption, and condemnation which pretends to penetrate the mystery of their hearts. True silence is an expression of love. . . .[6]

---

6. *The Rule of the Society of St. John the Evangelist* (Cambridge, MA: Cowley Publications, 1997), 54.

Silent retreats take different forms. Some hardy souls (and bodies) go off backpacking by themselves in the wilderness. Sometimes for safety's sake they join with a companion, similarly committed to retreat. Some find a quiet cabin by themselves near a lake, by the ocean, or in the woods. More and more retreat houses and monasteries have hermitages available, where one can camp out alone for several days at a time, either preparing one's own food or joining others for an occasional silent meal, or some combination. These self-directed retreats require strong inner resources. A generation ago "preached retreats" were the norm, and they are still popular and abundant. Some preached retreats are silent; others are not. In either case, a leader offers a few addresses each day intended to instruct, inspire, and encourage the prayer of retreatants. Since the real director of any retreat is the Holy Spirit, the addresses may well provoke further reflection and prayer. But it may also turn out that the Spirit prompts another sort of prayer altogether, and following this stimulus implies no negative judgment on the leader.

Finally, recent decades have seen the rise of individually directed retreats. In this style of retreat we meet daily with a director, in a session lasting anywhere from about fifteen to fifty minutes. Such retreats can be particularly beneficial for those who cannot find suitable spiritual direction where they live. During retreat, the focus of direction is on the retreatant's prayer. Directors help discern the graces or temptations at work as retreatants describe their experience of God—or apparent lack of experience—during their periods of meditation or throughout the retreat day. The director usually proposes a focus of prayer for the coming day, often suggesting a passage of Scripture for meditation. The guidance available in a directed retreat keeps us moving through the retreat, avoiding the likelihood of getting "stuck." The director's skillful discernment is reassuring. With greater confidence about God's ways with us, we can respond more unreservedly to the graces coming to us through the retreat.

Ten days before his sudden death in Bangkok, Thomas Merton was in Ceylon visiting a remote and abandoned Buddhist

shrine. There he experienced what he called an "aesthetic illumination" that completed his inner journey. Although he had been
sent to Asia by his superiors to attend a couple of conferences, in
many respects the trip served as something of a retreat for him. It
was certainly a pilgrimage. Gazing at the colossal statues of sitting and reclining Buddhas, he was struck by "the silence of the
extraordinary faces. The great smiles. Huge and yet subtle." What
overtakes him is the recognition that

> The rock, all matter, all life, is charged with dharmakaya . . .
> everything is emptiness and everything is compassion. I don't
> know when in my life I have ever had such a sense of beauty
> and spiritual validity running together in one aesthetic illu-
> mination. Surely . . . my Asian pilgrimage has come clear
> and purified itself. I mean, I know and have seen what I was
> obscurely looking for. I don't know what else remains but I have
> now seen and have pierced through the surface and have got
> beyond the shadow and the disguise.[7]

We read this extraordinary testimony piercingly aware of
something Merton could not know as he entered this account
into his personal journal: that he would be dead less than a
week later, struck down by electric shock from a faulty hotel
fan. Yet who can doubt that the illumination that seized him
in Polonnaruwa fulfilled not only his Asian pilgrimage but
his life's? The son of a painter, Merton was keenly sensitive to
beauty his entire life, whether in literature, painting, sculpture,
or nature. Beauty held a sacramental power for him. His jour-
nals and other writings are filled with reflections on the arts.
An avid photographer, for whom photography was a path to
contemplation, he took photos throughout this final journey of
his, including pictures of the Buddhas that moved him so deeply.
God speaks to us in our native language, and in this case God
spoke to him through the silent, subtle, massive yet peaceful
beauty of those imposing figures.

7. *The Asian Journal of Thomas Merton*, ed. Naomi Burton, Brother Patrick Hart, and
James Laughlin (New York: New Directions Books, 1975), 235–236. The journal entry is
for December 4, 1968; the event described took place on December 1.

At the conclusion of a retreat, we do not yet understand its significance. It will take weeks, months, or perhaps the remainder of our lives for the direction of the graces to become apparent, if it ever does. At the end of the retreat, the concerns we initially brought along may or may not have resolved. It might not matter anymore. In the same journal entry, Merton testifies to having come upon the one thing needful—the insight that allows everything else to fall into place:

> All problems are resolved and everything is clear, simply because what matters is clear.

After retreat, we return to our workaday world with our perspective purified and sharpened: "what matters is clear." The monumental problems of the world and the complexities of our own lives have not gone away, but we can now view them with transfigured vision. We have encountered Christ in ways we could not have planned. And we know the risen Lord goes before us, as he promised his disciples, as we face whatever awaits us in the future. We will meet Jesus there, too. With St. Paul, we are eager to press on. We are not yet complete and we have work still to do—inner work and outer service. The twists and turns of our journey will bring us back, one way or another, to the paschal mystery that marks our life in Christ:

> I want to know Christ and the power of his resurrection and the sharing of his sufferings by becoming like him in his death, if somehow I may attain the resurrection from the dead. Not that I have already obtained this or have already reached the goal; but I press on to make it my own, because Christ Jesus has made me his own. (Phil. 3:10–12)